D1594724

Hybrid Identities and
Adolescent Girls

CRITICAL LANGUAGE AND LITERACY STUDIES
Series Editors: Vaidehi Ramanathan, *University of California, USA*; Bonny Norton, *University of British Columbia, Canada*; and Alastair Pennycook, *University of Technology, Sydney, Australia*

Critical Language and Literacy Studies is an international series that encourages monographs directly addressing issues of power (its flows, inequities, distributions, trajectories) in a variety of language- and literacy-related realms. The aim with this series is twofold: (1) to cultivate scholarship that openly engages with social, political and historical dimensions in language and literacy studies and (2) to widen disciplinary horizons by encouraging new work on topics that have received little focus (see below for partial list of subject areas) and that use innovative theoretical frameworks.

Full details of all the books in this series and of all our other publications can be found on http://www.multilingual-matters.com, or by writing to Multilingual Matters, St Nicholas House, 31–34 High Street, Bristol, BS1 2AW, UK.

Other books in the series

Collaborative Research in Multilingual Classrooms
Corey Denos, Kelleen Toohey, Kathy Neilson and Bonnie Waterstone
English as a Local Language: Post-colonial Identities and Multilingual Practices
Christina Higgins
The Idea of English in Japan: Ideology and the Evolution of a Global Language
Philip Seargeant
Language and HIV/AIDS
Christina Higgins and Bonny Norton (eds)
China and English: Globalisation and the Dilemmas of Identity
Joseph Lo Bianco, Jane Orton and Gao Yihong (eds)

CRITICAL LANGUAGE AND LITERACY STUDIES
Series Editors: Vaidehi Ramanathan, Bonny Norton
and Alastair Pennycook

Hybrid Identities and Adolescent Girls
Being 'Half' in Japan

Laurel D. Kamada

MULTILINGUAL MATTERS
Bristol • Buffalo • Toronto

Dedicated to Jonah,
the six girls of this study
and all the other families like ours in Japan

Library of Congress Cataloging in Publication Data
A catalog record for this book is available from the Library of Congress.
Kamada, Laurel D.
Hybrid Identities and Adolescent Girls: Being 'Half' in Japan/Laurel D. Kamada.
Critical Language and Literacy studies
Includes bibliographical references and index.
1. Identity (Psychology)--Social aspects--Japan--Case studies. 2. Racially mixed
children--Japan--Ethnic identity. 3. Language and culture--Japan--Case studies.
I. Title.
HM753.K34 2009
305.235'208905052–dc22 2009033792

British Library Cataloguing in Publication Data
A catalogue entry for this book is available from the British Library.

ISBN-13: 978-1-84769-233-7 (hbk)
ISBN-13: 978-1-84769-232-0 (pbk)

Multilingual Matters
UK: St Nicholas House, 31–34 High Street, Bristol, BS1 2AW, UK.
USA: UTP, 2250 Military Road, Tonawanda, NY 14150, USA.
Canada: UTP, 5201 Dufferin Street, North York, Ontario, M3H 5T8, Canada.

The policy of Multilingual Matters/Channel View Publications is to use papers
that are natural, renewable and recyclable products, made from wood grown in
sustainable forests. In the manufacturing process of our books, and to further
support our policy, preference is given to printers that have FSC and PEFC Chain
of Custody certification. The FSC and/or PEFC logos will appear on those books
where full certification has been granted to the printer concerned.

Typeset by Techset Composition Ltd., Salisbury, UK.
Printed and bound in Great Britain by Short Run Press Ltd.

Contents

List of Tables and Figures

Tables

Figures

Transcription Conventions

?	(in text) rising intonation, question
(?)	undecipherable speech
(laugh)	laugh
CAPITALS	loud enunciation
,	(comma) continuing intonation (utterance not completed)
bold print	Japanese transcribed into Romanization (the actual speech) (Hepburn System of Romanization)
italic print	the English translation of the Japanese
regular print	the actual speech in English (not a translation)
(explanation)	explanation or clarification in parenthesis (not the actual speech)
(.)	pause less than one second
(..)	pause longer than one second
"quotation marks"	words enclosed in quotation marks indicate quoted speech, emphasized lexis, voice of someone else or self at an earlier time
[*English translation*]	English translation of Japanese embedded in an English segment
[implied meaning]	implied, but unspoken, meaning
[...]	ellipsis: omission of one or more lines of the excerpt

Pseudonyms are used for all names:

A = Anna, H = Hanna, M = Maya, N = Naomi, R = Rina, S = Sara
L = researcher, ? = (in the speaker column of transcripts) one of the six girls was speaking, but which girl was speaking was unclear, ?s = (in the speaker column of transcripts) two or more of the six girls were speaking or laughing simultaneously, but which of the girls was unclear.

Acknowledgments[1]

First and foremost, this book could not have been written without the enthusiastic cooperation and input from each of the six participants and their families whom I owe a dept of gratitude. I wish to specially thank the mother of one of the girls who initially introduced me to the five other families and assisted me in arranging the first meeting.

I would like to express my deepest gratitude to Mark Sebba for his guidance and words of wisdom from the earliest stages of this study. I would also like to extend my humble appreciation to Jane Sunderland who has helped me through every stage of this project with her rigorous and critical attention to detail along with her enthusiasm, warmth, generosity and friendship. From the start, I also thank Greg Meyers and Norman Fairclough, for their support, wisdom and guidance in opening my mind to an incredible world of discourse analysis.

I am extremely grateful to Bonny Norton whose works have had a tremendously inspirational influence on me and the course that this book was to take, long before I had even met her. I would also like to thank Yasuko Kanno who was helpful to me in subtle but profound ways, by going before me and generously helping me to see how it can be done.

I also want to acknowledge my colleagues in Japan in the Bilingualism Special Interest Group of the Japan Association for Language Teaching, who offered me feedback on my work at various stages, particularly Mary Goebel-Noguchi. Also Tim Greer, as always giving of himself, even with a broken right arm, carefully typed out pages of suggestions for me on an early draft of the book. My brother, Ed Nudelman, and Masataka Yamaguchi also generously spent hours proofing early drafts of the book and offering insightful critique along with needed encouragement.

Special thanks go out to Margaret Wetherell and Nigel Edley for taking their precious time on several occasions to rigorously go over my work, providing me with invaluable insight into some complex and fascinating aspects of discursive psychology. Likewise, I am deeply indebted to Judith Baxter for carefully proofing various segments of my work and discussing the essential aspects of Feminist Post-Structuralist Discourse Analysis.

This project could never have evolved into the shape of the book that it is without the supportive and helpful staff of Multilingual Matters, in particular Anna Roderick. I also extend my heartfelt thanks to Julia Menard-Warwick and Janet Shibamoto-Smith who finely read the first draft of the manuscript and offered tremendously helpful suggestions throughout.

Closest to home, I express my thanks to two people who had to put up with a working mom with three agendas: my husband for his patience and support and my mixed-ethnic son who was the main catalyst in the decision to pursue this topic. Finally, I want to express a lifetime of thanks to my mom, physically separated from me by an ocean for most of my adult life, but always right there next to me in loving support, who nurtured in me the courage to challenge myself and to keep going at all odds.

Note

1. Grateful acknowledgment is made to *Time Asia* for permission to reprint on the cover of this book (and also in Appendix 2, Line no. 1) an illustration by Cecelia Wong that appeared in *Time Asia* (March 11, 2002: 22). All rights reserved. Reprinted by permission of Time Asia and Cecelia Wong. Also to the Horikoshi Police Department in northern Japan for permission to reproduce the text and illustration of their police report (Figures 2.1–22.4) which was publicly distributed throughout the city of Hirosaki in June, 1999.

Preface

Much contemporary writing on identity has focused on the benefits of hybridity, where identities are fluid, flexible and indeterminate, and global citizens draw on diverse influences to construct new, multilingual identities. Even countries such as Japan, which has had a history of emphasizing monolingual homogeneity within an ideology of Nihonjinron (see Kubota 2002), have started to shift toward a more open identification with multiplicity. Young people, Maher asserts, are rejecting fixed ascriptions of cultural identity and are instead playing with notions of metroethnicity, 'a hybridised "street" ethnicity deployed by a cross-section of people with ethnic or mainstream backgrounds who are oriented toward cultural hybridity, cultural/ethnic tolerance and a multicultural lifestyle in friendships, music, the arts, eating and dress' (Maher, 2005: 83). As Maher notes, 'Cultural essentialism and ethnic orthodoxy are out. In Japan, metroethnicity is in. Cool rules' (Maher, 2005: 83).

As the title of Kamada's book, *Hybrid Identities and Adolescent Girls: Being 'Half' in Japan* suggests, however, the hybridity celebrated from some perspectives cannot be worn quite so lightly. On the one hand, as Kamada shows, the adolescent girls in her study may be able to take up positions that trade on their novel status as children of mixed background, to move across identities, to take up positions within new discourses within Japan. And yet, as Young has long reminded us, hybridity has always had its darker side, suggesting not only the possibility of mixing but also that the mixing is of pre-given elements of hybridity 'whose tensions and divisions it re-enacts in its own antithetical structure' (Young, 1995: 27). So here, as the other half of Kamada's title suggests, we also have the notion of being 'half', the idea that these young people are less than whole, part of a mixture that renders them half Japanese and half something else. And while young Japanese people may be getting into metroethnicity, they are equally capable of talking of others as 'half' (or perhaps the slightly preferable, but also problematic 'double'). Kamada's book shows how a group of young girls navigates this difficult territory.

The tensions lived out by these girls – between being half and being hybrid – capture at another level the tension between structuralist and poststructuralist conceptions of language, identity and culture – distinctions that are of great interest to contemporary applied linguistics. The structuralist view that a person can be 'half' assumes an essentialist position with regard to the symbolic systems and practices that structure people's lives. In the case investigated in this book, Kamada found that what it means to be Japanese, for many citizens, is associated with a pre-given and unchanging set of characteristics, defined by language and ethnicity. The notion of hybridity, on the other hand, indexes poststructuralist notions of multiplicity and contestation. As poststructuralist scholars attest, what it means to be insider–outsider; us–them, male–female is a constant source of negotiation as language practices are defined and resisted. Kamada embraces Bhabha's (1994) view that all forms of culture are continually in a process of hybridity, a 'third space' that enables other positions to emerge. As Bhabha argues, third spaces, while bearing the traces of the practices that inform it, give rise to new forms of meaning and representation. It is precisely such new forms of meaning and representation, associated with adolescent girls in Japan, which Kamada investigates with great skill and sensitivity.

While Bhabha developed his groundbreaking ideas in the relative comfort of prestigious tertiary institutions, Kamada traveled the length of Japan, over a period of several years, to interview six girls in their homes and local communities. What distinguished these six girls from their peers was that each had one parent who was white and English speaking, and another parent who was Asian and Japanese speaking. Kamada sought to investigate how these young women, who were 12 years of age at the beginning of her study, discursively constructed their hybrid identities in the context of Japan. In undertaking this intriguing study, she has contributed to a growing body of research in applied linguistics that seeks to investigate how young people negotiate hybrid identities in contexts that are often unfriendly and unwelcoming. However, while scholars such as McKay and Wong (1996) in the USA, Duff (2002) in Canada and Miller (2003) in Australia have investigated the changing identities and language practices of students who have been geographically displaced, and are newcomers to the local language, Kamada's students all held Japanese nationality from birth, were fluent speakers of Japanese and were all relatively proficient in English. Nevertheless, like many displaced youth, they were all engaged in daily battles for respect and recognition both inside and outside the classroom. Kamada's research, like that of Rampton (2006) in the UK, thus provides a particularly unique lens through which to examine the challenges faced by adolescents worldwide whose ethnic identities and bilingual language practices diverge from the local norm. Of central interest in Kamada's study is how the girls experienced practices of marginalization, and how they negotiated, contested and resisted them.

Bhabha's distinction between cultural difference and cultural translation helps to locate Kamada's study within a wider analytic framework. While cultural difference references debates on diversity, cultural translation challenges the very notion of cultural content, taking the position that cultural practices construct their own systems of meaning and representation. What it means to be 'half' or 'gaijin' in Japan, for example, cannot be easily translated, though these constructs had very particular meanings for the girls in the study. To be positioned as 'half', for example, while problematic for many of the girls, was nevertheless preferable to being positioned as 'gaijin'. Further, as Bhabha notes, the understanding of difference cannot be accommodated within a universalistic framework. When asked, therefore, 'What kind of person do you consider yourself to be?' the girls responded, unequivocally, 'it depends on the place'.

What other insights, of relevance to applied linguistics, does Kamada gain from these six remarkable young women? Clearly, the girls learnt from a very young age that 'the nail that sticks up gets hammered down'. How the nail is 'hammered down', however, was not only constituted in and by language ('they just like stare at me and go "gaijin, gaijin"'), but was marked by gendered practices. While boys were more likely to be 'loud' and say 'really bad things', girls 'don't come right out with it', and are more likely to ask, 'Are you American?' As Rina noted, 'if you're girls they just let you be, but if they're boys they might bully you'. Many applied linguistic scholars have found that the linguistic practices of any given community can serve to either include or marginalize other members of the community, with profound implications for identity and human possibility (Kanno, 2008; Norton, 2000; Ramanathan, 2005; Toohey, 2000). It is not surprising then that these girls all sought affiliations outside of their school contexts, and that their bilingual friends, or what Anna called her 'double friends', were an important source of support.

Kamada also draws attention to the ways in which the identities of these young women changed over time, in ways that expanded possibilities for their future. In poststructuralist theories of identity, language practices are considered to play a crucial role in constructing diverse subject positions for speakers, and Kamada's data powerfully captures changing language practices experienced by the girls over a period of several years. While all the girls agreed that they 'hated' being positioned as 'half' when they were younger, and wanted to 'darken' their hair and be more 'Japanese', their perception of their difference changed as they began to appreciate the symbolic capital associated with being bilingual, and having access to English, in particular. As Sara said, 'everyone thinks it's good, and a lot of people tell me that it's good, and now even I am beginning to think that'. Rina, likewise, noted, 'I have many choices for my future and bilingualism kind of um expands my future'. Associated with a shift in their perceptions of difference was a concomitant re-evaluation of the source of the problem of marginalization. Rather than resisting their own embodied identities, the girls began to see their tormentors as undesirable and 'totally disgusting people'.

While Kamada's research thus concludes optimistically, and applied linguists and language teachers can take some comfort from the finding that girls in the study were able to shift from 'half' to 'hybrid' over the course of adolescence, there is no room for complacency. Certainly, to the extent that some notion of metroethnicity may now be cool (Maher, 2005), or young rap artists may celebrate being 'double' or 'freaky' Japanese (see Pennycook, 2003), a space has opened up to be different. And yet, as the research of scholars such as Kanno (2008) highlights, English language in Japan has a very privileged position; it has become, as Piller and Takahashi (2006) note, a language of status and desire, and those associated with the language – typically white Westerners – are similarly accorded a very particular set of privileges. If the girls in Kamada's study had not been positioned as 'American', their hybrid identities may have remained devalued and their social positions marginal. Kamada's study challenges language teachers and applied linguists to constantly interrogate the assumptions about language, identity and culture that we bring to our classrooms, and the practices we observe among students. While theories of diversity and difference can help us to conceptualize our work, it is the stories of young people that make struggles for social change particularly salient and urgent.

Bonny Norton, Alastair Pennycook
and Vaidehi Ramanathan
June 2009

References

Bhabha, H. (1994) *The Location of Culture*. London/New York: Routledge.
Duff, P. (2002) The discursive co-construction of knowledge, identity, and difference: An ethnography of communication in the high school mainstream. *Applied Linguistics* 23, 289–322.

Kanno, Y. (2008) *Language and Education in Japan: Unequal Access to Bilingualism.* Basingstoke: Palgrave Macmillan.

Kubota, R. (2002) Japanese identities in written communication: Politics and discourses. In R.T. Donahue (ed.) *Exploring Japaneseness: On Japanese Enactments of Culture and Consciousness* (pp. 293–315). Westport, CN: Ablex Publishing.

Maher, J. (2005) Metroethnicity, language, and the principle of cool. *International Journal of the Sociology of Language.* 175/176, 83–102.

McKay, S. and Wong, S.C. (1996) Multiple discourses, multiple identities: Investment and agency in second language learning among Chinese adolescent immigrant students. *Harvard Educational Review* 66 (3), 577–608.

Miller, J. (2003) *Audible Difference: ESL and Social Identity in Schools.* Clevedon: Multilingual Matters.

Norton, B. (2000) *Identity and Language Learning: Gender, Ethnicity and Educational Change.* Harlow: Pearson Education Limited.

Pennycook, A. (2003) Global Englishes, Rip Slyme and performativity. *Journal of Sociolinguistics* 7 (4), 513–533.

Piller, I. and Takahashi, K. (2006) A passion for English: Desire and the language market. In A. Pavlenko (ed.) *Bilingual Minds: Emotional Experience, Expression and Representation* (pp. 59–83). Clevedon: Multilingual Matters.

Ramanathan, V. (2005) *The English–Vernacular Divide: Postcolonial Language Politics and Practice.* Clevedon: Multilingual Matters.

Rampton, B. (2006) *Language in Late Modernity: Interaction in an Urban School.* Cambridge: Cambridge University Press.

Toohey, K. (2000) *Learning English at School: Identity, Social Relations and Classroom Practice.* Clevedon: Multilingual Matters.

Young, R. (1995) *Colonial Desire: Hybridity in Theory, Culture and Race.* London: Routledge.

Chapter 1
Constructing Hybrid Identity in Japan

... my son is being verbally abused and discriminated against because his name sounds foreign and he looks a little different. There are one or two children in his class with extreme influence over the other children who say to my son in Japanese, 'Foreigners are stupid! Die foreigner!' They consistently use the word 'stupid' and 'die'. How can Japanese children be so cruel and ignorant of children who are different? My son has been biting his teeth at night and scraping them back and forth while he sleeps and fears where he can go around school without being tormented by the children. Some children have even thrown rocks and sand at him for no reason at all except that he is different. Furthermore, they take his things and throw them back and forth teasing him ... If his stress level gets so high because of this problem we will have no other course of action than to withdraw him from the Japanese school

November 1998. From an e-mail sent over the BSIG[1] e-list from an American father of an elementary school child in Japan of Japanese and white mixed-parentage

My daughter just sees herself as a Japanese girl who has a strange, bicultural Dad

November 2001. From an Australian father of a 12-year-old child in Japan of Japanese and white mixed-parentage

Importance and Timeliness of the Study of Hybrid Identity in Japan

I have lived in Japan for over half of my life as a 'white' foreign woman – a *gaijin*. I originally ventured to Japan in 1975 for a few years to explore an exotic Eastern culture and to teach English. In the early 1980s, I returned to Japan on a Japanese scholarship to study education at Osaka University. After nearly a decade living on my own there, I married a Japanese man. In a few years we had a child – a mixed-ethnic son who soon came to assume an ethnic identity differing from both of ours.

1

I was born, raised and educated in America, and then came to live in Japan, as a foreign country, out of choice. I have worked hard to acquire good, but not perfect, Japanese language skills and to understand and adapt to the rules, mores and practices of a complex Japanese society while dealing with my foreign status. While I have had my own struggles with adapting to life in Japan as a foreigner, my son's situation is categorically different. He is not a foreigner; he is Japanese. Japan is his homeland; Japanese is a native language for him.

The first quotation above is from a letter that appeared spontaneously over an e-list of the (Japan) Bilingualism Special Interest Group (BSIG) in 1998 from a desperate father of a mixed-ethnic child attending a Japanese elementary school. It carried the impact of a bombshell on the list members (me included) who make up an English-speaking foreign community in Japan, mostly with Japanese spouses and mixed-ethnic children. A huge flood of discussion emerged in a manner that the e-list had never seen before as mail flew back and forth for weeks. Suddenly it seemed everyone had a story to tell of their child, of someone they knew, or of themselves. Several people had the story to tell of their child, who upon entering the Japanese school system found herself/himself for the first time suddenly called *gaijin* (foreigner) by classmates.

I had my own story to tell of my unpreparedness as a 'white' American mother in dealing with racialization of my son, experienced on both sides of the Pacific, in America as well as in Japan. I was amazed as I personally witnessed how cruel very small children can be to each other. In Japan, my son was made to feel different and teased for his stand-out curly hair and thought of as a 'White' foreigner. Perhaps this is what made it all the more shocking for me when during a brief residence in a suburban American school; I personally witnessed some elementary school boys racializing my son as Chinese, using depreciatory language. It was the first time for me to feel the sting of racialization in America first hand.

Many parents on the e-list in Japan expressed the extreme shock and disappointment felt by their children in Japan in being constituted as *foreigners* in their homeland. Up until that point in their lives these children had considered themselves to be Japanese, just like their best friends whom they had played with in their neighborhoods since they were big enough to walk. After all, one of their passports officially verified their Japanese nationality; their first (and for some, only) language was Japanese; and one of their parents was Japanese, along with Japanese grandparents, cousins, uncles and aunts.

The online discussion was so impassioned and rich that we decided to put together a monograph on the topic of ethnic bullying in Japan in order to address many of these problems and to help others in similar situations. Someone was appointed as editor and articles were requested of the list members who had so energetically shared their private experiences, their journeys and their solutions to problems.[2] Most of the members of this BSIG e-list are English-speaking foreign nationals concerned with issues of how to instill bilinguality in our mixed-ethnic children in a society where bilinguality and minority language education is not an option for most such children within the Japanese educational system (see Kanno, 2004, 2008).[3]

Suddenly *multilingualism* was not the only issue that I and others in this community in Japan had to consider. Now the notion of hybrid *identity* had entered our thinking, and we could not retreat from considering complex questions as our children started growing up. I began to realize that these questions needed to be empirically researched in order for us to know how to understand and deal with raising mixed-ethnic children (to aid parents), devise curriculum and provide counseling (to aid educators), offer answers to immediate questions (to aid children personally dealing with issues of identity and social marginalization), and facilitate better communication between members of the foreign community in Japan and their Japanese neighbors.

This was the catalyst that drew me to this topic at a time when there was nearly no research at all undertaken on the topic in Japan. Members of this foreign community in Japan had zealously demonstrated the importance of the need to understand the hybrid identity of their children being raised in Japan.

This particular research community of mostly 'white' foreigners married to Japanese, who have been residing in Japan for two or three decades now, represents pioneers of a new segment of Japanese society. While ethnically mixed children of international marriages have existed in Japan since before World War II, up until recent years they have not been seen in large numbers, making these children of today the first ever generation of a *sizable* (and growing) community of such children to appear in various regions around Japan, particularly in the larger cities. The impassioned timeliness and importance of this topic had been demonstrated and this e-list discussion clarified the need for a study on the hybrid identity of these children.

The second quotation above illustrates the feelings of another sort of 'white-foreign' parent of a mixed-ethnic child in Japan. This was written by a father, who perceives his daughter as *not* having any particular issues with her 'biculturality'. This quotation, along with the first one, represents just two diverse ways in which parents of such children in

Japan understand their children's ethnic identity. However, how the parents view their children and how the children themselves construct their own identities do not always match, and are not fixed attributes. What this book examines is how the children themselves actually constitute their own identities and position themselves within various contexts in their daily interactions with others.

An Emerging Hybrid Identity in Japan

This book examines how six adolescent girlfriends in Japan discursively construct their *hybrid* identities within the context of Japan. While the term *hybrid* can assume many nuances, the focus of this book is on children of mixed-parentage born and raised in Japan. While children of Japanese and South American (mostly Brazilian) mixed-parentage have been one of the fastest growing ethnic groups in Japan in recent years, in this study I narrow the focus to specifically examine children with one Japanese parent, and one non-Japanese (white-foreign) parent who was born and raised in an English-speaking environment of Britain, the USA or Australia. (The reasons for this decision are presented in the section 'A focus on Japan and on children of Japanese and "White" mixed-parentage' [p. 8].) While in many ways, these participants might just seem like 'the (Japanese) girl next door' and that is how they often see themselves (and as illustrated in the second quotation above), their associations and solidarity with each other form an important part of their identities within their own communities as well as within the larger Japanese community.

The first generation of a sizable community of these mixed-ethnic children (referred to as 'half' in Japanese) has emerged in Japan in recent years, challenging the long-held myth of Japan as a single-race society (*tan'itsu minzoku*). However, in spite of such changing demographics, the discourse of Japan as homogeneous still continues to inform political, social and educational practices in Japan. One of the main objectives for undertaking this study is to explore how racialized, ethnicized and gendered practices are discursively taken up and represented or rejected by members of this new community of children of mixed-parentage. The argument I make is that this examination will lead to a conceptualization of how apparently delimiting and constraining discourses might, in fact, be open to a reconstruction that is more positively enhancing. I further argue that while social 'othering' may serve to isolate and marginalize a certain group of mixed-ethnic minorities, hybridity may also lead to an identity of privilege and heightened self-esteem in the same individual according to the accessibility of certain more empowering alternative discourses. In this study while I foreground the examination of ethnic identity, I also explore gender identity, particularly the intersection of ethnicity and gender.

The girls are all the same age and in the same grade at different schools in a geographically broad community. They consider each other to be 'best friends' and have been associated through their foreign parents' network of friends and associations since pre-school or earlier. This study, conducted over the span of their early adolescence (ages 12–15), problematizes how they take up, represent or reject racialized, ethnicized and gendered practices in their daily encounters with others.

What is particularly interesting about this group of mixed-ethnic youths – and what is shown in this book – is that while these girls often struggle to positively maneuver themselves and negotiate their identities into positions of contestation and control over marginalizing discourses that disempower them as 'others' within Japanese society, paradoxically, at other times within alternative more empowering discourses of ethnicity, they also enjoy a celebrated status that they discursively create for themselves. This book shows how these girls come to celebrate their individual mixed-ethnic cultural capital and how, through this construction, they are able to negotiate their identities positively as they come to terms with their constructed hybrid identities of 'Japaneseness', 'whiteness' and 'halfness/doubleness'.

Another main aim of this book is to 'give space to the competing voices of participants' (Baxter, 2003: 72) who might otherwise be silent or silenced and whose stories might otherwise not have been known. This book has a storyline throughout that follows these six girls out of childhood and into the rapid physical and mental/emotional growth years of early adolescence. It analyzes spoken data, collected over several years, during a time when these girls were highly conscious of being in the public gaze and at a time when they were often confronted with issues of acceptance and popularity at their schools. Adolescence is a time of extreme self-consciousness in terms of not only ethnic identity, but also newly emerging gender awareness and gender identity.

There is a pervasive Japanese proverb, which warns of diversity or difference getting squashed:

The nail that sticks up gets hammered down. (*Deru kui wa utareru*)

This proverb implies that those who fail to work hard enough to avoid standing out in Japan either must certainly face being pressured into conforming or, where that is not possible, can expect to face some kind of 'othering' (or bullying)[4] by their peers. While these girls work very hard to conform to Japanese behavioral norms, conforming to the norms of physical appearance is something beyond their agency, as they recurrently attract the stare and notice of others due to their conspicuous 'ethnic' features. Within this context, a major question central to this book arises: how do these girls constitute themselves on the basis of their *physicality*? Within this Japanese proverb, facial and bodily features differentiate people of non-Japanese ethnicities from the mainstream as *'nails that stick up'* (as foreign-looking outsiders who stand out conspicuously). This study explores how the participants work to positively position themselves in the constitution of their hybrid *embodied* identities, which they are unable to *hammer down* (conform, transform) into the physical 'embodiment' of 'Japanese'.

The search for an appropriate term

This book deals with mixed-ethnicity and mixed-ethnic identities in the context of Japan. My long struggle to find an appropriate term to use to refer to participants of this study became a process of elimination. I realized only after I began the study that the term *bicultural*, while applicable, was not specific enough, in that it does not clearly distinguish between bicultural children of two (biological) *Japanese* parents who have lived overseas, with that of *bicultural* girls in this study who have one (biological) *non-Japanese* parent who was raised outside of Japan and one (biological) Japanese parent who was raised in Japan. The term *bilinguals* also does not fit these girls, as not all of them were comfortable or highly proficient in using their minority language; all of them spoke Japanese as their primary language – or one of their primary languages. While in this study all of the participants' non-Japanese parents were 'white' and English speaking, I further resisted the use of the term *biracial* to refer to these girls, partly because of the association of 'race' with the 'black/ white' model of 'racism', which grew out of a particular historical context in the West. Also, the notion of the validity of the concept of 'race' itself has been highly questioned (see the section 'Introduction: Ethnicity, Ethnicism and Racialization' [p. 16]). Rather than using binary categories of *bicultural, biracial, bilingual* or *dual-ethnic*, in this book I was looking for a more neutral, non-binary term that signified a mixing of (uncountable) ethnicities.

At first, I also rejected the use of the concept (within post-colonial theory) of *hybridity* or *hybrid identity* to refer to the girl participants of this study, as it is a very unfamiliar term in Japan and it seemed to convey an unpleasant, non-human connotation. However, in the end, I finally decided to use these terms, particularly when I was referring to the participants' 'hybrid' identities and *not* to them personally as 'hybrid' people. The term *hybridity* – which in its simplest form means *mixing* (Bhabha, 1994) – has been widely used in post-colonial contexts in Europe, North America and Oceania. Within post-colonial theory (e.g. Bhabha, 1990, 1994; Werbner, 1997; Werbner & Modood, 1997; Young, 1995), studies examining hybrid identity have looked at how people have dealt with ambivalent identities caused by a mixing of cultures, races, ethnicity and languages.

While I had been searching for a term that the participants, in referring to themselves, might use, what became apparent was that most of the time these girls did not particularly use *any* specific term to describe themselves. When given examples such at *multiethnic, double, half, Eurasian* and so forth, and then asked to write down what they would prefer to be called in either English or Japanese, all of them wrote down that they just wanted to be called by their given names.

The word *hybrid*, in recent years, has been associated with a variety of notions such as a new kind of energy-efficient *hybrid* car, originally engineered and manufactured in Japan, that simultaneously runs on both gasoline and electricity (or bio-fuel); a better quality of *hybrid* plant created through mixing of lesser strains; a *hybrid* computer operating system that can handle mixed systems; and *hybrid* identities of human beings who inhabit a 'third-space' identity inclusive of – and yet separate from – either the first or second 'spaces' of their two ethnically diverse parents. In all of these *hybrid* notions, there is a connotation of a product coming into being of something different and *better* than the components that make it up. The 'reclaimed' *hybrid* nuance of an upgraded quality, combined with the notion of difference (and in the case of *people*, a connection with the notion of ambivalence), was indeed just the concept that I was looking for to describe the six girl participants of this study. Thus, in the end, I decided to use this term in this book in this positive sense to describe the identity of the participants.

Throughout this book, I also use several other terms to refer to the participants. One such term is *mixed-ethnic*, which I use especially in contexts where I directly refer to the girls themselves. Interchangeably with these other terms, I also use *a child of Japanese and white mixed-parentage* in order to describe these girls more specifically based on their two parents' differing ethnicities.[5] Below, I present several *Japanese* terms, which I also use to refer to these girls.

Japanese terms: Halfness, doubleness, foreignness/otherness

This section briefly looks at the Japanese words for 'foreigner/outsider' (*gaijin* and *gaikokujin*[6]), 'half' (*haafu*) and 'double' (*daburu*). Both of the

Japanese words, *gaijin* and *gaikokujin*, are commonly used today to denote the meaning of 'foreigner' or a person outside of the category of Japanese (an outsider).

The predominant Japanese word in common usage to refer to mixed-ethnic people in Japan today is *'haafu'* (from the English word 'half'). While a *gaijin* is usually thought of as someone born and brought up overseas with an imperfect (or non-fluent) knowledge (or acquisition) of Japanese language and culture, a *'haafu'* person is generally thought of as someone born and raised in Japan of one Japanese parent, often fluent in the Japanese language, knowledgeable of Japanese culture and commonly educated (for at least part of the time) in local schools along with their Japanese peers. However, the mixed-ethnic girls of this study were also frequently constituted as *gaijin* by Japanese people who are often unable to clearly distinguish between mixed-ethnic Japanese and non-Japanese (foreign) people.

While many Japanese people today use the word *haafu* for lack of an alternative Japanese word (without particularly intending to attach a social stigma), many foreign-raised parents of such children have preferred to refrain from using the word *haafu* to refer to their children, as it seems to imply a negative, deficit connotation that constitutes these individuals on the basis of foreignness or *incomplete Japaneseness* (see Kamada, 2005a, 2006a). Within the foreign community in Japan over the last few decades, a rejection and deconstruction of the use of the word *haafu* has led to the spontaneous reconstitution and creation of an alternative word *'daburu'* (derived from the English word 'double'), implying an additive nuance (see the section 'The "Momotarou Paradigm": The *Oni* (Beast) as Foreign "Other"' [p. 36]).

Participants and the Research Site of Japan

This section looks at the various reasons behind the selection of particular participants and the research site, and explains why I felt a network of adolescent girls residing in Japan with Japanese and 'white-foreign' mixed-parentage would represent a fruitful epistemological site in which to study *hybrid* and gendered identities.

A focus on Japan and on children of Japanese and 'White' mixed-parentage

A major reason for selecting Japan and this group of participants relates to my own personal involvement and membership in this group.

As mentioned above, I am a 'white-foreign' American woman who has been living continuously in Japan for the latter half of my life. Since shortly after the birth of our son, our family has been residing in a rural region of northern Japan where we have sometimes felt like pioneers in a frontier, where foreigners, international marriages and mixed-ethnic Japanese children are still rare. My son was in the lower grades of elementary school when I began this study.

In spite of my rural residency, I have been very active in multilingual and multicultural research and discussion within a loosely connected Japanese and English-speaking (bilingual) community of 'foreigners' throughout Japan, many of whom have mixed-ethnic children. For several decades, I have been addressing the issues relevant to myself, my family (including my own mixed-ethnic son) and this foreign community. We have been concerned with questions of ethnic social discourses, languages and identities affecting our children who have been raised in Japan by one Japanese parent and one non-Japanese English-speaking parent.

Although it is partially for these personal reasons that I have chosen to investigate children of this specific mix of ethnicities who may not be the most representative or the largest group of mixed-ethnic children in Japan, this does not mean that I particularly wish to exclude children of other mixed-ethnicities in Japan from this discussion. It is my hope that this research will not only have significance beyond Japan, but will also locally enhance the understanding of Japanese people, particularly making them aware of the dominant discourses of ethnicity in Japan and their influence on the constitution of the identities of all mixes of ethnicities of peoples living among them. I also hope to inform members of the other various ethnic communities there.

My personal involvement with Japan is not the only reason why Japan makes an interesting context in which to study hybrid identity. Japan is only recently beginning to be examined as a multiethnic culture where a prevailing hegemonic view of Japan as a monoracial, monocultural, monolingual society dominates and impacts social practice throughout Japanese politics, education and the media. Compared with highly multiethnic and multicultural societies such as the USA and Britain, non-Japanese and mixed-ethnic individuals are still relatively rare in Japan. It is for this reason that the struggle for mixed-ethnic adolescents to be individually accepted and recognized equally as Japanese citizens, permanent residents, short-term or ambiguous residents by members of the society where they reside becomes an extremely timely topic in the context of Japan. While British and North American studies have paved the way for research into ethnic identity and social struggle (e.g. Heller, 1999, 2001; Katz, 1996;

Norton, 2000; Wetherell & Potter, 1992), it is also important to explore hybrid identity based on the specific characteristics and context of Japan.

Children attending Japanese schools

While studies have looked at hybrid identity construction and bilinguality in the context of immersion or international schools in North America (e.g. Cummins, 1991; Heller, 1999, 2001), Japan (e.g. Bostwick, 1999, 2001; Greer, 2001, 2003) and elsewhere (e.g. Skutnabb-Kangas, 1981, 1999), this study fills a gap by looking at the construction of identity of children of mixed-parentage who attend regular Japanese schools. I was interested in examining children whose families had made a conscious decision to raise their children by assimilating and integrating them into Japanese society in a relatively permanent manner by electing to send them to regular local Japanese schools in spite of the availability of international schools in their community (where such attendees tend to seek higher education overseas and often also future employment and residence).

By attending Japanese schools (both private and state), these girls are *not* afforded the protected security available to mixed-ethnic children attending international schools where 'ethnic difference' is the norm. The girl participants of this study nearly always use Japanese to converse among themselves, and unlike children attending international schools, who often code-switch (Greer, 2001, 2003), they rarely switch into English when conversing among themselves.

Girls and adolescents

Drawing on research conducted in gender and feminist studies (e.g. Bloustien, 2001; Bucholtz, 1999; Coates, 1999; Litosseliti & Sunderland, 2002; Sunderland, 2004, 2006), I felt that examining the talk of girl participants would offer at least as good a picture, if not better, of gender construction as that of boys, or of boys and girls together. I felt that girls, when gathered together with their friends, would be more expressive and interactive and would carry the talk beyond my specific questions than boys. I wanted to create an atmosphere where the participant friends would feel comfortable to express themselves freely. In order to utilize a network of friends, this necessitated selection of a single-sex group. Including me, a network of females seemed the most obvious selection.[7]

I selected *adolescent* girls, commencing from their pre- or early adolescence. This seemed to be an under-investigated group that could offer tremendous insight into the process of identity construction, especially when observed over time, as the shift from childhood into adulthood is a time of extreme change in terms of both physical and mental maturation (Coates, 1999; Walton *et al.*, 2002). I felt that late-adolescent children or adults would not exhibit such rapid changes over the same duration of time. Compared with children of elementary school age or younger, I thought that early adolescents would have a better grasp of language as a means to articulate and express themselves and would be more sophisticated language users who used language to achieve various discursive functions over younger children. It is precisely the use of discursive functions that I intended to investigate.

Central Questions

This study takes up three central questions, which examine (1) tensions and dilemmas of hybridity, (2) celebration of hybridity and (3) intersection of hybridity and gender (at the site of the body). These three questions and their sub-questions are explained in detail below.

Concerning *dilemmas of* hybridity, as mentioned above, a pervasive Japanese proverb warns that those who fail to work hard enough to avoid being *the nail that sticks up* (standing out or being different) in Japan either must certainly face being hammered into conformity or, where that is not possible, will leave themselves open to some kind of 'othering' by their peers. Within this context, we might ask how these mixed-ethnic girls 'take control of' and negotiate this ethnic *othering* in Japan. Related to this, we might also ask *how* these girls discursively construct their own categories of hybridity for themselves, for example by taking up, contesting, or (re)constituting this ethnic 'othering'. As well, we might also ask how and in what contexts they constitute their Japaneseness or their Whiteness.

I wanted to consider whether mixed-ethnic girls in Japan identified their ethnic selves in contradictory ways, and if so, in what ways. Extending the question of *how* participants deal with these dilemmas of othering, I also wanted to examine the specific discursive tools that these mixed-ethnic girls in Japan might use to give accounts and represent themselves in relation to their ethnicity. I wanted to explore an as-yet under-examined model of ethnic identity in the context of Japan, a country that has not been thought of as multiethnic until recently. In this context, as mentioned above, it is the 'whites' and 'mixed-whites' (among others) who are racialized as marginal. So to summarize, the first central question is

(1)   Are there any tensions or dilemmas in the ways children (adolescent girls) of Japanese and 'white' mixed-parentage in Japan identify themselves in terms of their ethnicity?

If so, what are they and how do these girls constitute themselves?

Next, unlike the majority of mixed-ethnic peoples represented in the post-colonial model in Europe, these girls have *two* (socially constructed) *dominant* heritages in their make-up: their indigenous Japanese heritage and their 'white', Western [super-power nation] heritage. They speak the indigenous Japanese majority language as their first language while also claiming access to the high-status English minority language, native to one of their parents. They have all been educated in local Japanese schools. Along with this, through their foreign-born parent, they have a world available to them beyond Japan, which provides them with access to greater choices, information and connections (including family) overseas, not generally accessible to their Japanese peers. They have two nationalities and two passports.[8] I wanted to explore if this notion of *double dominance* was a feature discursively constructed and enjoyed by these girls or not. If it was, I wanted to investigate *how* girls of this study might discursively create cultural, symbolic and linguistic capital of bilinguality and biliteracy, along with other forms of economic and social capital. In summary, the second central question (and sub-question) is posed as follows:

(2)   How, if at all, do children (adolescent girls) of Japanese and 'white' mixed-parentage in Japan *celebrate* their ethnicity?
       How, if at all, do they construct ethnic (and gendered) cultural, symbolic, linguistic and social capital for themselves on the basis of their hybrid identities?

Finally, adolescence is a time of extreme self-consciousness in terms of not only ethnic identity but also newly emerging gender awareness and gender identity (Orenstein, 1994). In examining the ethnic identities of these girls, the question arises as to how these girls connect their gender identities with their ethnic identities? Related to this 'ethno-gendered' intersection of gender and ethnicity is the question of how these girls constitute themselves on the basis of their *physicality*? With facial and bodily features setting them apart from the mainstream as '*sticking-up nails*', how do they discursively work to positively position themselves in the constitution of their mixed-ethnic *embodied* identities that they are often unable to *hammer down* into the physical form of 'Japanese'.

In assessing hybrid identity, I wanted to consider if and how these girls identified themselves based on their physical appearance – their 'lived-body-selves' (Thapan, 1997a) – what I refer to as their *ethnic embodiment*.

I wanted to examine how they positioned themselves and performed their hybrid identities on the basis of their constituted appearance. I felt that this question of embodiment (and gender identity) analyzed within a feminist poststructuralist discourse analysis (FPDA) framework might significantly contribute to a novel way of also examining ethnic identity. In summary, the third central question asks:

(3)   How, if at all, do children (adolescent girls) of Japanese and 'white' mixed-parentage in Japan discursively identify themselves in terms of their positioning and performances based on their *gendered* and *ethnic embodiment* (their ethnicized body selves)?

Structure of this Book

This book is comprised of eight chapters, of which the first three provide background to the study and data collection. The four middle chapters, Chapters 4–7, provide detailed analysis of various data extracts in problematizing the main issues and the central questions of this book. The final chapter summarizes and concludes the book. An explanation of Chapters 2–8 is outlined in more detail below.

Chapter 2 (*Examining Discourses of 'Otherness' in Japan within a Multi-perspective Discourse Analysis Approach*) locates this study within a multi-perspective social constructionist discourse analytic framework. This chapter outlines the theoretical and methodological applications of post-structuralist discourse analysis (PDA), FPDA and discursive psychology (DP). Studies of race and ethnicity are examined. Racial superiority discourses and the notion of 'othering' in Western societies are compared with Japan. Particular social discourses in the context of Japan presented in this study are discussed here. Finally, a contemporary Japanese text example is analyzed, illustrating how these discourses actually occur in Japan.

Chapter 3 (*The Participants and the Data Collection*) describes the six participants in detail and outlines the methods used for data collection and the process of analysis of the data. This chapter further addresses the connection between the theoretical framework and the selection of particular data in order to answer the central questions. Issues of ethics and reflexivity are also addressed here.

The data analysis and the significant findings from the analysis addressing the central questions are discussed in Chapters 4–7.

Chapter 4 (*Negotiating Identities*) problematizes the issue of 'othering' in an endeavor to explore how the girls take up, negotiate, contest and (re)constitute ethnic 'othering' by people in their world. This chapter also looks at ethnic identification through the discursive tensions and dilemmas of intersecting discourses that the participants draw on.

Chapter 5 (*Claiming Good Difference; Rejecting Bad Difference*) examines how the girls deconstruct the notion of difference as *bad* and position themselves within alternative discourses in which 'difference' or diversity is constituted positively as *good*.

Chapter 6 (*Celebration of Cultural, Symbolic, Linguistic and Social Capital*) looks at and problematizes how these girls celebrate their ethnicities through their construction of cultural capital.

Chapter 7 (*Discursive 'Embodied' Identities of Ethnicity and Gender*) focuses on the discursive intersection of ethnicity and gender. How these girls identify their hybrid embodied identities through their positioning and performances within discourses of ethnicity and gender at the site of the body is explored.

Chapter 8 (*Discursive Construction of Hybrid Identity in Japan: Where has it Taken Us?*) concludes the book by re-examining the major analytical problems of this study. This chapter also summarizes the discursive changes that these girls undergo over the several-year time-span of the study as they grow out of childhood into adolescence and develop a greater ability to draw on a wider range of alternative discourses. How this work contributes to our knowledge of hybrid identity is addressed here. Finally, thoughts for change and future directions conclude the book.

Summary

In this chapter, I have discussed the catalyst for undertaking the study, emphasizing the importance and interest in the topic. In order to situate this study within the context of Japan, the terminology that I selected for use throughout the book to signify ethnic and racial 'otherness' and 'othering' for both English and Japanese words was introduced. Next, I presented an overview of the reasons behind the selection of adolescent girls of Japanese and 'white-foreign' mixed-parentage who were attending Japanese schools. The research framework and the central questions to be explored in this book were then outlined: tensions and dilemmas of hybridity, celebration of hybridity and intersection of 'embodied' ethnicity and gender at the site of the body. Finally, the structure of the book was laid out, chapter by chapter.

In the next chapter, I provide further background for this study by reviewing studies on the social construction of 'otherness'. I introduce various discourses of ethnicity and gender appearing as linguistic traces in participants' speech and within the epistemological research site of western Japan. Finally, I illustrate how these ethnic discourses actually occur by examining the text of a police report in Japan calling for Japanese citizenry to report 'suspicious-looking' foreigners.

Notes

1. The BSIG is a sub-group of the Japan Association for Language Teaching (JALT). JALT is an academic organization in Japan with some 3000 members who are mostly English-speaking foreigners residing in locations all over Japan or are Japanese teachers of English, many of whom have children of international marriages. The BSIG is comprised mostly of a community of over 200 English teachers in Japan who are also researchers and parents making up a network of assistance, support and research in the acquisition of bi-/multilingualism of multicultural and mixed-ethnic children (see <www. bsig.org/>). I have been a member of this e-list and a founding member of the BSIG since its inception (1990). I have also been an officer in the BSIG for nearly as long.

2. The resulting BSIG monograph, entitled *Bullying in Japanese Schools: International Perspectives* (Gillis-Furutaka, 1999), was very successful and sold extremely well at its debut at the 1999 International JALT Conference in Shizuoka, Japan (see <www.bsig.org/monograph/mon7.html>).

3. Kanno (2004) examined how the educational system in Japan is overdue in addressing language minority children. She looked at the identities of a group of language minority children who comprised an exceptionally high ratio of 40% of the student population of a particular elementary school in Japan. The staff tended to blame these students and their home lifestyles for their failure to fit their identities into the existing school structure. Kanno (2008) also explored the unequal access to bilingual education in Japan, concluding that schools contribute to linguistic stratification of bilingual students of differing economic classes. Privileged students are nurtured to participate in the elite global community, whereas underprivileged students (at other schools) are nurtured to participate in an impoverished community. (For more on Kanno, see also Kamada, 2006b.)

4. There appears to be a very close link in Japan between 'othering' and bullying in the context of Japan (see Gillis-Furutaka, 1999).

5. In other publications, I have also used the term *multiethnic* to refer to this group of participants (see Kamada, 2004, 2005a, 2005b, 2006a, 2008).

6. Another Japanese honorific term of respect used to refer to a foreigner is *gaikoku no kata*, which literally means 'a person from a foreign country'. This usage appeared in only one instance in the data, where it was used to purposely express sarcasm and emphasis (see Extract 4.4).

7. To test some of these notions and compare results, I also conducted one semi-structured interview with two adolescent boys of Japanese and 'white' mixed-parentage (see Kamada, 2009). I later decided not to use the data and analysis for this book, not because it was not rich and interesting, but because of space limitations (see the sections 'Boys' data' and 'Implications for Future Research')

8. Japanese law allows Japanese nationals to possess two passports (dual nationality) only up until age 22, when they are expected to choose one and abandon the other. Recently, a proposal has been submitted to a governmental panel calling for the Nationality Law to be revised to allow offspring of mixed-parentage with one Japanese parent to possess dual nationality.

Chapter 2

Examining Discourses of 'Otherness' in Japan within a Multiperspective Discourse Analysis Approach

Introduction: Ethnicity, Ethnicism and Racialization

This chapter focuses on the theoretical and methodological foundations upon which this study is based. Selected in order to analyze how gender and ethnic identity are performed in living practice among mixed-ethnic girls in Japan, I show how these theoretical notions are linked with specific dominant and alternative racial, ethnic and gender discourses occurring in the context of Japan. Before commencing with this discussion, I begin, first of all, with a discussion of the terms *ethnicity* and *race*.

I conceptualize *ethnicity* as an identifying affiliation with a group of people (usually with a name attached) that an individual assumes within a certain context. Along with a shared past history, ethnic links of commonality might also include other aspects of personal heritage and identification such as shared: language, religion, worldview, nationality, family, birthplace or historical place of origin. Shared ethnicity may also include similar physical features, hair color and texture, and skin color. However, not all of these conditions need to necessarily coincide together for a person to associate oneself with a particular ethnicity. At any moment one's ethnic affiliation may change as the individual may choose to foreground or background their various ethnic affiliations and subjective positions depending on context and interactions with others. Ethnicity, as with other aspects of personal identity (such as gender, social class, sexual orientation) is just part of one's identity making up a person's multiplicity of selves.

Many people think of *ethnicity* as being synonymous with *race* or as a 'euphemism' for race (Ratcliffe, 1994); however, differences between the two concepts have also been clarified. 'Highly visible markers' such as skin color and facial features can become associated with labels that sustain 'ethnicity' (Aguirre & Turner, 2001). It is, however, particularly *the notion of race* that has historically been connected with discourses of 'biologically inherited traits' such as skin color and physical features whereas 'ethnicity' has generally been used to refer to a cultural group 'with an actual or commonly perceived shared ancestry, with language markers, and with national or regional origin' (Fenton, 1999: 4). The connection of *race* with slavery and colonial control, along with the ideology of 'racial' differences, has commonly come to be associated with the black–white binary. The argument of 'race' as a scientific discourse to categorize people has been rejected as an erroneous pseudo-science (e.g. Fenton, 1999; Ratcliffe, 1994; Young, 2000) in that DNA analyses have shown evidence of more genetic variation *within* so-called 'racial' groups than *between* them. Nonetheless, *racism* and the process of *racialization* continue to be reproduced in societies.

The discursive reproduction of racism among members of the white elite and their use of commonsense rhetoric to talk about minority groups has shed light on how racism gets discursively reproduced in people's everyday talk (e.g. van Dijk, 1987, 1993; Wetherell & Potter, 1992). In contrast to this examination of the rhetoric of people in powerful positions, I was interested in exploring the *effects* of racism by looking at identities and subjectivities of *marginalized 'others'*. I use the notion of racialization (or racism) to include ethnicism as a social practice (see Aguirre & Turner, 2001; van Dijk, 1987). While having some parallels with Western postcolonialism, Japan, situated in a different historical context as both an Asian 'former colonial power' and as 'a seven-year occupied country', offers a novel site to investigate racialization and ethnicism, where it is the 'whites'[1] who are racialized and 'othered'. In the context of this study, situated in Japan, the category of 'white' was found to often correspond with other ethnic group features such as language, place of birth, religion or worldview and so forth. Thus in this book, when I refer to the category of 'white', I am assigning an ethnicity rather than a race.

The next section briefly examines the poststructuralist movement, which provides the ideological framework for the discourse analysis approaches that I have selected in order to examine ethnic identity.

From Structuralism to Poststructuralism

The theoretical framework of this study comes out of the poststructuralist response to the notion of the fixed nature of 'structures' or 'truths'.

For the poststructuralist, all 'structure' is only temporarily fixed within certain contexts and environments, where structures can always be challenged and transformed depending on the context. The structuralist Marxist, Louis Althusser (1918–1990), had established how our true relationships in the world and our representations of reality are distorted by imaginary relationships. These 'realities' are controlled by the ideology and language of such institutions as the police, schools, the media and churches. Althusser (1971) argued that ideology functions for individuals through his notion of *interpellation*, explained as the process where people become 'transformed' as *subjects* through a process of being 'hailed' by someone. He demonstrated this in his famous example of a police hailing someone, 'Hey, you there!' (Althusser, 1971: 174). In a person's response to being hailed, that person is *interpellated* as an ideologically constituted subject who becomes positioned in the hailing.

But there are problems with Althusser's model when we try to address the notion of people's *inability* to resist being interpellated into subject positions. Foucault (1972, 1979, 1980a, 1980b), a student of Althusser, attended to this, by incorporating the notion of *agency* into the theory of subjectivity. Foucault (1972) also explored how 'reality' or 'truth' is constructed, ascribed power and taken up within societies (and also contested) through the construction of knowledge by the means of language use. Power and knowledge are joined together in discourse. Power gives form to the production of 'knowledge' and 'truth', which can never be accessed in an absolute form, as they are only representations.

Laclau and Mouffe (1985) also contributed to poststructuralist thought in their modification of Althusser's theory. The subject is not just positioned by a single discourse, but comes under the influence of various, different and often *competing discourses* simultaneously (Laclau & Mouff, 1985). When opposing ideologies come into conflict (such as a 'discourse of homogeneity' and a 'discourse of diversity'), this struggle is said to be temporarily resolved by *hegemonic interventions* in which the more powerful discourse comes to dominate (Laclau & Mouffe, 1985). It will maintain its hegemonic position until other opposing discourses emerge to challenge and overtake it.

A Multiperspective Approach

A poststructuralist framework allows for *multiple perspectives* to be heard alongside one another. This *multiperspectivism* fits well with the basic constructionist view of 'perspectivism' in bringing together several different theories and methods in creating different forms of knowledge (Phillips & Jorgensen, 2002). Here, I mainly draw on the multiperspective approaches of *poststructuralist discourse analysis* (which includes *feminist poststructuralist discourse analysis*) and *discursive psychology*[2] and to some extent *critical discourse analysis* (hereafter, PDA, FPDA or (F)PDA, DP and CDA, respectively).

One of the features that attracted me to FPDA is its versatility as a multiperspective approach that works 'supplementarily' with other methods by promoting a 'plurality of versions' heard alongside one another (Baxter, 2003). Rather than taking the stance that one discourse analysis method is 'better' than another, FPDA allows for an interplay of different perspectives (Baxter, 2002a, 2002b). FPDA, CDA and the integrative trajectory of DP (e.g. Edley & Wetherell, 1997, 2008) all promote a synthetic approach that accommodates and integrates both Foucauldian macro-social discourse analysis along with a more fine-grained linguistic analysis of data. These approaches analyze what people are discursively *doing* in their talk, their actions, interactions and other forms of semiosis such as gestures and eye movement.

While having more similarity to CDA than other approaches, FPDA differs from CDA in several major aspects (Baxter, 2008). Firstly, FPDA has an epistemological, 'transformative' agenda rather than a critical/ emancipatory agenda in which it is less interested in exposing unequal relationships and injustices. FPDA is more interested in understanding complex and shifting power relationships and identities within and across given contexts. Whereas CDA often examines oppositional power relationships, FPDA gives space to a range of different perspectives. Furthermore, FPDA differs from CDA in that it is *anti-materialist* in tendency in that speakers are seen as only existing inside of discourses, 'where one discourse is always negotiated, challenged, evolved and adjusted through the lens of other discourses' (Baxter, 2008: 248).

Within FPDA, subject positions offered by different discourses are often competing, sometimes contradictory, usually provisional and constantly shifting so that few individuals are uniformly powerful or powerless (Baxter, 2008). Adolescents can be particularly 'unfixed' in this respect, in their exploration and experimentation with different subject positions and identities (e.g. Bloustien, 2001; Coates, 1999; Eckert, 2000). While adolescents explore and experiment with a range of subject positions and identities, they at the same time often find themselves being positioned in fairly rigid ways by dominant cultural discourses. Coates (1999) found in her longitudinal study of the talk of teenage girls (from ages 12 to 15) that as girls mature, their talk begins to take on a wider range of voices and discourses, which constrain, rather than liberate them as these discourses come into conflict.

In this study, I mainly draw on the two approaches of FPDA and DP as there are many common features particularly evident between these two frameworks, aside from the promotion of multiperspectivism. These commonalities are taken up in the following section.

Commonalities of FPDA and DP

This section looks at commonalities in the two approaches of FPDA and DP and discusses how these frameworks are combined in this study.

Constructionism and deconstructionism

Both FPDA and DP (also CDA) are framed in *constructionism*, which views any description of the world as possible and as having the possibility of being altered or countered with other descriptions (Gergen, 1985, 2001). As an epistemology, constructionism diverges from Western Modernism where knowledge was taken to be reflections of the world in the brain, like a mirror. The constructionist view of the world is the opposite as Gergen illustrates below:

> The world does not produce our concepts; rather our concepts help us organize the world in various ways. The botanist, landscaper and real estate agent see my yard differently because they each approach the scene with different mental categories. (Gergen, 1999: 11)

Constructionism rejects any claim to an 'absolute truth or knowledge', as no claim can be neutral and free of its historical and social context. Thus constructionists employ reflexivity upon themselves in their own analysis and construction of events. Drawing on constructionism within both FPDA and DP, my purpose in this study was *not* to try to understand the participant girls' 'true' nature or 'what really happened', but rather to examine how they talk about themselves and construct versions of reality, in what situations and for what functions (see Wetherell *et al.*, 2001a, 2001b).

I was interested in examining the 'commonsense vocabularies and resources' (Potter & Wetherell, 1987: 57) that the girls use in ordinary speech to explain their 'realities' of their worlds. These versions of reality are not always 'neutral descriptions' but serve functions such as blaming, using excuses, praising, condemning, accounting for error and claiming of 'the truth'. DP looks at how people rhetorically give accounts and use discourse by drawing on commonsense notions in order to construct their realities, referred to as *interpretive repertoires*. DP also examines how people often draw on two conflicting repertoires (*ideological dilemmas*) in their speech (see Billig, 1987/1996, 1991, 1997; Billig *et al.*, 1988), where on the one hand they display prejudiced repertoires, while simultaneously employing other rhetoric to appear not prejudiced (Wetherell & Potter, 1992). The purpose is not to focus on the 'attitude-system' of speakers; rather, it is important to highlight 'how the themes of ideology are instantiated in ordinary talk' and how people carry the 'ideological history of discursive themes' into the present (Billig, 2001: 218), in order to decode how these practices are being applied to the present.

DP has developed many analytical tools and models useful in a combined micro-discourse analysis approach, such as the application of the *discursive action model* (Horton-Salway, 2001; Potter, 2003; Potter & Mulkay, 1985). This model has three components to it: *action* (what people do with language – how actions are accomplished and how people attribute causes to events); *fact and interest* ('[which examines] how people construct accounts in a way that makes them appear solid and factual, how they attend to other people's's accounts as motivated by self-interest' [Horton-Salway, 2001: 155]); and *accountability* (actions such as blaming, denying, placing responsibility, refuting and exonerating).

Constructionism draws on Bakhtin's (1984) notion of *double-voicing* and *the utterance* in which people construct their meanings of 'reality' by taking up voices in the present as they draw on historically constructed discourses and repertoires already in the world. Double-voicing refers to a single discourse in which two voices appear, which have two intentions. The use of someone else's discourse comes to serve one's own purpose as they adapt it into their own speech (Bakhtin, 1984). While every utterance that is spoken is novel, at the same time utterances draw on cultural and historical ideologies, which are established commonsense 'natural' ways of thinking and behaving in a society (Billig, 2001). These ideologies, which have come to be viewed as ordinary and taken for granted, include unequal treatment of its members and have long been a part of language, discourse and consciousness of society.

Both DP and FPDA have an interest in *deconstructive criticism* based on theories of Derrida (1973, 1976, 1978). Derrida's notion of *deconstructionism*, which is the basic foundation of discourse analysis, tries to show how the structures formed in discourse, which we take as general 'truths', are politically produced and distributed by people with privileged access to power and control. By pulling apart and *deconstructing* the 'commonsense' structures, the political processes that hold them together can be revealed – for example, of unequal hierarchical oppositions such as 'man and wife'; or constructions of associations, such as the connection of a certain 'race' of people with *laziness*, or of the connection of foreigners with the increase in heinous crime.

Deconstructionism has a special place in FPDA in that it allows a new way of interpreting texts by offering 'a method of questioning and decentering the hierarchical oppositions that underpin gender, race and class oppression' (Baxter, 2003: 24). To *deconstruct* a fixed representation or term is to scrutinize, challenge and 'problematize' it. Along with a *deconstructionist* approach, *self-reflexivity* and selecting a specific *feminist focus* are the two other central principles of FPDA (Baxter, 2003).

The following section examines how both approaches of FPDA and DP analyze identities in terms of how people *subjectively position* themselves.

Subjectivity and the discursive subject positioning of selves

Another important analytical concept that I utilize within both (F)PDA and DP is the notion of *subjectivity* and the taking up of a *subject positions* (also *positioning*). Subject positions are unfixed, constantly shifting identities taken up by people in their talk or 'ways of being'. These positions that people create for themselves and others may be those historically available or they may be newly created in their talk. In this study, it is of less importance as to *which* identity is constructed and taken up in positioning by the participant girls, than that of *how, why* and in *what contexts* the girls construct their identities.

The term 'identity' in cognitive psychology has been reconceptualized as *subjectivity* (e.g. Mama, 1995; Norton, 2000; Weedon, 1987). Similarly, the unfixed concept of 'positioning' has been used to replace the static concept of 'role' in social psychology (e.g. Davies & Harré, 2001; Hollway, 2001). Throughout this book, I use the notion of *subjectivity* and *position(ing)* to include a range of unfixed, contextually contingent shifting identities. Once people take up certain positions, they come to see the world from that viewpoint. When people interact, they do so based on their present positioning within a certain context, which is constituted by their entire history 'as a subjective being' composed of all of their numerous past positions within various discourses (Davies & Harré, 2001). The multiplicities of selves include both interactive (constitutive) positioning in which a person can be positioned by another and also the exercise of personal choice or agency in which a person may position oneself (Davies & Harré, 2001).

The next section looks at the overlap in the frameworks of FPDA and DP in the way that they both provide a venue for addressing the concerns and agendas of the marginalized and often silenced 'other' in society.

Examining gender and other political perspectives

While both (F)PDA and DP resist determinism and 'grand narratives', they both allow a space for research that takes a particular political perspective. PDA is interested in fluctuating power and fluctuating positioning and focuses on how people are *multiply* positioned, or multiply position themselves or others, in interconnected, interwoven and often competing, social discourses (Baxter, 2002a, 2002b) (see also Sunderland & Litosseliti, 2002). Later, Baxter reformulated PDA 'to incorporate an explicit feminist focus' (Baxter, 2002a: 840) to which the word 'feminist' (FPDA) was added. The FPDA focus is to uncover the gender discourses that emerge within the discursive practices of the speakers and examine ways in which women or girls come to be positioned as not only powerless, weak and marginalized at times, but also powerful and in control at other times. It is concerned with the analysis of 'gender as a site of struggle' (Baxter, 2003) and highlights the often silenced voices of women and girls. Other perspectives may also be taken up in FPDA along with feminist concerns.[3]

While DP does not necessarily champion feminism, it can and sometimes does (e.g. Edley, 2001; Edley & Wetherell, 1996, 1999; Kamada, 2008; Wetherell & Edley, 1998). Within a DP approach, Edley (2001) examined how *masculinity* is constantly done or 'accomplished' through discursive interactions and negotiations with others. Edley's (2001) study showed how 'lived' ideologies or the commonsense notions or 'wisdoms' of culture can be very contradictory and competing in message by revealing the 'ideological dilemmas' in people's talk.

Through a process of examining the characteristics and social practices associated with relevant discourses, and the ways in which they are taken up or rejected in specific contexts, FPDA directs the focus on women and girls away from the 'second wave feminist perspective' as *powerless victims* and instead views them 'as *potentially powerful* in terms of their multiple positioning within different discourses' (Baxter, 2003: 41, my italics). In this study, I have taken FPDA a step further to also include the *ethnically* marginalized and racialized 'other' who is likewise sometimes seen as a powerless victim, but at other times as potentially empowered.

The next section examines the Foucauldian notion of how *discourses* inform the ways in which people position themselves in their day-to-day interactions with others and how they represent the world from particular perspectives within both FPDA and DP.

Discourses and the discursive construction of identity

I begin this section by clarifying a distinction between the use of the term *discourse* (such as spoken language) and the (sometimes) plural term *discourses* (such as social discourses). I draw on Fairclough's (2003) definition of *discourses* as a form of social practice and as perspectives or ways of representing processes, relations and structures of the world including thoughts and beliefs. Fairclough noted that the singular term *discourse* '(in what is widely called "discourse analysis") signals the particular view of language in use' (Fairclough, 2003: 3) such as language expressed through people's talk, writings, drawings, photographs and other semiotic forms of meaning making. The term *discourses* (or social discourses) refers to broad, macro-ideological concepts, which Fairclough illustrated as 'particular "discourses" such as the "Third Way" political discourse of New Labour' (Fairclough, 2003: 4) (see also Fairclough, 2000).

The notion of the *discursive construction* of (some kind of) identity refers to the position that individuals or institutions assume in the development (or contestation) of ideologies that they construct (or deconstruct). They do this as they draw on *discourses* that they express through the means of their *discourse* (their talk, writings, body movements). Just as the relationships between *discourses* compete, conflict and dominate one another, so do relationships between people (Fairclough, 1999, 2003). People may also choose to contest, alter or question already existing discourses or they may create new repertoires or discourses to (re)constitute themselves in a novel manner that may herald change.

FPDA, DP and CDA all examine language (or discourse) as a means to understand how people represent the world in their talk, their written texts and other forms of semiotic meaning making – often from particular perspectives. While DP uses the specific terminology of 'interpretive repertoires' and 'ideological dilemmas', this is not unlike 'discourses' as used in FPDA and CDA. *Interpretative repertoires* have been defined as 'basically a lexicon or register of terms and metaphors drawn upon to characterize and evaluate actions and events' (Potter & Wetherell, 1987: 138). Edley (2001), who uses an integrative macro-Foucaldian and micro-analytic approach to discourse analysis within DP, defines the very close the relationship between the terminologies of *discourses* and *repertoires*.

Both concepts invoke the idea of repositories of meaning; that is, distinctive ways of talking about objects and events in the world ... both ... see this fact as having the same major implication; namely, that in becoming native speakers, people are enticed or encultured into particular, even partial, ways of understanding the world. In short, they are committed or tied to the concept of ideology. (Edley, 2001: 202)

Baxter suggests that 'what counts as discourse' can be determined by paying attention to both a *synchronic* 'detailed, micro-analysis of stretches of text' (Baxter, 2008: 251) and a *diachronic* (ethnographic) analysis over a long period of time where patterns and changes can be observed in the context of certain social groups (see the section 'Research Plan' [p. 56]). Baxter's (2003) four-point framework for *locating discourses* in particular contexts provides a useful framework for identifying discourses affecting a particular epistemological site. Analysts should search for: words repeatedly used by the participant; commonly emerging themes; links apparent in the interactions between participants; and the contradictions apparent in their interactions (Baxter, 2003: 138).

With this as a guide, I have identified several *dominant* and *alternative* macro-level discourses (or repertoires) of ethnicity in Japan appearing in the dataset. These are explained in the sections following.

Discourses and Repertoires of Ethnicity in Japan

The discussion above established the interchangeability of the notion of 'repertoires' within DP and 'discourses' within FDPA and CDA in representing commonsense ideological notions. Following Edley, I use the terms *discourses* and *(interpretive) repertoires* interchangeably, in that they are both used to signify similar worldview perspectives. In this book, for the sake of simplicity, for the most part, I will refer to these ideologies or social practices as *discourses* rather than *repertoires* (see Tables 2.1 and 2.2).

Sunderland (2004) argued that anyone can identify and name a discourse after a bit of analytic work, although she also emphasized that reflexivity is important in documenting discourses. From a constructionist viewpoint, names of discourses are arbitrary, unfixed and unclosed *interpretations* and hence are always 'provisional' or 'contingent'.

As introduced in the section above, in this study, diachronic (ethnographic) and synchronic (micro-analytic) methods were used together to identify a range of provisional discourses in the data of the girls by observing them, their families, their community and their spoken data over a long period of time. Through this process of discourse identification,

Table 2.1 Dominant discourses of ethnicity in Japan and examples manifested in speech

Dominant discourses of ethnicity in Japan	*Dominant discourses of ethnicity manifested in speech in Japan*
'A discourse of homogeneity' denies ethnic diversity in Japan. 'Japaneseness' is conflated with nationality, race, ethnicity and language	'Japan is a homogeneous country/society' 'Japan is a monolingual country/society'
'A discourse of conformity' promotes the disagreeableness of standing out as different. People must work hard to *perform* or *appear* within norms, or expect to be 'hammered down' into conformity	'The nail that sticks up gets hammered down' (a Japanese proverb)
'A discourse of *gaijin* otherness' denies that people with non-Japanese features could be Japanese citizens or that they could understand Japanese customs, language or behavior	'*Gaijin* are not Japanese (citizens, 'race', ethnicity)' '*Gaijin* cannot speak Japanese' '*Gaijin* speak English' '*Gaijin* cannot use chopsticks'
'A discourse of (hybrid) halfness' is a deficit, subtractive discourse which constitutes mixed-ethnicity as incomplete Japaneseness	'She/he (person of Japanese and white mixed-parentage) is *haafu* (half)'

Source: Adapted from Kamada (2008) with permission from Palgrave MacMillan.

I have provisionally identified and arbitrarily named seven discourses of ethnicity in the girls' ethnographic site and in their data (Kamada, 2005a, 2008). They are as follows:

- a discourse of homogeneity;
- a discourse of conformity;
- a discourse of *gaijin* (foreign) otherness;
- a discourse of halfness;
- a discourse of diversity;
- a discourse of interculturalism;
- a discourse of doubleness.

Along with these discourses, I have also identified two ethno-gendered discourses in their data:

- a discourse of foreign attractiveness;
- a discourse of foreign grotesqueness.

Table 2.2 Alternative discourses of ethnicity in Japan and examples manifested in speech

Alternative discourses of ethnicity in Japan	Alternative discourses of ethnicity manifested in speech in Japan
'A discourse of diversity' recognizes and allows for the positive constitution of *difference* as enhancing and valuable	'Japan is a multiethnic, multilingual, multicultural society'
'A discourse of interculturalism' promotes the value of intercultural savvy as cultural capital: ability to speak a foreign language, having access to global information; being able to use the Internet in other languages; having connections, relatives or close friends overseas	'People are different than they appear'
'A discourse of (hybrid) doubleness' is a deconstruction of the deficit notion of 'halfness' created by parents in order to offer their mixed-ethnic children a more empowering discourse of ethnicity	'She/he (person of Japanese and white mixed-parentage) is *daburu* (double)'

Source: Adapted from Kamada (2008) with permission from Palgrave MacMillan.

The major (provisional) dominant and alternative discourses affecting this epistemological site of Japan are presented in the left-hand column of Tables 2.1 and 2.2 (see also Kamada, 2004, 2005a, 2005b, 2008). Listed in the right-hand column are examples of how these discourses are manifested as 'commonsense' expressions in people's present-day speech in Japan. While these utterances are 'reconstructed' and 'prototypical', they are frequently encountered in Japan in people's speech, in the media and in written texts.

Below, I discuss in more detail the relevant *dominant* and *alternative* macro-level discourses of ethnicity, which have been identified in the data of the participants.

A 'Discourse of Homogeneity'

A *discourse of homogeneity* emerged repeatedly in the data as the most dominant discourse. The participants made constant references (usually in contestation) to the commonly held notion of Japan being seen as a mono-racial, monoethnic, monocultural, monolingual society (see Befu, 2001; Lie, 2001). The girls used the lexis of 'homogeneity' (*tan'itsu minzoku*) to contest the notion of a 'one-people Japan'. They also talked around the subject of homogeneity and the problems with being ethnically non-Japanese in Japan.

This *discourse of homogeneity* has long been identified as a dominant discourse having a broad effect on social, political and educational social practices in Japan (Befu, 2001; Denoon *et al.*, 1996; Lie, 2001; Maher & Macdonald, 1995b; Miller, 1982; Noguchi, 2001; Noguchi & Fotos, 2001; Parmenter, 1997; Weiner, 1997b). Underlying this discourse is the denial of the existence of ethnic diversity in Japan in place of a narrowly defined standard of 'sameness' in terms of both *enacting Japaneseness* through actions that people *perform* as well as *looking Japanese* in appearance.

Japan's colonial period of territorial conquest, with movements of Japanese people going outside of Japan and outsiders shifting into Japan (as Japanese subjects), created a discourse of ethnic heterogeneity in which, 'Japanese ethnonational identity became crystallized via encounters with the colonized others' (Lie, 2001: 109). What resulted from this was a Japanese sense of hierarchical superiority over the colonized peoples with Japanese at the top, followed by Koreans and Chinese, and with Southeast Asians and Pacific Islanders at the bottom (Lie, 2001). This legacy transformed the prewar and wartime discourse of heterogeneity into a post-war ideology of homogeneity with the collapse of the Japanese empire at the end of World War II (WWII) and the relinquishing of colonial control. Post-war rapid economic growth also contributed to the spread of the notion of homogeneous nationality. Then in the 1980s, with the increase in foreign unskilled workers entering Japan, rather than allowing a discourse of multiethnicity to emerge, a *discourse of Japaneseness* came to strengthen a notion of the lower class 'other' in contrast to the middle-class (or classless, homogeneous) Japanese, according to Lie (2001). To allow a discourse of multiethnicity to dominate in Japan would be a weakening of national cultural assets: 'cultural capital of Japanese, in other words, is to embody and enact Japaneseness' (Lie, 2001: 166).

Another example to illustrate linguistic traces of the appearance a discourse of homogeneity in Japan can be seen in what is referred to as the *stem-race hypothesis*. This Japanese-produced hypothesis claimed that 'Japanese racial purity' has been maintained by the subjugation, assimilation and then disappearance of all the differing racial groups living together on the Japanese islands throughout centuries of history dating back in an unbroken 2500-year lineage with the Imperial Household, leaving the pure Japanese blood in tact (Robertson, 2001). This notion served as a justification for the 'multiracial prehistory of Japan … [not to] … interfere with the nationalist ideology of a monoracial Japanese culture' (Robertson, 2001: 4). Like the pseudo-science of other racial superiority discourses, this stem-race hypothesis to account for Japanese purity of blood has been scientifically upturned in recent years with DNA technology. Nevertheless, the notion of Japanese 'blood' as pure and unique continues to be reproduced within this discourse of homogeneity.

A contemporary example of the discourse of homogeneity being put into social practice by the Japanese Ministry of Education (then *Mombusho*), pointed out by Parmenter (1997), was the denial of heterogeneous plurality in Japanese schools. In a blatant negation of the existence of foreign-born schoolchildren in Japan, one section of the 1989 *Mombusho* guidelines on moral education for middle school students reads:

> 生徒たち日本において生をうけ、これはでに育まれてきた。そのこ
> とを考えるならば、自分というものを知るために、まず、自分の国
> のこと、自分の国のあゆみを知ることが必要となる。

> Students [in Japanese schools] were born and have been brought up in Japan. Thinking in that way, in order to know themselves, it is necessary first for them to know about their own country and their own country's course of history.[4]

The Japanese government continues to effect educational practices and policies today along this line of thought within a discourse of homogeneity. This is in spite of the evidence revealing that students *not* born and brought up in Japan are appearing in ever increasing numbers in Japanese schools (see Kanno, 2004, 2008).

East/West colonial racist discourses

The production of racist discourses stressing the racial purity and superiority of the colonizers is seen to be a feature of both the Western and Japanese experience of colonialism. The Occidental 'discourse of white-racial supremacy' has a parallel in the Oriental context of Japan in the 'discourse of Japanese racial purity' and cultural superiority emerging during its colonial period. In the West, supremacy theories placing white people as innately racially superior to Africans or Asians served as justification for the exploitation and enslavement of black peoples through the proliferation of a pseudo-scientific discourse (Christian, 2000; Mama, 1995). The notion of *white-racial supremacy* was not only taken as commonsense, or a 'God-ordained truth' (Mama, 1995: 94), but also as 'being substantiated and legitimized by the emerging sciences ... all of which reified racist sentiments which accorded with imperialist interests, giving them the incontestable status of scientific truth' (Mama, 1995: 94, 95). Though these Western and Eastern discourses came about through different historical processes – several centuries of the slave trade and the creation of global empires in the case of the West, and in the case of Japan a relatively short period as an imperial power, the end result was quite similar: the marginalization and dehumanization of the subject races. As a former colonial power, Japan can be seen as a 'former-colonial-power' society, albeit in a fundamentally and contextually different way than that of the West.

A competing 'discourse of diversity'

Competing with the above *discourse of homogeneity* and struggling to be heard alongside of it, traces of a contesting alternative *'discourse of diversity'* were also seen occurring throughout the data with references to the positive constitution of *good* difference as empowering and valuable. In their work to contest the above marginalizing dominant discourses, the participants of this study made frequent use of this alternative discourse.

This discourse allows for the positive constitution of difference as enhancing and valuable. Recently in certain situated contexts in Japan, standing out as superior, creative or special has come to be heard as *good* difference. Within the elementary schools, the *Monkashou* (Ministry of Education, Culture, Sports, Science and Technology) has recently been promoting the catchphrase repertoire *'minna chigatte, minna ga ii'* ('Everyone is different, and everyone is okay'. or 'All people in their differences are all good'). While this discourse allows for the acceptance of social diversity as enhancing and valuable, the *Monkashou* has not yet provided educators with training or curricula in how to actually implement this discourse into operationalizable educational practice. Recently, a struggle has been ensuing in Japanese government concerning *which* ideological agenda to promote in school curricula in order to address the effects of the troubles of modern society on schools. Notions of diversity and acceptance of difference continue to compete with the promotion of (neo) nationalism and a nationalistic ideology for priority in the school curriculum.

A 'Discourse of Conformity' and Enactment of Japaneseness

Intersecting with a *discourse of homogeneity*, linguistic traces of a *'discourse of conformity'* could also be seen repeatedly occurring in the data. References to acting or looking *different* were numerous, as were references to the consequences of non-conforming actions, appearance, speech patterns and ethnicity/foreignness. The girls repeatedly used the lexis of *hamideru* (to stand out), *hamiru* (to stand out [slang]), *hamigo* (the kid that stands out [slang]), *hamitteru hito* (standing out kid [slang]), in their numerous narratives about school life.

This notion of standing out is deeply rooted in Japanese society and is expressed in the popular Japanese maxim, *Deru kui wa utareru* (the nail that sticks up gets hammered down) mentioned in Chapter 1. This saying illustrates the taken-for-granted 'commonsensical' notion of the disagreeableness of standing out as different.

Conforming to group harmony and *using restraint* have always been highly valued social practices. LoCastro refers to this Japanese notion of restraint (*enryo* in Japanese) as one of 'three characteristic behaviors of Japanese interpersonal communication' (LoCastro, 1990: 121) (along with moderation and empathy). Acting outside of strictly defined behavioral norms or just *looking different* challenges the status quo and is seen as an act of non-conformity. Thus, as expressed in this proverb, individuals must work hard to avoid allowing themselves to stand out in Japanese society, by constantly attending to the exercise of restraint within this discourse, which I have identified as a *discourse of conformity* (see Kamada, 2005a, 2005b, 2006b, 2008). Even in recent times, prominent Japanese leaders and ordinary people alike continue to draw on this discourse in their social and linguistic practice.[5]

I use the phrase '*enacting Japaneseness*' to represent what I would refer to as the 'doing being Japanese' aspect of this discourse of conformity. 'Enacting Japaneseness' occurs when individuals position themselves within a discourse of conformity based on commonsensical notions of 'proper' Japanese behavior. As will be illustrated below, the girl participants of this study take up *both* positionings – that is, of enacting Japaneseness within a discourse of conformity, as well as positionings in which they reject conformity.

Whiteness, halfness and Japaneseness

The socially constructed category of 'Whiteness' in Japan and Western countries is built on different historical trajectories. Within the post-slavery, post-colonial context of America and Western Europe, 'Whiteness' has often been seen as the unmarked racial category in juxtaposition to the black, 'foreignness' category, referred to as 'opposite and unequal' (Trechter & Bucholtz, 2001: 5). Whiteness can also take on a macro-ideological position as the *only* racial category in a particular context (such as in America), thus denying or '*whiting out*' other racialized subject positions (Trechter & Buchholtz, 2001: 5).

In contrast, in the post-war, former-colonial-power and post-occupied context of Japan, it is the category of 'Whiteness' that is equated with the marked and foreignness category. The Japanese word *gaijin* generally translates as 'foreigner' or 'outsider', but it is often nuanced as 'White/ Caucasian' (or non-Japanese looking) person regardless of nationality or context. 'Whiteness' is also associated with the notion of 'super-power' nation, of English as a dominant world language, and often of physical beauty and strength. At the same time, *gaijin* 'White' people are often marginalized and 'othered' in Japan as essentially different, and positioned as outsiders perpetually unable to ever intrinsically understand the essence of Japanese society, language or customs.

While the category of 'Whiteness' is constructed differently in Eastern and Western contexts, both can be taken as power-ideological constructs that necessarily include the 'Other'. The notion of 'Whiteness' is constructed in relation to non-whiteness, just as the notion of 'Japaneseness' has also been closely linked with the foreign/outsider (usually Western and 'White') as the 'antithetical representation of the essence of Japaneseness' (Kowner, 2002: 171) (see also Donahue, 2002a, 2002b). After Japan's devastating loss of WWII, according to Lie (2001), a dominant homogeneity discourse of Japaneseness (*nihonjinron*) created a cultural essentialism expressed as a view of the world narrowed down into binary categories of 'we Japanese' and 'the Western (White) Other'. This Whiteness category in Japan also includes *haafu* (half) people of Japanese and White mixed-parentage (see the section 'Discourses of "Halfness" and "Doubleness"' [p. 34]).

A 'Discourse of *Gaijin* Otherness'

Intersecting with the above discourses, I have also identified a '*discourse of gaijin (foreigner) otherness*'. As will be shown in the analysis chapters (Chapters 4–7), even though the mixed-ethnic participants were born/ raised in Japan, have a Japanese parent (and other Japanese relatives), hold Japanese nationality/citizenship, and speak Japanese as their first or only language, they often talked of how they were constituted as *gaijin* (foreigner/outsider), or how they felt 'gaijinized' (Iino, 1996).

This section looks at the social construction of 'otherness' in Japan and examines how Japanese have defined themselves in the post-war era against the foreign 'other'. The social and historical background against which the notion of the 'ethnic other' emerged, took shape, developed, and today continues to be reproduced in Japan is problematized, in order to understand the background of the contemporary dominant '*discourse of gaijin otherness*'.

The term *gaijin*, while generally translated as 'foreigner' or 'outsider', is used in some contexts to synonymously refer to white/Caucasian people. Japanese people have a tendency to use the word *gaijin* even outside of the context of nation as an ethnic insider–outsider category, similar to how Jewish people refer to non-Jews as *gentiles*. The word *'gaikokujin'* (literally, 'a person from a foreign country') is a more formal, more polite form than the commonly used, rougher term *'gaijin'*. However, as Darling-Wolf pointed out, even though *gaikokujin* is a more polite form, 'few Japanese use it, even to a foreigner's face' (Darling-Wolf, 2003: 169).[6]

The mixed-ethnic participants of this study were often positioned not only as *haafu* but also as *gaijin*[7] (or *gaikokujin*) (see Chapter 4). Both intersecting discourses of *gaijin* otherness and homogeneity deny that Japanese citizens with non-Japanese ethnicity or with mixed-ethnicity exist in Japan, creating several common stereotypical expressions used in people's talk and actions, such as *'gaijin* are not Japanese (citizens, race, ethnicity)', *'gaijin* cannot speak Japanese', *'gaijin* speak English', *'gaijin* cannot use chopsticks' and *'gaijin* cannot eat certain Japanese foods'.

Nihonjinron and racial superiority: Constituting Japaneseness and constituting 'the other'

Japanese identity construction in post-war years has been largely influenced by a genre of literature (and television commentary) referred to as *Nihonjinron* (literally, theories on Japanese people). Central to *Nihonjinron* was the inclusion of the 'othered' westerner in contrast to Japanese. Kowner (2002: 171) argued that during this time it was through comparing themselves with a constructed image of foreigners/outsiders that Japanese identity could be formed. This *Nihonjinron* literature sought to place Japan and Japanese people as hierarchically superior by essentializing what it means to be Japanese and proclaiming that Japan, Japanese people, Japanese language, the Japanese brain and so forth are exclusively unique in the world (e.g. Suzuki, 1975, 1978; Tsunoda, 1978).

Nihonjinron ideology was integrated with a *discourse of Japaneseness* which constructed Japan as an homogeneous society where anyone who was not 'pure' Japanese in terms of race, ethnicity, nationality, language and class was referred to as the 'other' or the 'outsider' – a worldview narrowed down into binary categories of 'we Japanese' and 'the other' (Lie, 2001). This 'us–them' racial discourse founded on the marginalized and stereotyped 'other' is not limited to the Japanese model. Yuval-Davis has defined a similar model of the 'us–them' divide outside of Japan as a construction of 'biological, cultural, religious, linguistic or territorially based boundaries as signifiers of a fixed, deterministic genealogical difference of "the other"' (Yuval-Davis, 1997: 193).

As a genre of literature and as a social discourse, *Nihonjinron*, according to Befu, was an attempt to answer the question, 'Who are we Japanese?' (Befu, 2001: 3). Kubota (2002) referred to *Nihonjinron* as a 'self-Orientalism', which emphasized cultural differences based on ethnicity and exoticism. In examining Said's (1978) notion of Orientalism, Kubota defined the essentialist construction of the Orient or the exotic Oriental as 'something that the West is not. The image is that we are this and they are that, creating Western authority over the Orient' (Kubota, 1999: 17). The production of *Nihonjinron* was seen as a way to 'rescue' Japanese from an identity crisis brought on by Westernization and as a way for Japanese to globally assert themselves politically and economically (Kubota, 1999). Befu (2001) attributed the proliferation of the *Nihonjinron* literature as arising from a symbolic vacuum in Japan after WWII, which touched on almost all aspects of life, including ecology (creating the discourse that Japan's small size is responsible for its love of miniaturization), subsistence economy (creating the discourse that Japan's wet-rice culture resulted in its tightly knit communities) and Japanese management (creating the discourse that Japan's economic success was attributable to its homogeneity and monolinguality).

The appearance of *Nihonjinron* literature coincided with Japan's highly inflated 'Bubble Economy' (1986–1991), which tended to statistically distinguish Japan as economically superior by world standards during this period. After some of this literature was translated into English in the 1970s, western-produced literature *supporting Nihonjinron* began to appear (e.g. Reischauer, 1978; Rohlen, 1983; Vogel, 1979), which then instantly created a backlash of challenge and critical analysis of the literature, which disputed the homogeneity myth and challenged the essentialism and myths of the *Nihonjinron* pseudo-science (Miller, 1982). Then after the burst of the economic bubble, new alternative discourses of diversity emerged challenging essentialist notions of homogeneity, by focusing on the richness of *ethnic diversity* in Japanese culture (Maher & McDonald, 1995a); the historical *multiculturality and diversity* of Japanese society (Denoon *et al.*, 1996; McCormak, 1996a); *minority groups* within Japan (Weiner, 1997b); and the historical *multilinguality* of Japan (Maher, 1995; Maher & Yashiro, 1991, 1995; Noguchi & Fotos, 2001).

Discourses of 'halfness' and 'doubleness'

An important feature of post-colonial theory is the concept of hybridity and hybrid identity, which deals with how the mixing of cultures, races and languages affects identities (Bhabha, 1994). The hybrid identity is further complicated as the hybrid individual finds him-/ herself in an in-between or a 'third space' (Bhabha, 1994) in which he/ she must overcome being stereotyped and subjectified within the colonial discourse as degenerate in terms of racial origin (see also Ching, 1998, 2001).

The hybrid identities of the mixed-ethnic girls of this study were complex and unfixed. Traces of two discourses of hybridity – *'a discourse of halfness'* and *'a discourse of doubleness'* – could be identified through both ethnographic work and, in particular, in the data analysis of the lexis the participants used in referring to themselves in terms of their mixed-ethnicity. All six girls were seen referring to themselves as both 'half' (*haafu*) and as 'double' (*daburu*). This is interesting in that while the word *'haafu'* is commonly used in Japanese society to refer to mixed-ethnic people, the word *'daburu'* is for the most part limited in usage to the English-speaking foreign communities in densely populated areas where this grass-roots term originated.

Haafu is a fairly new word, which came into common use over the last half century in Japan after WWII.[8] In applying Sacks' (1972) membership categorization analysis to the referent *haafu*, Greer (2003) found his 'multiethnic' (*haafu*) participants both identifying with this referent as well as contesting it, due to it belonging to more than just one category of 'standard relational pair' or category. Greer found that when the speaker was not Japanese that reference to *haafu* tended to belong to the category of 'Japanese'. However, when the speaker was Japanese, it tended more to belong to a subset of the category of *'gaijin'*, usually connoting 'White' foreigner.

Taken in this way, the use of *haafu* by Japanese constitutes mixed-ethnic individuals on the basis of foreignness, 'Whiteness' or 'half-Japaneseness'. Although this is just one of many of the ambiguous ways in which it might be interpreted depending on the interlocutor and the situation (see Greer, 2003; O'Hearn, 1998), I have identified this particular usage of the construction as a trace of a discourse and refer to it as a *discourse of 'halfness'* (see Kamada, 2005a, 2005b, 2006, 2008).

Most Japanese people consider *'haafu'* to be a neutral term and deny that its use implies racialized or derogatory connotations in referring to Japanese-mixed-ethnic people. However, recently many foreign-raised parents of such children in urban areas have contested and reconstituted what they consider to be a 'discourse of deficit' (Sunderland, 2004) or subtractive 'discourse of halfness'. These parents have promoted a new 'discourse of doubleness' by referring to their children as 'double' (*daburu*) instead of 'half'.

All three of the girls with foreign mothers reported in interviews that their mothers had encouraged them to reject the use of '*haafu*' in referring to themselves and instead to refer to themselves as '*daburu*' in order to empower them in an additive, anti-racist manner. The other three girls in the study with foreign fathers were also aware of the word and likewise used it often throughout the meetings and interviews.[9] However, not all mixed-ethnic children particularly position themselves using the referent *daburu*, and some feel that it seems to imply that they have to live up to a standard of being doubly 'good and talented' (Singer, 2000; see also Greer, 2003; O'Hearn, 1998).

While the production of this new reconstituted discourse of *doubleness* grew up spontaneously within this community over the last couple of decades, it remains limited in use in Japanese society as a whole. The promotion of this discourse by parents of mixed-ethnic children in Japan represents an attempt to incorporate an anti-racist discourse into their parenting styles and choices. The occurrence of the integration of anti-racist discourse into parenting styles by parents of mixed-ethnic children raised in predominantly white societies has also been reported on (Katz, 1996; Mama, 1995). This use of *daburu* among the participants of this study manifests as a linguistic 'trace' (Talbot, 1995; Sunderland, 2004) of the contesting discourse.

The following section looks at an example of the impact of (initially governmental) practices involving the conscious production and distribution of a genre of propaganda voicing a discourse of the foreign 'other' as demonic. Discourses of embodiment are drawn upon to portray an enemy beast as the uglified non-Japanese 'other' within an extreme genre of *Nihonjinron*.

The 'Momotarou Paradigm': The *Oni* (Beast) as Foreign 'Other'

Minami's (1994) coinage of the term '*fascist Nihonjinron*' was used to refer to an even stronger nationalist association of *Nihonjinron* with Japan's wartime and pre-war (1920s–1940s) imperialism (Kubota, 2002). This stronger discourse of Japaneseness, constructing the foreign 'other', was put into practice before and during WWII. It was exemplified by the use of a popular traditional Japanese folktale in order to indoctrinate schoolchildren in a racialized anti-Westerner ideology.

This folktale, called *Momotarou*, or 'Peach Boy', is a favorite traditional Japanese story, told in many dialects and versions all over Japan (see Kawai, 1996). Momotarou is a mere boy who overpowers intruding beastly sub-human characters, called *oni* (*beast* or *ogre*). *Oni* have appeared in Japanese folk mythology from as far back as Japan's earliest text in *The Kojiki* (712 AD). *Oni* are depicted as muscular and anthropomorphic, but also as horned and barbaric sub-human beasts. They are traditionally pictured with very large noses and hairy faces, in contrast to characterizations of Japanese people as civilized folk with usually hairless faces and much smaller noses.

From the Russo-Japanese War (1904–1905), comic images were distributed of Momotarou defending Japan against the Caucasian 'Northern devils' from Russia who were represented by *oni* (Onishi, 1989). Then in the 1930s, Momotarou was again depicted as a boy war-hero in paintings, leaflets and magazines, but it was especially during WWII that this popular fairytale was used to inculcate a nationalistic discourse (Klaus, 1991). It was universally distributed in state school readers and in various forms of media such as animation and comics. In 1943, a propaganda film, entitled, *Momotarou: Solider God of the Seas*, was commissioned by the Japanese Naval Ministry with the instruction of depicting Westerners as *oni*.

Referred to as *The Momotarou Paradigm*, an entire genre of media was produced and dispersed throughout Japan in the form of articles, movies, cartoons and so forth in which the heroic Japanese child overcomes the beastly foreign intruder, much larger and stronger than himself (Dower, 1986). The Momotarou character was depicted as youthful and vigorous while the *oni* was a portrayal of Anglo-Westerners as 'demons with a human face' (Dower, 1986: 255) and as 'the pure Self and the incorrigibly evil Other' (Dower, 1986: 255). Following Dower, Antoni writes, 'In films and caricatures of this type, Momotarou appears as a youthful and strong embodiment of the "new" Japan, in sharp contrast to Americans and the British, who are presented as aging and feeble "demons with a human face"'(Antoni, 1991: 166). Below, I return to this *Momotarou Paradigm* to demonstrate how discourses of the foreign 'Other' are still intertextually drawn on today (see the sections 'A "discourse of foreigner grotesqueness"' [p. 44] and 'The "embodied" other' [p. 52]).

A 'Discourse of Interculturalism'

In recent years, another discourse, which I have identified in the dataset, is what I call a *discourse of interculturalism*. 'Interculturalism' is a word I use to represent a quality, consciousness or proficiency, which enables people to communicate well with and understand peoples of other 'different' cultures. The evaluation in modern-day Japan of the high social value of interculturalism has given rise to this discourse. The mass media has also drawn on and promoted this discourse in advertising. In a television commercial for a language school airing during the data collection period, the Japanese word for interculturalism, *ibunka*, was invoked. In the advertisement, Japanese people, non-Japanese people and an alien from outer space were shown speaking in various languages (not their own), including a Japanese local Kansai dialect (see Extract 6. 10). In a stretch of data, a participant in this study (Rina) was seen identifying with this commercial. She narrated the sequence shown on television and told how it can help to spread the notion of interculturalism in Japan and in so doing contribute to her empowerment as a person having more than one culture. Rina summarized the commercial as follows (data from the Hot Springs meeting):

> K: **de kansaiben o hanasu uchuujin tsutte, 'ma, ibunka chuuno kana?'**
> *and then the Kansai-dialect-speaking alien from space says, 'well, ain't that intercultural?'*

This discourse of interculturalism has historical borrowings from earlier discourses of 'openness to the outside world' (emerging just prior to the beginning of the Meiji Period [1868–1912]) and *kokusaika* or 'internationalization' (emerging during the Bubble Economy [1986–1991]) (see McCormack, 1996b). These earlier discourses have for the most part been advanced through institutional top-down promotion and practices via such media as the *Mombusho's* Guidelines on Education during the postwar period. The concept of *kokusaika* during the late 1980s was taken to embrace both the pride of Japanese traditions (including pride in its economic prowess) as well as the struggle for participation as an equal member in the industrialized and international community of the West, particularly the USA (Kubota, 2002).

Up until recently, the notion of *interculturalism*, as a social practice promoted in education, business and politics through both spoken and written contexts, had meant Japanese people communicating and interacting with other 'foreign peoples' outside of Japan or with foreign 'guests' coming to Japan. The notion of interculturalism occurring *within* the social structure of Japan itself is a new concept that, as a competing alternative discourse, conflicts with and creates tension with a discourse of homogeneity. Japanese people, for the first time, have to confront the idea that within Japan itself, diversity is increasing in terms of not only ethnicity and race, but also in terms of gender, class, religion, sexual orientation and academic/intellectual abilities.

The next section introduces the notions of 'doing gender' (West & Zimmerman, 1987, 2009), 'doing difference' (West & Fenstermaker, 1995) and ethno-gendered 'embodied' discourses.

'Doing Gender', 'Doing Difference' and Ethno-Gendering

West and Zimmerman's (1987) journal publication, 'Doing Gender', stimulated a major conceptual shift, overturning and replacing the static concept of *sex roles* as human traits that people possess, with a new theoretical notion of *gender* as something that individuals *do* in everyday interactions with others. This notion continues to strongly impact theoretical thought as pointed out by Jurik and Siemsen (2009) who wrote that this article is 'the most cited article ever published in *Gender and Society*, a journal that ranks among the top publications in sociology and women's studies' (Jurik & Siemsen, 2009: 72).

West and Zimmerman (1987, 2009) begin by establishing distinctions between the notions of *sex*, *sex category* and *gender*. *Sex* is determined at birth based on biologically accepted notions of classifying newborns as males and females, usually on the basis of genitalia. *Sex category* is achieved through a person's display proclaiming their membership in a particular category which might not always be the same as their sex. *Gender* is how a person manages their activity within normative notions of actions and attitudes, which are thought to be appropriate for that person's sex category. West and Zimmerman (2009) state

> ... sex categorization involves the display and recognition of socially regulated external insignia of sex – such as deportment, dress, and bearing ... The relationship between sex category and gender is the relationship between being a recognizable incumbent of a sex category (which itself takes some doing) and being accountable to current cultural conceptions of conduct becoming to – or compatible with the 'essential natures' of – a woman or man. We conceptualized this as an ongoing situated process, a 'doing' rather than a 'being'. (West & Zimmerman, 2009: 113, 114)

The following section looks at the related notion of 'doing difference'.

'Doing difference'

In their attempt to address social inequality through the concept of 'doing gender', West and Fenstermaker (1995) and West and Zimmerman (2009) have extended the notion of 'doing gender' to a broader framework to include *race* and *class* along with *gender*. People 'do difference' in situated interactions with others as gender, race and class 'difference' is simultaneously accomplished through their discursive actions.

West and Fenstermaker (1995) make three arguments concerning the 'doing' of gender before going on to discuss the interrelated connections with race and class. Their first point is that gender is a situated accomplishment of people who manage their conduct in relation to societal norms expected of the two sex categories. Their second point is that this accountability is an interactional accomplishment which allows others to notice (West & Fenstermaker, 2009: 21). Their third point is that in the 'doing' or making something accountable, it is not only interactional, but also institutional 'whereby situated social action contributes to the reproduction of social structure' (West & Fenstermaker, 1995: 21). As far as race is concerned, while 'racial categorization' differs from 'gender categorization' in some respects, 'appearances' are often taken by people to indicate some essential human condition. West and Fenstermaker (1995) state that race is also a situated accomplishment that is not merely a static trait. It is something that is done or accomplished in interaction with others (West & Fenstermaker, 1995: 23). Like gender, the accomplishment of race is unavoidable. West and Fenstermaker summarize their stance on the accomplishment of race as follows:

> The accomplishment of race consists of creating differences among members of different race categories – differences that are neither natural nor biological … Once created, these differences are used to maintain the 'essential' distinctiveness of 'racial identities' and the institutional arrangements that they support. From this perspective, racial identities are not invariant idealizations of our human natures that are uniformly distributed in society. Nor are normative conceptions of attitudes and activities for one's race category templates for 'racial' behaviors. Rather, what is invariant is the notion that members of different 'races' have essentially different natures, which explain their very unequal positions in our society. (West & Fenstermaker, 1995: 25, 26)

West and Fenstermaker also showed how class is accomplished and that race, gender and class are situated accomplishments that may be experienced simultaneously depending on the situation. Understanding how people are simultaneously gendered, raced and classed can explain how inequality works in interaction based on social institutions and historically created and accepted social norms. Later, in the analysis chapters, I show how 'doing gender' and 'doing difference' are accomplished by the adolescent girl participants in the study through examination of their talk.

The following section specifically looks at my conceptualization of the simultaneous accomplishment of gender and ethnicity (or *race*, in the lexis of West and Fenstermaker). However, before beginning this discussion, I digress briefly to explain my usage of the term 'embodiment'.

Embodied identities

The word 'embodiment', as used in this book, signifies how individuals make sense of themselves discursively through their positioning and actions (or 'doing' embodied identity) at the site of the body – their *'lived body selves'* (Howson, 2005; Thapan, 1997a). This *lived body* has been conceptualized as a 'site of knowledge and experience', which diverges from the sociological notion of 'the body as a reified object (of processes, forces, theory)' (Howson, 2005: 39).

The body has also been seen as an important aspect of human identity which is not simply a given, but something over which one can exert their own agency (Thapan, 1997b). While the body has symbolic and cultural value which may differ across cultures, and is thus also 'defined, shaped and constrained by society ... a person is also an agential body, in communication, and negotiation, with significant others in everyday life' (Thapan, 1997a: 1, 2).

Following West and Zimmerman (1995), the body has also similarly been conceptualized as an *event* in an act of 'becoming' through continuous and multiple practices and interactions with others in 'doing' embodied identity, rather than as an object in which the body is described (Budgeon, 2003: 52). This notion of the body goes beyond understanding 'what women's bodies mean' to 'what women can do' (Budgeon, 2003: 52).

Embodied aspects of *ethnic* physical features and phenotypes have been one of the central themes examined in the construction of ethnic identity. The term 'pigmentocracy' was used to refer to the varying degrees of darkness of skin (Mama, 1995: 102, 103). Black women participants constituted themselves within limited and dominant 'white European' discourses of beauty, '"good hair" means European hair, "good nose" means straight nose, "good complexion" means light complexion' (Mama, 1995: 103). Le Page and Tabouret-Keller referred to the construction of 'Negro' phenotypes not only in terms of skin color but also 'lips, nose, hair' (Le Page & Tabouret-Keller, 1985: 227).

Bloustien (2001) examined how adolescent girls come to view themselves through their talk about their bodies. Bloustien took up such themes as body watching and bodily praxis as a mode of knowledge, and other themes such as touching, body shape and food to demonstrate how and why girls do 'bodywork' through their 'serious play' in which they come to deal with enigmas and gaps between the ideal 'other' and themselves.

Japanese organizations have contributed to producing 'modes of embodiment' of temporary female workers in Japan (Gottfried, 2003). Practices associated with body management in their work such as requiring work uniforms (generally a white blouse, and dark colored jacket and knee length skirt; sometimes also a hat and white gloves), use of feminine language and gestures, bowing and showing deference, age restrictions and other controls on the body were shown to limit these women's position in society.

Ethno-gendering

The intersection of gendered and ethnic identities in the context of Japan is one of the central focuses of this study – what I refer to as _ethnogendering_ and what is very similar to West and Fenstermaker's (1995) conceptualization of 'doing difference', except that I prefer to use the term _ethnicity_ while they use the term _race_.

This conceptualization involves the simultaneous accomplishment of gender and ethnicity and is analyzed by examining the relationship between how the girl participants accomplish and manage their gender and ethnic 'differences' and how their actions or displays within certain situated interactions might come into conflict with how they are seen or constituted by others.

This section looks at _ethno-gendered_ discourses in Japan. Within this research 'site' of Japan, and at work within the data, various gendered discourses were provisionally identified or co-constructed through the course of this research. Linguistic traces of a 'discourse of advantaged femininity' and a 'discourse of female social flexibility' are observed in the data (see Chapter 7). Other discourses that I identified in the talk of the girls in this study include a discourse of 'if you've got it (some attribute), flaunt it' and 'if you flaunt it (some attribute), you deserve whatever reaction you get from people'. Clark (1998) found a similar 'blame the victim discourse' appearing in UK tabloid news reports of sexual violence.

This study particularly focuses on ethno-gendered discourses of _ethnic embodiment_. Here I refer to how the subjective 'lived-body/self' is further specifically constituted on the basis of a marginalized _ethnic_ self in relation to other dominant ethnic embodied discourses. In the following sections, I discuss two ethno-gendered discourses of embodiment in Japan. See Table 2.3 for these discourses and examples of expressions heard manifested in people's speech or texts in Japan.

A 'discourse of foreigner attractiveness'

In this and the next section, I examine linguistic traces of two discourses of embodied ethnicity in Japan also seen occurring in the research

Table 2.3 Ethno-gendered discourses of embodiment in Japan and examples manifested in speech

Ethno-gendered discourses of embodiment in Japan	*Ethno-gendered discourses of embodiment manifested in speech in Japan*
'A discourse of foreigner attractiveness' or 'a white-Western female beauty discourse' positions 'white' Westerners (and offspring of Japanese/white mixed-parentage) as more attractive than Japanese or Asians	'Westerners have (attractive) "high" noses (*hana ga takai*), or prominent features/deep-set eyes (*hori ga fukai*)' 'Westerners have good body style' (females: nice hips, breasts, legs; males: hunky chest, broad shoulders, tall)
'A discourse of foreigner grotesqueness' 'uglifies' the foreigner who is stereotyped as big, fat and hairy or of having a big nose	'Westerners are hairy-like animals/ beasts' 'Westerners have big noses' 'Westerners are big and fat'

site – what I have arbitrarily named: a *'discourse of foreigner attractiveness'* and a *'discourse of foreigner grotesqueness'*. These discourses are both gendered and racialized (see Kamada, 2005a, 2008).

First, I examine an ethno-gendered *discourse of foreigner attractiveness* (or a *'white' Western female beauty discourse*) within the context of Japan. Linguistic traces of this discourse were seen occurring within the spoken data of the girl participants of this study. This discourse places foreigners or people of Japanese and white mixed-parentage as more attractive than Japanese people in general on the basis of various 'body' features such as facial shape, body shape and skin and hair color. This discourse of foreigner attractiveness is widely distributed by the Japanese media and in advertising where 'white foreigners' are often used for their 'beauty' value especially to promote entertainment or consumer products.

While not specifically referring to this as a discourse, Darling-Wolf (2003) also examined 'foreigner attractiveness', but in her study this notion appeared in the talk of *Japanese* women in reference to 'white foreigners'. Darling-Wolf (2003) established that Western images via the media have influenced modern-day Japanese women's conceptions of foreign attractiveness (Darling-Wolf, 2003). She examined, from a feminist perspective, how 29 Japanese women in Japan negotiate and construct attractiveness as influenced by Westernized media representations. She found all of her Japanese women participants positioning white-Westerners as more physically attractive than Japanese. She quotes her participants who draw on various related discourses:

> 'Westerners have a very nice [body] style …' (Takako); … 'They have good appearance, big eyes, high noses' (Reiko); 'Westerners are more beautiful, they are tall, have high noses, big eyes, and a good sense of style' (Nishimura-san); 'compared to Japanese women, they are more elegant, they look more excellent than the Japanese' (Chieko); … 'They have good [body] style, you know, compared to Japanese models, they have nice breasts, nice hips, longer legs' (Abe-san). (Darling-Wolf, 2003: 165, 166. Darling-Wolf's brackets, quotations and parenthesis)

Many of Darling-Wolf's (2003) Japanese participants constructed a hierarchy in which they placed 'whites' at the top, 'halves' in the middle and Japanese at the bottom. Several of her participants referred to 'foreign' or Caucasian features of a 'high nose' (*hana ga takai*) or a 'deeply sculptured face' (*hori ga fukai*), which constructs not only *attractiveness*, but also *foreignness* (or Caucasian features). Some of Darling-Wolf's (2003) participants used the descriptor 'good body style' to positively describe a 'foreign' female's shapely figure and large breasts (also a 'foreign' male's hunky full-chest, broad shoulders and tall stature). Many Japanese glossy fashion magazines (such as *Nikita* [for women] and *Leon* [for men]) exclusively use 'white foreigners' as models (instead of Japanese) in order to create this 'nice body style' image for their Japanese readers. While these representations of the exotic white foreigner 'beautify' the 'foreigner', they also serve to objectify (Foucault, 1979) the foreign (often female) body. Perhaps, as well, they might also serve to marginalize the Japanese speaker – at least in the context of a white interlocutor.

A 'discourse of foreigner grotesqueness'

The above ethno-gendered '*discourse of foreigner attractiveness*' conflicts with another competing discourse, which I have identified as a '*discourse of foreigner grotesqueness*'. The notion of 'the foreigner as grotesque' first began to emerge in Japan at about the same time that Caucasian foreigners (almost exclusively males) began to noticeably appear in Japan at the end of the 19th century. Woodblock prints from the late Edo and early Meiji periods (1868–1912) have portrayed European and Americans with large, unattractive noses and voluminous hairy bodies. Later, war propaganda from the early 20th century portrayed the grotesqueness of Caucasian lineaments in terms of facial and bodily hair, as well as facial and body shape (Dower, 1986). These and similar representations have been used *to uglify* the stereotyped foreigner (big nose, big body, fat, hairy) and continue to 'ethnically embody' and constitute non-Japanese people as grotesque in contemporary texts such as media reports, comics and police reports (see the following section 'The Social Construction of *Gaijin* in Japan Today'). Here within this 'discourse of foreign grotesqueness', the *uglified* foreigner (often male), as with the *beautified* white foreigner (often female), the body is ethnically objectified and gendered and described apart from the person.

The girl participants from this study revealed a body consciousness in which they struggled to resist a disempowering 'discourse of foreigner grotesqueness', and instead worked to position themselves within an interconnected, but empowering, 'discourse of foreigner attractiveness' (see Extracts 4.16a–c and 7.1) (see Kamada, 2009).

The Social Construction of *Gaijin* in Japan Today

As an example to illustrate how *gaijin* (including *haafu/daburu*) people are socially constructed today in Japan within some of these discourses provisionally identified above, I analyze the text of a local Japanese police report.[10] Although this particular writing was printed in Japanese and distributed in June 1999 to every home in a relatively small rural city in northern Japan where I was residing (population: 170,000), in recent years, these kinds of police reports have been appearing all over Japan. I here draw on the work of the critical discourse analyst, Fairclough (2001), and mainly focus on the *social problem* aspect of his analytical framework and for reasons of space leave aside most of the *micro-linguistic analysis* of the text.

The text

The text of the police report was part of a one-page police bulletin entitled, *Patarouru Horikoshi*,[11] consisting of five separate police news items each accompanied with cartoon-like illustrations (see Figure 2.1).

One of these news items is focused on here (translated from the Japanese), entitled: 'Cooperate in preventing illegal residency and illegal labor of foreigners' (see Figure 2.2).

Following is a Romanized version of the Japanese (Figure 2.3) and an English translation of the text (Figure 2.4).

Even a cursory analysis of this text points to the significance of certain historical discourses of xenophobia and homogeneity, identified above and also evident in the *Momotarou* paradigm, which still appear

Figure 2.1 *Patorouru Horikoshi* (Horikoshi Patrol)

Figure 2.2 Police report with illustration

Patorouru Horikoshi Heisei 11 nen 6 gatsu go

(1) Gaikokujin no Fuhou Taizai Boushi ni Gokyouryoku o
(2)   Fuhoushuro
(3) Rainichi gaikokujin no fuhou taizaisha ni yoru
(4) satsujin goutou nado no kyoaku hanzai de
(5) Nihonjin ga higaisha tonaru keesu ga
(6) fuetekiteimasu.
(7) Sumiyoi Aomori-ken o tsukurutame
(8) keisatsu de wa zenryoku o agete torikundeimasu.
*(9) Fushin na gaikokujin o mikaketa
*(10) gakikokujin ga kyousei roudou saserareteiru
(11) nado no jouhou ga arimashitara,
(12) oshirasekudasai.

(Cartoon speech bubble): Kiretemasuyo!

Figure 2.3 Romanized Japanese transcript of 'Horikoshi Patrol'

Horikoshi Patrol, June 1999 Issue

(1)   Cooperate in Preventing Illegal Residency of Foreigners
(2)   Illegal Labor
(3)   As a result of illegally overstaying foreigners coming to Japan
(4)   fiendish crimes such as murder and burglary
(5)   in which Japanese have been victimized
(6)   have been increasing.
(7)   In order to build a comfortable place to live in Aomori Prefecture
(8)   we police are doing our utmost to grapple with this.
•(9)   If you see suspicious looking foreigners [or]
•(10) foreigners forced into labor
(11) or if you have any other information
(12) please inform us.

(Cartoon speech bubble): It has expired!

Figure 2.4 English translation: Transcript of 'Horikoshi Patrol'

intertextually in this text produced and distributed in present-day Japan. I discuss the linguistic traces of the appearance of these discourses in the sections below.

The social problem

This discussion focuses on Fairclough's (2001) method of CDA, in which the analyst sets out to, first of all, *identify the social problem*. In order to do so, this section discusses the social order surrounding foreigners residing in Japan and some background of their coming to reside in Japan.

According to the Japan Ministry of Justice and Immigration Bureau report on population (June 2008), as of the end of 2007, there were 2.15 million registered foreigners residing in Japan, making up 1.69% of the shrinking population of Japan of 127.7 million. While still small percentage-wise (compared with America at 11.1% and Germany at 8.9% of population in 2005) (JINF, 2008), the number of registered foreigners in Japan has increased by 50% compared with a decade ago (*The Japan Times*, June 4, 2008). Although not all-inclusive, broadly, I have classified present-day foreigners in Japan into three categories based on historical and ethnic factors, which are explained below in order of historical appearance in Japan.

The first and largest group consists of (Far-East) Asian foreigners such as Koreans and Chinese who have resided in Japan in large numbers since before or during WWII and whose facial features are indistinguishable from Japanese. The Japan census report for 2007 listed 55.8% of all registered foreigners as 'coming from' China, North Korea and South Korea (Japan Ministry of Justice and Immigration, 2008). A majority of these 'foreigners' who 'came from' these countries overseas were actually born and raised in Japan. The numbers of registered Korean foreigners in Japan have decreased over a decade due to the fact that they do not include the 153,103 naturalized Japanese citizens mostly made up of Korean and Chinese ethnicities (see Debito Arudou, 2009). Koreans were the largest group of registered foreigners in Japan in 2006 at nearly 600,000 or 28.7% of foreigners, closely followed by Chinese, but this was reversed at the end of 2007 when Chinese became the largest group of foreign residents in Japan at 28.2% followed by Koreans at 27.7% (Japan Ministry of Justice and Immigration, 2008).

During Japan's period as a colonial power, Asian colonial subjects were forced to take Japanese citizenship. Over two million Koreans were conscripted (as Japanese subjects) to work in Japan as laborers in factories and mines. Although many Koreans were repatriated back to Korea after the war, by 1946 there were still around 650,000 Koreans left in Japan. Then, in 1952 when Japan signed the San Francisco Peace Treaty and became a sovereign nation, the Koreans living in Japan were stripped of their Japanese citizenship. While many ethnic Koreans residing in Japan have since reclaimed Japanese citizenship, many of their children and grandchildren, who were born in Japan and speak only Japanese, still do not have Japanese citizenship (many having rejected the idea of assimilation out of choice) and these second- and third-generation 'foreigners' still struggle for social rights (see Hanazaki, 2000; Kang, 2001). Those Koreans who were brought to Japan forcibly during Japanese colonial rule and their offspring today have been given a 'special' permanent resident status.

The second main group of foreigners in Japan consists of (mostly white) North Americans, Europeans and Australians who began appearing in large cities in Japan after WWII, and whose native language is generally a well-placed foreign language such as English (or another western European language). Their reasons for coming to Japan include missionary work, academic study, pursuit of Japanese arts and employment such as foreign language teaching, marriage and so forth. This second group is by far the smallest of the three. The Japan census report for 2007 lists only 51,851 foreigners from America (2.4% of total registered foreigners) as the largest nationality represented in this second group of foreigners. American servicemen residing within Japan-based American military bases have also been present in Japan since the end of WWII, although they enjoy a special status and are not counted in official Japanese statistics as 'foreign residents' in Japan.

Members of the third and newest – as well as fastest-growing – group of foreigners have mostly come from developing countries of Southeast Asia (Philippines, Vietnam), the Middle East (Iran, Iraq), East Asia (Pakistan, Bangladesh) and South America (Brazil, Peru). Following the Chinese and Koreans, the next largest populations of registered foreigners in Japan are Brazilians, Filipinos and Peruvians. According to the 2007 Japan census report, 316,967 Brazilians made up 14.7% of registered foreigners in Japan. One of the newest groups to appear from the 1990s is the *Nikkeijin* (literally, second-generation Japanese) who are predominately Brazilian and other overseas 'second-generation' Japanese-heritage 'returnees' to Japan. Most *Nikkeijin* have entered Japan as unskilled laborers, with little or no Japanese language proficiency, creating a new 'underclass' (Weiner, 1997a). The tremendous need for cheap unskilled labor, created by the economic bubble, coincided with a leveling off of Japan's population growth. This resulted in a sudden large influx of this third group of foreigners to fill this employment void by taking jobs that young Japanese had come to shun, referred to as the three Ks: *kitanai, kiken* and *kitsui* (the three Ds in English: dirty, dangerous and demanding). While not explicitly stated in the text of this police report and veiled in the illustration as well, it is particularly members of this third category who are designated here.

Mixed genres and tensions

Tensions are created in this police text in the mixing of genres. It is at the same time a genre of a crime report, an official document, a mass-media information sheet and a kind of 'wanted poster' with an attached 'police-sketch', of sorts, served by the illustration. The police who have produced this leaflet have designated it as a local patrol report genre, promoted in its name, 'Horikoshi Patrol'. The 'wanted poster' genre acts as a community appeal by asking the citizenry not only to 'cooperate' by 'informing' the police, but also asking them to make a decision on *who* may be a 'suspicious looking foreigner'. Although it is a police report targeting 'illegal foreigners' in Japan, in effect all foreign-looking people residing in Japan could potentially fall suspect and be constituted by the (Japanese) citizenry as 'suspicious' based on their 'foreign' appearance – including the mixed-ethnic girl participants of this study.

The ethnic 'other' order of discourse in Japan

In their framing of *multiperspective approaches,* where theoretical schools of discourse analysis can be combined into one framework, Phillips and Jorgensen (2002) propose the idea of applying Fairclough's (1995) and Chouliaraki and Fairclough's (1999) notion of an *order of discourse.* Identifying an *order of discourse,* or discourses relevant to a certain problem in a particular social field, is useful in establishing a complex range of available discourses and genres that participants might draw upon. According to Phillips and Jorgensen (2002), this framing works well within the three discourse analytic approaches that they investigate: Potter and Wetherell's (1987) DP, Laclau and Mouffe's (1985) PDA and Fairclough's (1992, 1995) CDA. Phillips and Jorgensen (2002) underscore the importance of the tensions and meanings involved when opposing discourses are invoked at the same time. For the purposes of this study, I here examine the order of discourse of mixed-ethnicity and foreign 'otherness' in Japan. Using the language of Japanese discourse, I examine the order of discourse surrounding the words/notions *gaijin* (or *gaikokujin*) and *haafu.* This order of discourse is reflected not only in this police-report text, but also appears in the spoken data of the mixed-ethnic participants of this study who are likewise constituted within tensions of the same opposing discourses.

The dominant discourses

Dominant hegemonic discourses of ethnicity in Japan identified above, which affect the participant girls of this study, also permeate this police-produced text. Dominant and often xenophobic discourses appearing in this police-report text can be seen as follows:

- A homogeneous society is a safe society. (A heterogeneous society is not.)
- Japan is a homogeneous society.
- Foreigners coming into Japan are the cause of instability and crime.
- People with physical features distinguishing them as non-Japanese (*gaikokujin*) may be suspects who should be watched or reported to police.
- People who have non-Japanese features are *not* Japanese (citizens), but are foreigners.
- Foreigners are/may be suspicious, untrustworthy troublemakers.
- Foreigners (or foreign-looking people) should be reported to police if they *appear* suspicious.
- Foreigners disrupt the status quo ('our Japanese' harmony).
- Foreigners are the perpetrators of fiendish crimes (murder, burglary) (in which Japanese are victims).

- Foreigners not only *act* differently (from 'us Japanese'), but they also *look* very different (from 'us Japanese') (as depicted in the illustration).
- Foreigners are victims ('keep watch for foreigners who are forced into labor').

Missing or alternative discourses

Not included in this police report are alternative discourses, which are *missing* here. Such discourses are those marginalized voices, which are not heard; but from the standpoint of many marginalized ethnic groups in Japan, *should* be heard. These could be thought of as follows:

- Foreigners (*gaijin / gaikokujin*) and mixed-ethnic (*haafu / daburu*) people contribute positively to society.
- The cause of rising crime in Japan is *not* directly due to foreigners coming into Japan, and remaining as overstaying illegal foreigners.
- Japan is a heterogeneous, multiethnic society (country).
- Foreigners and mixed-ethnic people residing in Japan do *not* disrupt the status quo.
- Mixed-ethnic or non-Japanese (looking) people born (or residing) in Japan are *not* always foreigners.
- People having non-Japanese features may be Japanese (citizens).
- People having Asian features may *not* be Japanese.
- People having non-Japanese features may speak Japanese.
- People having non-Japanese (or Caucasian-like) features may *not* always speak English.
- Mixed-ethnic and non-Japanese people should be treated equal to Japanese people.

The 'embodied' other

The representation of 'foreigner(s)' by the Japanese word '*gaikokujin*' appears four times in this three-sentence text and appears more than any other single lexical item. However, we might question who this *gaikokujin* specifically refers to. The illustration accompanying the text depicts a respectable looking foreign gentleman dressed smartly in a business suit and necktie and holding a briefcase. He is drawn as a stereotypical 'white' foreigner *manga* caricature with an extremely oversized nose and light hair. This foreigner is standing in juxtaposition to a Japanese policeman, depicted with a small dot for a nose and dark hair. It is clear that the text does not refer to middle-class white foreigners as depicted, but instead refers to unskilled foreigner laborers described above in category three.

This creates a tension between what seems to be portrayed on the surface, and what is actually implied.

Whereas the text creates a discourse of how foreigners *act* differently from 'us Japanese', the illustration depicts how foreigners also *look* very differently from 'us Japanese' by illustrating the foreigner with a hugely oversized nose (about equal in size to his entire arm). The authoritative – but nonetheless, 'cutely' depicted – policeman is scrutinizing the foreigner's document. In a speech bubble, he states, 'It's expired!', which is framed with an exclamation point. While the policeman's eyebrows are raised expressing the emotion of surprise, the foreigner is seen with furrowed eyebrows indicating anxiety. Also a drop of sweat (a common Japanese *manga* symbol used to indicate stress, worry or anxiety) appears on the foreigner's forehead, insinuating his guilt.

We can begin to see how the *Momotarou* paradigm has carried over in this depiction of the 'demonic other' (Dower, 1986) represented in the parable of the *oni* (ogre) as the suspicious foreigner/outsider with the large nose and other un-Japanese-like 'racial' features such as hair color and texture, within a discourse of 'foreigner as grotesque'. The promotion and distribution of these discourses through similar means have been steadily increasing in Japan recently, making this kind of police report 'normal' and treated as routine.[12]

Summary

In this chapter, I laid out the multiperspective theoretical and methodological framework of this study. I have demonstrated the commonalities of the two compatible approaches of FPDA and DP and explained the underlying theoretical notions. The two approaches are clearly in a process of development, as the literature in the related fields continues to grow. Thus they are not fixed and static in how they can be used. What is evident is that they have much in common and are in no way contradictory.

I then turned to how the theoretical notion of *discourses* is applied to the site of Japan by examining a selection of provisionally identified discourses of ethnicity and 'othering' occurring in Japan (and in the data of the participants of the study). The production of the discourse of *Nihonjinron* and associated discourses was examined in terms of the relationship of the aftermath of the collapse of the empire of Japan and the resulting problems of difference, marginalization and hybridity. The shift from an ideology of *multiethnicity* and *heterogeneity* during Japan's period of colonial domination in Asia to a discourse of *homogeneity* in the post-war era has been attributed to the tremendous impact of the loss of the war and effects of the Bubble Economy. This was followed by a sudden infiltration of large numbers of 'lower class' unskilled laborers. With this, the ideology became popularized of Japan as a homogeneous, classless or (an entirely) middle-class society in which foreigners were not included. Essentialist notions of 'Japaneseness', which equated race, language and nationality, were deeply integrated with the construction of the outsider 'other'. Parallels were shown between Western ideologies of white-racial supremacy in post-slavery and post-colonial contexts to that of the Japanese racial purity discourse.

In order to illustrate the notion of how 'othering' has been constructed and reproduced in modern-day discourse in Japan, I examined the *Momotarou paradigm* with the *oni* as the foreign 'other'.

Finally, to illustrate how these historically situated discourses occur in current actual practice, the text of a locally produced police report that discursively constructs the 'illegal foreigner' in Japan from an institutional level was analyzed. I explored 'the social problem' in terms of the context in which the various groups of foreigners have come to reside in Japan. I discussed *the order of discourse* (Fairclough, 1995) surrounding the notion of *gaijin/gaikokujin* in terms of both dominant and alternative discourses of ethnicity in Japan. I explored how racist and ethnic constructions of foreigners in Japan – as constituted in the text – produce, reproduce and maintain dominant hegemonic relations of power, which marginalize such groups. These same discourses appearing in this police text affect the mixed-ethnic participants of this study, as they are often treated as *gaijin/gaikokujin*.

The following chapter introduces the participants of this study and the data collection process.

Notes

1. 'Whites' are *not* the only ethnic/racial group who have been racialized and 'othered' in Japan. Although this book focuses on 'whites', a broad range of other non-Japanese ethnicities in Japan have been subjected to various types of marginalization and discrimination (see Diene, 2006; Debito Arudo's (2009) website: www.debito.org/).
2. There are two major schools of DP – both of which use discourse analysis approaches and take up traditional psychological issues such as *identity*. The DP school, upon which this study is framed, is based mostly on the work of M. Wetherell, N. Edley and the early work of M. Billig and J. Potter, among others. It uses an integrative approach that includes a poststructuralist view of discourses combined with a fine-grained analysis of discourse. The other DP approach is strongly concentrated in the Loughborough School and relies heavily on the micro-analytic turn-taking approach of conversation analysis.

3. For example, I have also used FPDA to highlight the silenced voices of a similar pair of *boys* in Japan (see Kamada, 2009).
4. This quote is from the 1989 *Mombusho Guidelines on Moral Education*, translated and referenced by Parmenter (1997: 13).
5. The Governor of Tokyo, Ishihara Shintarou, in 2004 evoked this saying, while at the same time inducing what might be called a 'foreigners as cause of crime discourse' and 'foreigners as untrustworthy discourse'. Ishihara stated, 'Whether or not to hammer Japanese nails is not the issue. The issue is foreign nails. These cannot be trusted and must be walloped flat at every opportunity' (Dillion's [2004] translation).
6. In recent years, the use of the word *'gaijin'* has come to be recognized by the media as politically incorrect with negative connotations of exclusiveness. Because of this *'gaijin'* has been included on the list of terms to be avoided in state (public) documents and in the print and broadcast media and to be replaced with terms such as *gaikokujin* or *gaikoku no kata*. In general usage, however, the word *gaijin* continues to be commonly used.
7. The term *gaijin* (and sometimes *gaikokujin*) have generally been used to refer to 'white' foreigners, while Asian foreigners residing in Japan are often referred to by more specific names such as Chinese, North Korean and South Korean. Presently with the influx of a greater variety of ethnicities of foreigners coming into Japan, the terms *gaijin/gaikokujin* have come to refer to a broader range of non-Japanese people, making the nuance less 'ethnically' specific.
8. The word *haafu* is commonly used to refer to people of Japanese and white mixed-parentage and thus physically differentiable, in contrast to Japanese-Chinese or Japanese-Korean who are not physically distinguishable from 'pure' Japanese. In particular, members of these latter groups, who have a much longer history in Japan, were sometimes referred to by other, less-neutral, derogatory pejoratives from Japan's colonial period (1910–1945), such as *konketsuji* (mixed-blood kid), *konketsu* (mixed blood), *zasshu* (mongrel) and *ainoko* (cross-breed [in-between] kid). Recently, *haafu* has come to refer to a broader range of mixed ethnicities.
9. In contrast to these *girl* participants (who reside in an urban expanse with a large foreign population), in another study that I conducted, a similarly matched pair of Japanese/'white' *boys* (who reside in a rural northern region of Japan with few foreigners) never used the word *daburu* to refer to themselves. In interviews with the boys and their families, I discovered that, unlike the urban girls, the rural boys had never heard of the usage of *'daburu'* and never used it, nor was it used by any of their family members. Thus, when referring to themselves in the data, the boys instead only referred to themselves (or their ethnicities) as *'haafu'* (see Kamada, 2009).
10. The Horikoshi Police Department in northern Japan generously granted permission to reproduce the text and illustration of this police report.
11. This translates as Horikoshi Patrol. *Horikoshi* is a place name.
12. See Debito Arudou's website: <http://debito.org/> for examples of the production and distribution of documented 'racist' actions, practices and publications in Japan. Arudou, a naturalized Japanese of American origin, is an activist in Japan for the cause of human rights for non-Japanese and the passing of an anti-discrimination law.

Chapter 3
The Participants and the Data Collection

Introduction

This chapter examines the selection of the six participants of the study and looks at the community in which they are situated, their individual families and schools, and their relationships to each other. Here I outline the data collection process and discuss issues of translation, categorization and analysis of the data. Finally, I address questions of research ethics and reflexivity. I begin with a short introduction of the research plan.

Research Plan

In order to address the research questions of this study and to identify the relevant discourses appearing in this site, I conducted a two-tier research plan along the lines of FPDA (Baxter, 2008), which includes a *diachronic* ethnographic survey of the research site as well as a *synchronic* analysis of the data, including both 'denotative' or descriptive micro-analysis as well as 'connotative' interpretation of positioning within competing discourses (see also West, 2002).

The diachronic, ethnographic analysis involved observation and recording of the mixed-ethnic adolescent participants in Japan over a long period of time in order to examine their language and practices, including patterns of speech, actions and repetitions of topics and lexical terms. Aside from these ethnographic observations, field notes, interviews and other data collected, my insider knowledge of the data collection site (Western Japan) includes my own long residences living, working and raising my own mixed-ethnic child there.[1]

During the *synchronic* tier of the study, I conducted open-ended *semi-structured interviews*. Here I stimulated discussion on the topic of mixed-ethnicity, but allowed the participants' discussion to go in any direction in which they wanted to take it, in order to collect rich data on *their* topics. Some of the main questions I presented to the participants included: Is there bullying in your school?; Do you think there is ethnic discrimination in Japan?; Have you ever been ethnically/racially bullied?; What word do you use to describe yourself (your ethnicity, nationality, race)?; What is good about being 'half'/'double'?; Do you feel different from your Japanese peers?; Are you happy to have been born 'half'/'double'?; If you were born with two Japanese parents (rather than just one) how do you think your life would be different?

During the last meeting together, I also allowed the girls to 'play the role of the researcher' by having them each generate and present their own questions to the group (see the section 'Data Collection: Recorded Sessions'). As well, aside from questions, I had also prepared some pictures from magazines and other sources which I asked them to comment on. These included a local police report about foreigners, a cover photo of *Time Asia* magazine with attractive mixed-ethnic Asian/White girls and a Japanese children's book with three marked appearances of *'gaijin'* or 'White' people (see Appendix 2).

The English-Speaking Foreign Community in Morita, Japan

An intricate, but loose, network of English-speaking foreigners, connected through a web of associations and friendships was, for the most part, established by the generation of these girls' parents in the data collection area of the Morita (a pseudonym) region of Japan. These girls were brought up in a (foreign) community within a larger (Japanese) community, without the convenience of any specific venue or neighborhood, spread over a vast geographic area spanning five prefectures. While this area is linked by an efficient rail system, best friends in this group were often separated by a commute of over one hour. From the time these girls were small, they enjoyed regular events throughout the year where households similar to their own would get together like extended family and enjoy outings or reunions together. Especially, *fun* holidays (such as Christmas and Halloween) were often shared together with other such families as these girls grew up. Although not without much effort, coordination, and parental support and help, these girls often arranged sleepovers among themselves to increase their opportunities to meet each other.

English community networks

Produced and consumed by this foreign community are various English language events and art magazines; announcement and advertisement flyers; clubs and associations; language and recreation classes; and after-school-schools. One of the most predominant ways of linking this network of foreigners together is the word-of-mouth means of passing information from one person to another (including mobile phone, e-mail messaging and talk) to announce activities and get-togethers established by and for themselves.

One group that particularly helped to link the participants of this study and their families throughout their kindergarten and elementary school years was a grassroots organization established by the foreign parents in this community called KOMNES (kids of one or more native English speaker) (an equivalent pseudonym). As the name indicates, its original purpose was an attempt for foreign parents to bring their children together to encourage their English speaking. KOMNES usually meets once monthly for some kind of fun activity such as barbeques, Halloween and Christmas parties, camping trips, talent shows and other events. Parents take turns coordinating the various activities.[2] When the participants of this study were younger, they and their families had actively participated in the group and, for some of them, it was through KOMNES that they first met (see the section 'The girls' relationships to one another' [p. 65]).

Nearly 20 years before I began this study, for over five years, between 1982 and 1987, I lived in this community. During this residence, I came to understand the local dialect and culture as well as the foreign community there. In 1987, I relocated to another location within Japan. Then in 2000, I moved back into this community for one year and I renewed my friendships with some of my former foreign friends and acquaintances who had remained there since the 1980s. One of them, a British woman, later introduced me to her mixed-ethnic daughter who became the pivot of my research when she later introduced me to five other mixed-ethnic girls her age, comprising her network of friends.

The foreign parents

While often dealing with their own plights of 'othering', foreign parents of mixed-ethnic children in Japan face various issues in raising their children in Japan whose ethnicity differs from their own. This section looks briefly at some of these issues.

Though this study focuses on ethnic identity, social class is another factor affecting identity. All six girls of this study could be considered to be from middle-class families, with college-educated parents. Katz (1996) revealed how often race, ethnicity and gender intersect, bringing him to conclude that *class* may have even more influence on the choosing of partners than race (Katz, 1996). In examining the construction of racial identity of London-reared infant and toddler children of mixed-parentage through interviews with their mainly white mothers, Katz (1996) observed the white mothers' conscious decision to place themselves in a marginal position in their coupling with someone outside their own ethnicity. While in some cases 'black' culture held an exotic attraction for white women and a way to escape their rigid and sometimes dull British upbringing, it was not only race which affected their choices, but also such factors as personality, appearance, class and intelligence (Katz, 1996). Whereas the 14 women of Katz's study married outside their race, they all married within their same class, be it middle or working class. Middle-class values were extended to race in that middle-class parents wanted to build their child's self esteem in order to deal with whatever may arise in their lives due to their mixed-ethnicity, gender and other factors.

While the development of bilinguality seemed to be one of the biggest concerns of parents in this Japanese community as evidenced by their networking web, I found that some parents occasionally tended to gloss over the hybrid identity of their children as *ordinary* or *non-significant*. For example, at the start of the study, when I approached an Australian father of a potential participant about the possibility of including his daughter in the study, he voiced this notion of his daughter's 'biculturality' as being ordinary (see the second quotation at the beginning of Chapter 1). He referred to his daughter as someone who just sees herself as a Japanese girl who has a strange foreign dad, a notion I have heard voiced by foreign fathers of mixed-ethnic children in Japan on other occasions as well (see Kamada, 1995a, 1995b, 1997). This father emphasized that his daughter has other 'bicultural' girlfriends, not so much because they are all 'bicultural', but because they are truly good friends who also all have strange, 'bicultural' parents who also happen to be friends. Similar to this Australian father in my study, Katz writes of one of his participants, a white British mother of a mixed-ethnic child who did not particularly feel that her children self-identified as 'the other' or that they were perceived as different by society. Katz writes, 'At one extreme, Lucy saw her children as essentially "English", but with dark skins and an interesting background' (Katz, 1996: 126). (Later, in the analysis chapters, how the girls themselves actually constitute their ethnicity is examined.)

Although the families of these participants reside in a region with a relatively large foreign population of English speakers, many of them had few role models among them who had already pioneered the way, as most of them represented the first generation of cross-cultural families in this community. Katz (1996) also noted this lack of elder role models for the white mothers of black/white children raised in London, with each parent having only one or two friends or relatives in a situation similar to theirs. Katz (1996) suggested that this lack of role models also helped to account for the fluid, unstructured nature of their less defined role. As mentioned above, for the children in my study, the parents often seemed more concerned with minority-language (English) role models than with ethnic identity role models, although these areas often overlap.

The Six Participants: Families and Schools

While all of the girls attended regular Japanese schools, there was broad variation in the sorts of schools they attended, as well as diversity in their family make-up. Three of the girls have foreign mothers and three have foreign fathers who are all native speakers of English from America, Britain or Australia and who are all 'white'. One of the girls was presently living in a (Japanese) single-mother home during the data collection period. Following is a brief description of the six girls' family backgrounds and differing home and school communities to which they belong (see Table 3.1).

Rina

Rina's British mother came to Japan in her late twenties for the purpose of studying art in Morita. She met Rina's Japanese father during this time. He works at the Japanese branch of a famous, large international (not Japanese) company and Rina's mother continues to practice art while also teaching English freelance part-time. Rina has one brother who is one year younger than her.

Rina attended a Japanese state[3] school through sixth grade (age 12) and then entered a private Japanese middle school, called Minami Middle School (a pseudonym). Although it is not an international school, it has a very strong emphasis on English, with a student body consisting mostly of Japanese 'returnee' children who had lived abroad for several years and a few mixed-ethnic children like Rina. While Minami is nationally accredited as a Japanese school, it has an international sister-school situated adjacent to it, called Izumi International School (a pseudonym). Izumi was not fully accredited on the same status as a Japanese school when Rina first entered Minami.[4] Izumi is a separate international school with an

Table 3.1 Details about the participants

Pseudonym (sibling status)	Foreign parent: Japanese proficiency	Bilingual/biliterate proficiency of participant	Type of schools attended
1. Rina (One younger brother)	Mother: British Good (but not fluent) Japanese proficiency	Near-balanced bilingual and biliteracy proficiency: always uses English with mother	State elementary school. Private Japanese middle school: 90-min commute. Strong English emphasis: PE, art, music in English
2. Sara (Two younger brothers)	Mother: American Japanese fluency	Receptive bilingual: comprehends English, but speaks Japanese. Attended evening English classes for a few years. Uses Japanese at home	State elementary and middle schools in neighborhood
3. Anna (One younger sister)	Father: Australian Japanese fluency	Receptive bilingual: comprehends English, but usually speaks in Japanese. Uses Japanese at home	State elementary and middle schools in neighborhood
4. Maya (One older brother)	Father: American. Divorced, living separately in USA since Maya was six. Limited Japanese ability	Can express herself in English somewhat, but speaks slowly and uses limited vocabulary. Uses Japanese at home	Lived in America for three years (ages 1–4). State elementary and middle schools in neighborhood
5. Naomi (One younger brother)	Mother: American Japanese fluency	Near-balanced bilingual and biliteracy proficiency: always uses English with mother	State elementary and middle schools in a rural area. Only 11 students in school
6. Hanna (no siblings)	Father: American. Came to Japan after age 30 Not highly proficient in Japanese	Can express herself in English if pressed: father always uses English with her. She usually answers in Japanese	Private Japanese Catholic elementary school; private Japanese Protestant middle school

entire English medium of instruction catering mostly to children of missionary families, most of whom plan to attend university outside Japan, according to Rina. Although Izumi and Minami are separate, some activities and physical education classes are shared. As well, Minami's art and music classes are conducted in English, while all of the other classes are conducted in Japanese. Rina had to pass a competitive entrance examination to enter Minami and, like a large proportion of the students there, she has to commute by train, some 90 min each way from her home.

When I first met Rina at the end of her sixth and final year of elementary school, I felt her English speaking to be extremely proficient. She could be considered a near-perfect balanced bilingual in terms of speaking. Her English literacy ability is also extremely high. She told me that she prefers to read in English, even though she has always attended Japanese schools, except for 10 months spent in America where she attended a local American elementary school for part of first and second grades. Rina says that she also enjoys writing in English. (See Appendix 1 for an uncorrected transcript sample of Rina's English writing at age 12.)

Sara

Sara's American mother came to Japan in her early twenties to study at a university in Morita. During this time she met Sara's Japanese father. Presently, Sara's father works in the international office of a university, which often sends him overseas with students. Sara's mother works part-time as an English teacher at a high school. Sara has two younger brothers.

Due to the fact that Sara's mother is extremely proficient in Japanese and does not demand that her children use English with her, Sara and her other siblings use Japanese at home. Sara could be termed a *receptive bilingual*; she understands most of what is being said to her in English, but she is not comfortable, nor very proficient in English speaking. Sara's mother tried to ameliorate this problem by sending her to an English language school once a week. Sara attended it for about a year, but by middle school she lost interest and quit the school. Sara's reading and writing ability is higher on average than her Japanese peers who take English at school beginning from middle school (age 12). Sara has always attended regular state schools and by the last interview was attending a rather typical state middle school, located within walking distance from her home.

Anna

Anna's father is an Australian national who came to Japan originally as a high school exchange student. He has since reached total fluency in

Japanese speaking and literacy, while Anna's Japanese mother is highly proficient in English. Her father works as a scientist in a research institute. Anna has one sister who is three years younger than her.

Like Sara, Anna has always attended regular state schools and by the last interview was attending a state middle school. Anna attended a summer language program in Australia for a few weeks with Hanna during the data collection period.

As Anna's father is fluent in Japanese, like Sara's mother, he did not require his children to use English in the home. Thus Anna is not comfortable, nor very proficient in using English, although she expressed interest in improving her proficiency. Anna, like Sara, is also a receptive bilingual – she can understand some English that is spoken to her, but she is not comfortable in English production and will generally reply in Japanese if spoken to in English by her father. For the most part, she acquired her English reading and writing ability through her middle school English class, and her English proficiency is higher on average than her Japanese peers.

Maya

Maya's father is American and her parents met in the USA when Maya's Japanese mother went there to study English while still single. They got married and lived in the USA for four or five years during which time Maya's mother became quite proficient at English speaking. After that, they came to live in Japan where Maya was born. Then as a baby, Maya was taken with her family to live in the USA until she was three or four years old, during which time she began to speak English. Her family returned to Japan. Then, two or three years later, her father returned to the USA by himself after learning to speak a little Japanese, while the rest of the family remained in Japan. Since then Maya's mother has raised Maya and her brother (four years older than Maya) as a single mother. Maya has twice gone to stay with her father in the USA at ages 7 and 11, for one month each time. Last year, Maya's brother went to the USA, on a special school-sponsored program at his Japanese school, where he stayed with his father and attended a local school in the USA for one year. Maya's father continues to call and talk to her on the telephone (mostly in English) about twice a month.

Maya has always attended state schools in Japan. Now she can speak English fairly well, but her speaking is very slow and careful, and limited in vocabulary. Like Anna and Sara, her English reading and writing proficiency was mostly acquired in her middle school English class and is higher on average than her Japanese peers.

Naomi

Naomi's parents met in her mother's home country, America, and later moved to Japan where Naomi was born. Her Japanese father is a professional photographer and her mother is an English teacher and translator. Their home, located in an isolated area near a hot-springs resort, also occasionally becomes a 'word-of-mouth' (no advertising) 'bed-and-breakfast'. Naomi has one brother, three years younger than her.

Like Sara, Anna and Maya, Naomi also attends a Japanese state middle school similar in appearance, curriculum, facilities and teaching quality to most state schools in Japan. However, Naomi's school is unique in one aspect. As it is located in a very sparsely populated mountainous area of the Morita region, the entire middle-school student population totals only 11 students, outnumbered by a teaching staff of 14. Naomi was one of only five students in the first-year class (seventh grade); during that year there were no students in the third-year class. Naomi has attended elementary school classes in America for short periods of time (several weeks each) on a number of occasions while traveling overseas. She also attended a middle school in Australia for four months with Hanna during the data collection period.

Like Rina, Naomi is a near-perfect balanced bilingual (English/Japanese) in terms of speaking proficiency. Although Naomi's mother's Japanese speaking and reading proficiency is very high, she has been very conscientious about consistently using *only English* with Naomi and Naomi's brother in the home to ensure their bilingual acquisition. Naomi also has high English reading proficiency and she says that she enjoys and prefers reading in English for fun. She also enjoys writing in English.

Hanna

Hanna's American father traveled to Japan for the first time in his mid-thirties where he met and married Hanna's Japanese mother. He is presently working as an English teacher at a Japanese university. Hanna's mother works part-time as a receptionist at a doctor's clinic. Hanna is the only child.

While Hanna's mother was raised in the non-religious Buddhist and Shinto traditions typical of most Japanese families and her father was raised as a non-religious Jewish American, her parents chose to send her to a private Protestant kindergarten, a Catholic elementary school, and at the time of the last meeting Hanna was attending a Protestant middle school. The family selected the Christian schools on the basis of what they considered to be a good quality education. Both the elementary and middle schools, while private, are accredited Japanese schools with a Japanese medium of instruction and curriculum. Hanna proclaims herself to be Christian in terms of what she 'believes', although she has never been formally baptized.

Hanna's father is not very proficient in Japanese according to Hanna and he always speaks to her in English. While Hanna sometimes cannot understand him and she usually answers him in Japanese, she nevertheless has acquired a relatively good grasp of spoken English and she can express herself relatively well in English. Hanna can also read English texts at a higher-than-average level compared with her Japanese peers. Hanna attended a summer language program in Australia for a few weeks with Anna and later a middle school there for four months with Naomi during the data collection period.

The girls' relationships with one another

While all the girls attend different schools, some of them had attended the same kindergarten together. All of the girls have known each other since pre-school or earlier. Rina and Sara's mothers met while they were pregnant with the girls and later sent their daughters to the same kindergarten together. There, at the same kindergarten, Rina and Sara first met Hanna and Anna. Naomi has also known Rina and Sara since birth. Rina first met Maya when she 'suddenly appeared at KOMNES' (see the section 'English community networks' [p. 58]). Anna and Maya were best friends when they were in kindergarten, but now Hanna and Anna say they are best friends.

As it was Rina who introduced me to *her* network of friends, her relationships with the others are stronger than between some of the others of them. Rina and Naomi are best friends and get together about once a month, as do Rina and Sara. However, at the first group meeting, the girls informed me that Naomi seldom meets with Sara, Hanna or Anna. Sara also seldom meets with Hanna or Anna. Part of the reason is that, aside from the one hour or more in travel distance between many of them, they are all extremely busy with school and extra-curricular activities, as are most adolescents in Japan.

Data Collection: Recorded Sessions

This study spanned four grades of school, from the sixth grade of elementary school, through the three years of middle school. Clearly, the study has a temporal dimension of significance; however, it should be clarified that this study was not designed to be a longitudinal study, as I did not consistently trace each person in the same way over the duration of the study. At the first meeting, only one girl was present; at the second meeting three girls attended; at the third, fifth and sixth meeting all six girls attended; the fourth meeting consisted of two of the girls, without me present (see Table 3.2).

While these girls get together with each other from time to time in pairs or groups of three or more, there is no established setting where they meet regularly. It was thus necessary for me, as the researcher, to create venues in order to collect data: in restaurants, a community center and overnights twice at the home of one of the girls. This section details not only the group interviews that served as the main data used for analysis, but also other supplementary data collected and examined.

The main data used for this analysis are taken from six tape-recorded informal talk sessions with the participants. The names of the meetings, dates, grades at school, ages and numbers of participants are listed in Table 3.2.

I started the data collection with the idea of conducting *informal focus group* sessions (Barbour & Kitzinger, 1999; Krueger, 1998; Myers & Macnaghten, 1999), but I soon realized that for most of the sessions, I was instead conducting *semi-structured group interviews* (Wolcott, 1999). Kitzinger and Barbour (1999) define focus groups as

> ... group discussions exploring a specific set of issues. The group is 'focused' in that it involves some kind of collective activity – such as viewing a video, examining a single health promotion message, or simply debating a set of questions. (Kitzinger & Barbour, 1999: 4)

My purpose was not to particularly 'focus' on a particular type of activity; instead my intention was to stimulate talk through group discussion using some unstructured prepared questions, which allowed the topic of conversation to go in any direction the participants wanted to take it. I was also interested in collecting data that emerged spontaneously without reference to my predetermined questions. In order to create such a situation, during part of the last meeting, I asked each of the girls to *play the role of the interviewer* by making a question of their own to present to all of the girls to answer (including themselves). I found this to be an extremely effective means of collecting rich and interesting data, which for the most part, the girls themselves created. Wolcott writes, '*Semi-structured interviews* have an open-ended quality about them, the interview taking shape as it progresses' (Wolcott, 1999: 53). LeCompte and Schensul (1999) refer similarly to this type of interviewing as *open-ended interviews*.

Table 3.2 Meetings with the participants spanning four grades of school

Meeting name (approx. time)	Type of meeting	Date	Grade at school	Girls' names (ages)	Analyst present Y/N	No. of girls
Rina's house meeting (30 min)	Semi-structured interview	March 2001	Elementary school: sixth grade	Rina (12)	Yes	1
Café meeting (2 h)	Semi-structured group interview	November 2001	Middle school: first grade	Rina (13) Sara (13) Naomi (13)	Yes	3
Hot Springs meeting (3 h)	Semi-structured group interview	March 2002	Middle school: first grade	Rina (13) Sara (13) Anna (13) Maya (13) Naomi (13) Hanna (13)	Yes	6
Hanna/Anna meeting (30 min)	Spontaneous conversation	September 2002	Middle school: second grade	Anna (13) Hanna (13)	No	2
Birthday meeting (most of the day with taped sessions of over 3 h)	Several semi-structured group interviews	September 2002	Middle school: second grade	Rina (14) Sara (14) Anna (13) Maya (14) Naomi (14) Hanna (13)	Yes	2-4-5-6 (in four stages)
Last Reunion meeting (3 h)	Semi-structured group interview; spontaneous conversation	May 2003	Middle school: third grade	Rina (14) Sara (14) Anna (14) Maya (14) Naomi (15) Hanna (14)	Yes (but, not present during spontaneous conversation segment)	6

Two of the meetings in the dataset could not be called 'semi-structured group interviews', however, as they did not comprise a *group* of the girls. The first meeting took place between only Rina and myself and could thus be called a *'semi-structured interview'*. Another meeting took place between just two of the girls, who tape-recorded their talk upon my request, at a sleepover at one of their homes when I was not present. While this could not be called *naturally occurring data*, as they were consciously making a tape for me and my research purposes, it developed spontaneously rather than being directed by my pre-conceived categories and questions. Thus I refer to these data as *'spontaneous conversation'*. Also during part of the semi-structured interview of the last reunion meeting, for several minutes, while I was busy setting up the equipment, the girls spoke spontaneously among themselves in a similar fashion without my conscious presence, and thus I also refer likewise to that segment (see Extract 7.5).

I did not adhere to the commonsense principle of selecting *easily acces-sible* data. One of the reasons for this was that in the north of Japan where I reside, there are very few mixed-ethnic children and, at the time of the study, there were no international or immersion schools in northern Japan between Sendai (a few hours by train north of Tokyo) and Sapporo (in the northern-most island). Except for the first meeting, which took place while I was still residing in the Morita area, I traveled by airplane from the northern end of the main island of Japan to the Morita region for each of the other four pre-arranged group meetings. The data collection was costly in terms of these travel and other expenses such as venue fees, meals and small gifts, which I purchased for everyone at each meeting (as motivation and reward, but also considered customary practice in Japan).

Translation, Categorization and Analysis of the Data

Each of the tape-recorded sessions was transcribed using a transcrip-tion style close to ordinary English writing style, with a few specific conventions employed (see transcription conventions at the front of this book). A Romanization system of Japanese into alphabetic orthography, called the Hepburn System of Romanization, was used. Having resided in the data collection site for some five or six years during my early residence in Japan, I became extremely proficient in the understanding and use of the local dialect. I did all of the original translations from Japanese to English myself. In order to ameliorate situations where I was unable to decipher what was spoken in Japanese and also to insure accuracy of my translations, I had all of my translated transcripts checked by a native Japanese speaker who listened to all of the tape recordings that had

Japanese sections to check for errors or omissions. Efforts were made to translate the Japanese into English in a manner that was comparable to the informal language that the girls were using throughout most of the interviews. Where certain idiomatic speech, use of English loan words into Japanese, and gendered language forms were used, as a part of the analysis, throughout I have made efforts to explain the nuance and significance based on the original Japanese text.

The next step was to go through the entire set of data and look for occurrences that addressed the research questions. I compiled a list of main themes and discourses that were found to be repeatedly showing in the data (e.g. celebration of cultural capital, discourse of conformity, discourse of exclusion, racialization process, gendering). These were listed up and each given an arbitrary code symbol.

Then the entire set of data was examined and coded with these symbols marking repeatedly occurring themes and discourses. From the entire dataset, an abbreviated summary was compiled in the chronological order of the meetings, which included extracts considered significant based on the coded sections. In this condensed dataset, notations were made of where to find the extracts in the hundreds of pages of transcribed data from the recorded sessions, making it easy to handle and quick to locate particular passages in the data.

Later, themes were re-arranged and combined, some of which overlapped, into seven categories. For each category, searches were made through the abbreviated summary and relevant extracts from that summary were placed into the seven specific category files, with some extracts going into more than one file.

Finally, the categories were combined again into what became the four analysis chapters. The category of *isolation* came to comprise Chapter 4 (Negotiating Identities); the category of *difference* came to comprise Chapter 5 (Claiming *Good* Difference; Rejecting *Bad* Difference); the category of *cultural/symbolic capital* came to comprise Chapter 6 (Celebration of Cultural, Symbolic, Linguistic and Social Capital); and the categories of *ethnic embodiment* and *gendering* came to comprise Chapter 7 (Discursive 'Embodied' Identities of Ethnicity and Gender). I included the other two categories of *ideological dilemmas/contradictions* and *change* throughout.

Presentation of the data: Chronological versus topical

As mentioned above, this book is divided into categories or topics that are addressed in the four analysis chapters. However, in presenting the narratives of these girls, it was also my intention to try to present a coherent storyline of events. This necessitated the presentation of the data in a relatively chronological order. In order to address this conflict of chronological versus topical presentation of the data, I have tried to present the data within each chapter or section of a chapter in chronological order as much as possible. To a large extent, it has worked out that the topics that I discuss in the earlier analysis chapters appeared more predominantly in the earlier meetings while the topics taken up in the final analysis chapter predominantly came from the last meeting with the girls. Thus, while arranging the analysis chapters into different topics, I was more or less able to achieve a chronological storyline showing changes in the girls over time.

The Six Meetings

The main data collected for this study came from six tape-recorded sessions with the participants over the period of a few years spanning four grades of school (refer to Table 3.2). Throughout these six meetings, however, there is a degree of unavoidable inconsistency in representation of the participants as some of the meetings were not attended by all six of them (see the section 'The Unevenness of the Data Collected and Selected' [p. 74]).

Rina's house meeting

(Total time: about 30 min) The first meeting (March 2001), an informal *semi-structured interview*, took place with me and Rina (age 12), during the last week of her final year of elementary school (sixth grade) in a private room in her home.

Before the interview began, I had asked Rina to do a 'think-aloud protocol' (writing task) (see Hayes & Flower, 1983) of which my intention was to collect and analyze qualitative data on the relationship between bilinguality, thought processes and mixed-ethnic identity for a related paper, during the early stages of this study. The oral interview that followed the written task of the 'protocol' became much more central to my overall research plan for this study when I came to realize the richness of the spoken data. For the 'protocol', I asked Rina to choose among three topics, which I had previously prepared, and to write an essay in her minority language (English) while simultaneously speaking her thoughts aloud (in either of her two languages). (See Appendix 1 for a transcript of Rina's written text.) After completion of the writing task, I asked Rina if she would not mind talking with me awhile. She graciously accepted with the awareness that the tape recorder was still on. This interview was conducted totally in English.

Café meeting

(Total time: about 2 h.) The second meeting (November 2001), a *semi-structured group interview*, included three girls – Rina, Naomi and Sara (ages 12 and 13) – at a café over lunch near Rina's house. I had invited three other of Rina's friends to also join this meeting, but one of them was busy with a sports event, and the non-Japanese fathers of the other two girls, whom I had contacted, had both e-mailed me saying that their daughters were not interested in joining the meetings (see the sections 'The foreign parents' [p. 58] and 'Research Ethics: Adolescents, Their Parents and Privacy' [p. 76]). These girls had just recently left behind their elementary-schoolchild selves to now become pupils of middle school (seventh grade). This meeting started out in Japanese, but then switched back and forth between Japanese and English, with Rina and Naomi using English most of the time and Sara using Japanese for the most part.

After the meeting, upon Rina's mother's invitation, we all returned to Rina's house nearby for tea, so that I could discuss with the three (English-speaking, non-Japanese) mothers my research project (with the girls chatting together in another room). I had originally prepared an agenda for this parent meeting to try to gather some background information about the families. However, since Rina's mother had invited us as friends to her house, I did not feel it appropriate to tape record it and, for the most part, rather than me asking the questions, they all had many questions for me about the nature of the project. I had already known and been on friendly terms with Rina's and Sara's mothers and it was only Naomi's mother whom I was meeting for the first time. This meeting did not develop into an interview per se and many of my prepared questions were later addressed by the girls in recorded sessions and then transcribed with the other data. However, I felt that the tea meeting was very important and successful in that I was able to gain the mothers' understanding about my project and to establish rapport and trust among them.

Hot Springs (Onsen) meeting

(Total time: 3 h.) I continued to invite all six of the girls (via their parents) to this third scheduled meeting even though two of the fathers had previously told me that their daughters were not interested in joining (see the section 'Research Ethics: Adolescents, Their Parents and Privacy' [p. 76], for a discussion on research ethics). I felt like I did not want to purposely exclude them from the group activities if they so desired to join, so I approached the non-Japanese fathers again with another e-mail to invite their daughters to join. In the meantime, through the girls' own networking and talking among themselves, those who had attended the first meeting helped to encourage the others to join. It turned out that all six girls (all aged 13) showed up for the meeting (March 2002), perhaps partly due to the attraction of the venue selected for the third meeting. It was a sleepover at the secluded home of one of the girls (Naomi), which also occasionally served as a bed-and-breakfast (inn) near a hot-springs resort. Along with Naomi's parents and me, Sara's mother also stayed overnight and Maya's (Japanese) mother stayed until late. Perhaps part of the girls' willingness to be cooperative participants was the built-in rewards for them of participating. Our overnight agenda included dinner in a pizza restaurant and a dip in the hot-springs bath at the nearby resort hotel. The meeting, a *semi-structured group interview*, was conducted mostly in Japanese, but switched into English occasionally.

In order to stimulate discussion on mixed-ethnicity and othering in Japan, I had prepared some pictures from magazines that I presented for discussion (see Appendix 2). This technique of using photos and illustrations to stimulate discussion proved to be a very successful tool in collecting rich data on specific topics.

Hanna and Anna meeting

(Total time: 30 min) This *'spontaneous conversation'* session (September 2002) is different from the rest of the sessions making up the dataset of this study, in that this meeting took place between two of the girls (Hanna and Anna) without my presence. These data come from the transcribed talk from an audio-tape they made at a sleepover at one of their homes as they chatted together in bed after midnight on the evening before the Birthday meeting (see Extracts 5.10 and 7.1). Both girls are 13 years old. They are speaking in Japanese.

Birthday meeting

(Total time: most of the day [with taped sessions of over 3 h].) This fourth meeting that took place on Maya's birthday (September 2002) consisted of several *semi-structured group interviews*. Attendants eventually included all six girls (ages 13 and 14), but in staggered groupings as several arrived later due to various school sport-club obligations. The stages of the meeting and the amount of time for each segment are as follows: (1) Anna and Hanna arrive on time and we begin (about 40 min); (2) Later Naomi and Maya arrive to make a total of four members (1 h); (3) Finally,

Sara arrives to make a total of five girls (40 min); (4) We change venue for lunch and a birthday party. After lunch and a walk, we meet Rina who stays long enough for a snack at a third venue before the meeting ends (40 min). (By sunset, at the end of the day, with only Naomi and I left to wait an hour for her family to pick her up, we casually shopped and talked together.) This day's meeting was conducted mostly in Japanese but also switched into English at times.

During Stage 3 of this meeting when five girls were present, I gave them a written task in which I asked them to indicate on a piece of paper their affiliations, which we later discussed. I had them indicate their preferred affiliations by drawing their more important (in terms of priority) communities in larger circles and their less important affiliations in smaller circles. (I later had the sixth participant also address this question.) This data collection technique proved helpful in adding insight to the analysis of a related extract of spoken data included in this study (see the section 'Mixed-Ethnic Girl Friendships and Femininity Capital' [p. 162]; Extracts 6.9a and b).

Last reunion meeting

(Total time: about 3 h.) The girls, at the end of the Birthday meeting, had expressed their preference to return to the Hot Springs venue (Naomi's house) for a sleepover for the next meeting. Thus, I arranged a date (in May 2003), which the girls agreed to, and I set about booking the room with Naomi's mother. However, as three of the girls had their scheduled weekly lesson activities on that day, such as hip-hop (dance) lessons (which were priorities in their lives), it seemed that they would not make it there in time to join the interviews and that they would try to join in the sleepover later, after the interview had already finished. I was disappointed, but I decided to go ahead with just the three girls anyway, as it was the only opportunity available. However, at the pre-established meeting time of 3:00 pm, all six of the girls showed up exactly on time, as it turned out to be the *fifth* Saturday of the month when such lessons are routinely cancelled.

This meeting, a *semi-structured group interview*, also served as a reunion/homecoming party between four of the girls and two others, Naomi and Hanna, who had been out of Japan for the last four months in Australia where they had been attending a local school. It had been decided that they would return to Japan at semester's end to consider whether to continue with school overseas or to return to their schools in Japan. Hanna had decided to return to Japan for good, but Naomi decided not to return to her school in Japan and was coming home only for a vacation with plans to return to Australia for the beginning of the next school term.

This meeting was conducted in both languages, but mostly in Japanese. During part of this meeting, I provided them with materials and gave them the task of drawing their own self-portraits. I asked them to sign their pictures with their pseudonyms, which I had already selected for each of them (see their self-portraits in Appendix 3). There is a specific reference to one of the girl's self-portrait in one piece of spoken data used in this book (see Extract 7.5, Line no. 39). The self-portraits can be seen as constructions of the girls' identity which I examine in more detail in the section 'The self-portraits' [p. 199]. I also include the drawings in the appendix as a way of additionally introducing the six participants, without resorting to the use of photographs which compromise privacy.

The Unevenness of the Data Collected and Selected

While this book examines a network of six friends, the amount of data collected on each girl is uneven, as is the share of space given to each of the girls featured in the data selected for use in this book. There are several reasons for this. First of all, Rina appears more frequently than the other girls partly due to the fact that the other participants were introduced by Rina as her network of friends. The first meeting was conducted with Rina alone, making the volume of available data on Rina more than that of the other girls.

Aside from the volume of the data, some of the sound quality of certain speakers in the data was better than others. Since the sessions were not recorded on video, sometimes it was difficult to determine on the audio-tapes who was the speaker. Some of the girls were also more outgoing and contributed to more of the talk than others of them when they were all assembled together. For example, Anna and Sara, and to a lesser extent Maya, seemed more reticent than some of the others and did not assertively speak out as much as some of the other girls. Also Anna's and Sara's voices were low and not as distinctive as some of the other girls. During the transcription stage, there were many places where I could not determine with absolute certainty whether the speaker was Anna or Sara as their voices were similar. In situations where I could not determine with certainty which girl was speaking, on the transcripts in the column for the speaker, I placed a question mark (?). In contrast to the above mentioned girls, particularly the speech characteristics of Naomi, Rina and Hanna were very distinctive and easy to recognize. It is partly due to this reason that the easier to determine voices appear in the data of this book more than others, while the unclear speakers appear as question marks.

When all six of the girls were assembled together, Naomi, Rina or Hanna held the floor most often while Anna, Sara and Maya seemed to be less assertive in speaking out. Even though we used Japanese most of time and I tried to make the girls feel that Japanese should be the dominant language of our talk, the speech sometimes drifted into English. Part of the reason for the relative silence of some of the girls might be due to their lesser ability to use English compared to some of the others. In spite of this unevenness of the available data, I have tried to let the voices of the more silenced members also be heard. In my selection of the data to be used in this book, I have tried to allow space for each of the girls to be heard, albeit perhaps not always equal space.

Other Collected Data

Several other types of data were also assembled in the data collection process. This section explains each of these.

Audio-tapes made by the girls

At the end of the Hot Springs meeting, I had given each girl empty cassette tapes and had asked them to turn on a tape recorder while they were talking together in pairs or groups and to bring it with them to the next (Birthday) meeting. Influenced by a study conducted by Coates (1999: 124), I told the girls that if they said something that they did not want me to hear on the tape, they could just erase that part of it. Three girls (Sara, Naomi and Maya) who had slept over together at Sara's house on the evening prior to the Birthday meeting had attempted to make an audio-tape recording of their talk, but they had inadvertently forgotten to attach a microphone and the talk did not get recorded. Two other girls, Hanna and Anna, also slept over together the evening before the meeting and, as mentioned above (see the section 'Hanna and Anna meeting' [p. 72]), they made a 30-min tape recording of themselves. The sixth girl, Rina, had a volleyball competition the next morning, so she did not join in any of the sleepovers nor make a tape.

Correspondence with the parents and the girls

I exchanged well over a hundred e-mails during the data collection period with the girls and their parents. Originally, I contacted the parents to gain consent to include their children in my study. Later, I was able to correspond directly with the girls. There was also some regular postal mail that I sent out to the girls from time to time to insure that they received important notices such as meeting times, dates, places, maps, agendas and so forth. Nearly all of the correspondence that I sent out to the girls was written with the same information in both Japanese and English, as were the agenda lists for each of the meetings and all task instructions.

Field notes

I made field notes throughout the data collection period, especially whenever I had meetings or communication with the families or the girls. I used observations from these notes throughout the study in the process of identifying discourses affecting the particular epistemological site of Japan and analyzing the data. Some of the observations gleaned from field notes have been incorporated into this chapter as well.

Individual interviews

Individual interviews were conducted throughout the data collection period either in person, in e-mail, or during the meetings. Particularly, during the Birthday meeting gathering, which went on for the entire day in stages, I was able to conduct several personal one-on-one interviews with the girls. These interviews were recorded and transcribed along with the other data from the meeting.

Boys' data

I conducted one interview with two adolescent boys in Japan of Japanese and 'white foreign' mixed-parentage who were friends, with the purpose of comparing possible differences or similarities between groups of mixed-ethnic girls and boys (see Kamada, 2009). I transcribed, translated and examined their hour-long tape-recorded session. While some very interesting issues emerged in the data, I later decided not to use these data in this book, due to space limitations (see the section 'Implications for Future Research' [p. 225] for a brief discussion of the boys' data).

Research Ethics: Adolescents, their Parents and Privacy

This section looks at the question of research ethics and privacy. In order to use early adolescent girls as participants, I needed first to approach the parents of these girls to seek their approval before contacting any of the girls. I sent the parents a statement of my purpose, and a request for their cooperation in which I addressed issues of research ethics, such as issues of privacy and use of their personal information and what might be expected of their daughters.

As mentioned above, I received letters from two fathers who initially turned down my request. One of these fathers had apologized for the 'disappointing news' that his daughter adamantly did not wish to join my study, even though he himself was very enthusiastic and supportive, and had sincerely wanted his daughter to join. He stated that she had been going through a painful period on the issue of being bicultural and did not want to be reminded of it any more than necessary. In spite of this response, I had a feeling that if I could make the meetings valuable enough for the girls by addressing *their agendas* (of getting together and having fun), that I might later be able to encourage all six girls to join and to keep them wanting to attend again and again.

My project proposal had caused some tensions between parents and their children as the parents brought up the issue of 'mixed-ethnicity' (what we referred to in English at the time as 'biculturality') to their children – something that I had never imagined might occur. But it also brought home to me how delicate this issue could be for adolescents. Another father wrote to say that his daughter was not keen on making her ethnicity an issue, although his main reason for his refusal was a prior engagement for that day. A third girl was also unable to join for the first group meeting as she had a sports event on that day. Consequently, my project got off to a somewhat low-key start with a slimmed down group of three instead of six.

I was always very careful to respect the ethical issues associated with research on children and young people by first of all going through the parents for all contact with the girls. It was not until much later, after getting parental permission that I actually contacted the girls directly, but even then, I sent the same mail separately to the parents as well throughout the project. Before the start of the Hot Springs meeting, I again sent out invitation e-mails to all of the girls via the parents – including the parents who had said their daughters did not want to or were unable to participate the first time.

Fortunately, later, when Rina approached the three girls who had not joined, about attending the next meeting, which was to be a sleepover 'party' at Naomi's house, they not only attended, but were also extremely enthusiastic and expressive in their tremendously positive contribution to my project right from their first appearance. Also their parents were happy that they had decided to join. Nonetheless, planning each meeting was a laborious job in establishing the venue and arranging a time that would be convenient for all six families and their adolescent daughters simultaneously.

Although all of the families were highly supportive, cooperative and kind, it was very difficult coordinating the two factors of not over-inconveniencing the parents by involving them too much, and yet at the same time making them feel informed every step of the way. I knew that without the parent's positive consent, I would never be able to meet the girls. I felt very dependent on the cooperation of the parents in helping me with initial introductions and then later to help coordinate certain aspects of the meetings such as transportation and other aspects. Their support helped immensely as I was physically far removed from the location and I did not have access to a car while in the expansive Morita vicinity within which these girls resided. In the end, much of the corre-spondence that went on between these parents (and the six girls) and I eventually became very informal and intimate with us often signing our mail, 'love, [name]'.

During the data collection period, I sent around to each girl a Language Use Consent Form in both Japanese and English. I asked them to indicate on this form in writing their consent (or not) to use their spoken data (anonymously) in publications or in academic meetings. The girls all signed them and sent them back to me. I realized then that the information I collected, how I collected it and the ways in which I analyzed and displayed it, could be a potentially very sensitive issue. Throughout the process, I have been very conscious of issues of privacy and have tried to proceed cautiously when presenting my findings, although within this small community, even with the use of pseudonyms, it is often very difficult to do. My purpose throughout has been to empower this community and these individuals, rather than to damage or disempower them in any way.

Reflexivity: The Analyst Appearing in the Data

From the very start of this study, I made a theoretically directed decision to conduct qualitative research (see Mason, 2002; Silverman, 2005). The social constructionist position, upon which this study is theoretically based, rejects the notion that an external, objective reality can be quantified and fixedly determined. In contrast to this, qualitative research allows for a broader flexibility in the means in which to construct and measure 'know-ledge', which the social constructionist takes to be historically situated and contextually produced. I acknowledge, however, that the 'knowledge' that I create in this book is constructed through a process of continuous deci-sions made about which data to collect, which data to use and not use, and how to emphasize certain aspects of it over others. One might ask if my analysis is correct, or could the same data, analyzed in another manner by someone else, using other analytical tools and situated within different historical positioning, produce different results? I have tried to maintain reflexivity as an analyst regarding my own personal positioning. While my purpose in this book has been to highlight the voices of the participants where they otherwise might not have been heard, I have also tried to acknowledge the appearance of my own voice in the data. Throughout, I attend to reflexivity in my analysis by trying to show my readers that I have considered these issues and have tried to evaluate the data with all due clarity in representing the voices of the participants.

Often I found myself appearing in the data of this study, as my role in the co-construction of contextualized, constructed truth with these girls became apparent. My position as an English-speaking 'white foreigner' – whose ethnicity and place of birth differs from the participants – must also be accounted for and reflected upon. Also my mother tongue – English – differs from some of the participants. How might the voices of the girls have been different had I been a Japanese-speaking Japanese national? Yamaguchi (2005), a Japanese researcher living outside Japan, similarly looked at Japanese identities in America while reflecting on his position as researcher. He referred to his participants as 'Generation 1.5 Japanese' or 'people who immigrated to the US during their early life stages and have lost their native-like competence of Japanese or never attained it' (Yamaguchi, 2005: 269). Yamaguchi similarly attended to reflexive considerations concerning the influence of differences (in ethnicity and language) between the researcher and the researched, but from the opposite perspective of this study. Where my voice appeared in the data, I have tried to disclose myself as a co-constructor as much as possible in my analysis and not ignore the significance of my influence. Perhaps the girls might have expressed themselves differently had I stayed out of the interaction more and let them introduce their own topics and viewpoints without revealing my bias or my predetermined categories. Nonetheless, my role in this co-construction cannot be dismissed and thus my input becomes a part of the data itself. Throughout I, myself, become the seventh participant of this study.

Another question that I have reflected upon in this study is the obvious age difference between me, as analyst, and the girls as my participants. I was of the generation of their parents and I was furthermore acquainted with two of the parents before the start of the study and friendly with others of them after the study began. Due to these relationships, questions may arise as to what the girls might have been willing to share with me.

Nevertheless, it is also important to note, that except for the first meeting with just one girl (Rina), I had already moved out of this community and was living in another Japan location very distant from them.

The question of reflexivity is one that cannot be ignored in a qualitative study such as this (Charmaz & Mitchell, 1997; Hertz, 1997b; Wasserfall, 1997). Hertz emphasizes the importance of reflexivity in not only reporting, 'what I know', but also 'how I know it' during the entire process of the research (Hertz, 1997: viii). Throughout, I have tried to personally account for my own positioning and historical background, which I have brought to the research.

Summary

This chapter has examined the community from which the participants of this study emerged and the qualitative methodology employed. The six girl participants, while all attending regular Japanese schools and coming from families with one 'white foreign' parent and one Japanese parent, also had various individual differences between them in terms of their particular homes, schools and use of languages. Research ethics and matters of privacy are important aspects of research design that require careful attention from the start of the study. Questions of which data to select and the implications of the various choices made throughout the study are important issues that I, as analyst, had to consider, along with maintaining reflexivity in accounting for how I analyzed the data.

Notes

1. I have been residing (as an American foreigner) in Japan in various locations for nearly three decades. Among other localities in Japan, I lived for a total of six years in the (girl data) research site of Western Japan on two separate occasions. Presently, I have been residing in a relatively rural area of northeastern Honshu for over 17 years.
2. I, with my son (10 years old at the time), were also members of KOMNES (a pseudonym) while living in this community for one year. I took my turn as a parent in coordinating some of the activities.
3. What I have called a 'state school' is an elementary or middle school publicly established at the city/town/village level in Japan. In Japanese, it is called a *kouritsu gakkou*. (The British equivalent would be a 'state school'; the American equivalent would be a 'public school'.)
4. Izumi International School (a pseudonym) did later gain accreditation in 2003 when the laws changed. Students graduating from such English-language international schools were then finally allowed to apply to Japanese universities without first having to pass a separate high school equivalency examination.

Chapter 4

Negotiating Identities

Introduction: Negotiating 'Othered' Identities

This is the first of four chapters comprising the analysis section of this book. Here I examine, in detail, various selected extracts from the data that have particular relevance to the theoretical framework as laid out up to this point. I analyze linguistic 'traces' (Sunderland, 2004: 28; Talbot, 1995: 24) – features that suggest linguistic evidence of the existence of a certain discourse – of the various ideological worldviews or discourses identified in the previous chapter as they occur in the spoken data of the participants.

As mentioned earlier (see the section 'Research Plan' [p. 56]), the synchronic analysis stage of FPDA incorporates both denotative and connotative analysis. I begin by employing a denotative analysis of each extract. First, I examine details of verbal and non-verbal interaction in a non-evaluative manner. From there, through a connotative analysis, I connect how use of spoken language at the micro-level manifests intertextualized discourses at the macro-level (Baxter, 2008).

This and the following chapter address the first central question introduced in Chapter 1, restated here:

> Are there any *tensions or dilemmas* in the ways children (adolescent girls) of Japanese and 'white' mixed-parentage in Japan identify themselves in terms of their ethnicity? If so, what are they and how do these girls constitute themselves?

To begin with, this chapter explores how the six girls negotiate their ethnic identities (upon establishing that they do) by their constituting, contesting and taking control of 'othering' in their world. While this book is mainly concerned with ethnic forms of 'othering', there is a complex web of other factors also influencing the identification process of these girls as they pass through their adolescence. Many studies have focused on the identity concerns of adolescents (and specifically teenage girls) and how they perform inside of or outside of the norms of the in-groups at school (e.g. Bucholtz, 1999; Eckert, 1993, 2000; Finders, 1997; Orenstein, 1994; Simmons, 2002). This chapter looks at how these girls position themselves in the constitution of their identities through their tensions and struggles with the overlapping issues they face at school, particularly *isolation* in regard to both school-group exclusion/inclusion and *ethnic othering* as a result of their physical differences.

In particular here, I examine the discursive positions of 'being left out' and 'standing out' (*hamideru*, in Japanese) which emerged prominently in the earlier data. Also, I analyze how these girls take up, contest, take control of and (re)constitute this 'othering' within the various discourses available to them, along with the discursive functions they utilize in this process.

Isolation, Bullying and Being Left Out

This section looks at how one of the girls (Rina) dealt with issues of ethnic bullying and isolation within her various school settings. Gender issues also arise as Rina positioned *boys* as agents of this bullying. Here during the *Rina's house meeting*, at the end of her final year of elementary school (age 12), Rina is seen discursively creating several opposing constructions for herself which most of the other participants also articulated in later interviews. This extract starts out with me asking Rina why she had decided, for the following school year, to attend the private middle school, Minami (a pseudonym), a 90-min commute from her home, instead of the neighborhood middle school. The following extract and several that follow were taken from a semi-structured interview between Rina and I where we used only English. (See a list of the transcription conventions at the beginning of this book.)

(Extract 4.1) Rina's house (age 12): 'Very left out and isolated'

36 **L:** so what made you decide THAT school rather than a
            close-by-school?
37 **R:** well, the close-by school has a very BAD reputation for,
            you know, drinking,
38   not drinking, smoking, 'n drugs and stuff, so,
39 **L:** oh really? drugs?

40	**R:**	yeah, but that's about like five people and out of a hundred and that also,
41		but I felt that um, usually when I go into, to places or schools with people that are all
42		Japanese they kind of just like stare at me and go *'gaijin, gaijin'*,
43	**L:**	really?
44	**R:**	which makes me feel VERY left out and I become very isolated
45	**L:**	umm
46	**R:**	but when I went, the first time I went to Minami was when I was in fourth grade
47		and I walked in and I felt like I was at home, no one stared at me, no one asked me questions,
48		no one pointed, I just felt totally at home,
49		I didn't feel isolated
50	**L:**	I see
51	**R:**	yeah, and although most of the people were older than me, I just felt this was
52		the place that I've got to go to, and I've got to get in,
53	**L:**	uh-huh

Rina initially accounted for her decision to attend Minami Middle School by attributing a bad reputation to her local school. She began by building up an exaggerated 'reality' of her local school, by stating problems of drinking, smoking and drug use. But then Rina quickly withdrew her claim of there being a drinking problem at her school (Line nos 37–38), and then she further qualified the degree of drug use, when questioned, as consisting of a very small minority of students (Line no. 40). Within a DP approach, Horton-Salway (2001) refers to the building up of 'fact and interest' as one aspect of the *Discursive Action Model* where various discursive strategies are employed by speakers in order to make their accounts appear more factual and sound. Here Rina is using exaggeration to make her account more colorful and dynamic.

In her account of why she chose to attend Minami instead of a local school, Rina described her negative experiences at 'places or schools' where people stare at her and call her *'gaijin'*, racializing and isolating her (Line nos 41–42, 44). Rina used both past-tense verbs (I felt) to place the story in the past (Line no. 41), as well as verbs of present tense (when I go into; stare at me; makes me feel; I become isolated) to mark the continuation of the problem into the present (Line nos 41–42). Rina indexed ethnicity/race in using the lexis 'Japanese' (as a category to which she was excluded) and the intertextuallly voiced and un-translated pejorative *'gaijin'* (Line no. 42).

Rina imitated and at the same time contested this intertexual voice of Japanese people who constitute her as '*gaijin*' or 'foreign outsider'.

Rina drew on intersecting discourses to talk about how she was ethnically positioned. She was powerless at this point to resist being positioned as isolated, excluded and marginalized by name-calling classmates at school as well as by people outside of school who marginalized her as 'the other' based on her *gaijin* appearance within discourses of homogeneity, Japanese conformity and *gaijin* otherness. Inasmuch as Rina might try to conform to the norms of *behavior* at school, she could do nothing to change her ethnic *appearance*.

This account contrasts starkly with how Rina described her first experience later at Minami (Line nos 46–49), where no one stared or pointed at her. Rina found openness and acceptance within a discourse of diversity when the community shifted from that of a Japanese state school to that of a unique Japanese private school setting where mixed-ethnicity and 'differentness' become assets. She was able to reconstitute herself within alternative empowering discourses of ethnicity. Even difference on the basis of age ranking, which can sometimes be very rigid in Japanese society, was an issue that Rina brought up, but presented as *not* troubling for her at Minami (Line nos 51–52). Rina expressed both a desire to fit into Japanese society and be accepted as Japanese as well as a rejection of aspects of Japanese society.

In the following extract, Rina can be seen drawing on these same competing discourses of Japanese conformity and diversity to describe two other different educational communities in America to which she was affiliated, when her father was temporarily transferred to the USA with his family for 10 months. During this residence in America, Rina entered a local public (state) elementary school while she also attended a Japanese Saturday school. The extract begins with Rina describing the shift from a school in Japan to one in America.

Extract 4.2 (Rina's house) (age 12): 'Very open-hearted'

157 **R:** I was second grade, and I had just started Japanese school and had got lots of,
158 I felt isolated quite often then, but then I came to um, this American,
159 (Baxter) Elementary, and I felt that they were VERY open-hearted,
160 they welcomed me, they didn't leave me alone to do, to get on,
161 they helped me with places I didn't know and with their help I got good grades

162		and I felt it was very kind and I was very sad to leave,
163		but then I came back and found out that I could cope with school, but,
164	**L:**	you came back in third grade?
165	**R:**	I came back in second, I went in the end of first grade, first grade, December,
166		and I came back in September, and I felt I could cope quite a lot, yeah
167	**L:**	so, did you keep up your Japanese homework back there so you were OK?
168	**R:**	well, there was this, we went to this um, Japanese school
169	**L:**	Saturday?
170	**R:**	Saturday school and I REALLY didn't like it
171	**L:**	why?
172	**R:**	I don't know, but even though we were in a different culture,
173		they still seemed to leave me alone, ignore me
174	**L:**	I see
175	**R:**	I still felt isolated and left out, I really hated going there
176	**L:**	you felt like a gaijin, in a sense, in a Japanese school?
177	**R:**	yeah
178	**L:**	that's funny, wow
179	**R:**	and I,
180	**L:**	because all the other kids were Japanese?
181	**R:**	yeah, most of them were Japanese
182	**L:**	oh, I see
183	**R:**	and I felt very isolated and I hated it, the teachers weren't so comforting,
184		the work was OK, I didn't mind the work, but it wasn't,
185	**L:**	just the way you felt?
186	**R:**	yeah, I just,
187	**L:**	the way they were treating you, and stuff?
188	**R:**	yeah, I just didn't feel good, I didn't have any friends, some people invited
189		me to their house but, houses, but I didn't really have time to go, but, um,
190		the local school, I felt very pleased with and happy in and, yeah, I liked it

Examination of Rina's lexical choices to describe her two school settings reveals various tensions that she worked through in overcoming her sense of isolation in school. She used the word 'isolated' three times (Line nos 158, 175, 183), all in the first-person, past-tense form to refer to her feelings during her earlier elementary school years. Rina also used several other words to describe examples of these similar feelings of isolation in the context of a _Japanese school_ in America: 'leave me alone', 'ignore me' (Line no. 173), 'left out' (Line no. 175), 'I didn't have any friends' (Line no. 188). In the telling of her experiences of isolation, Rina also expressed 'strong dislike' (Line no. 170) and then twice used the lexis 'hate' to express an even stronger negative emotion (Line nos 175, 183).

Rina then switched to using lexes with positive connotations in referring to her contrasting experiences in an American public school: 'VERY open-hearted', 'they welcomed me', 'didn't leave me alone', 'helped me', 'very kind', 'I was sad to leave' (Line nos 159–162); 'pleased', 'happy' (Line no. 190). In referring to her changed feelings after her experience in the American school, she twice stated 'I could cope' [with school back in Japan] (Line nos 163, 166).

Rina began by accounting for why she was presently able to cope with the situation of isolation at her school back in Japan, based on her earlier positive esteem-lifting experience in an American school. Then the topic of conversation shifted as we started talking about a Japanese Saturday school that Rina also attended while in America.

Within the community of the Japanese Saturday school in America, Rina continued to feel lonely and isolated within a discourse of Japanese conformity. I helped co-construct this idea with her by suggesting that 'you felt like a _gaijin_, in a sense, in a Japanese school?' (Line no. 176). Within the larger context of America, one might expect the Japanese person to be considered the foreign 'outsiders' and the English-speaking Caucasians to be the 'insiders'. However, Rina's account discursively depicted this not to be the case within the context of the community of the Japanese Saturday school where she was positioned as the isolated outsider. This is what prompted me to treat her statement as remarkable with my comment 'that's funny, wow' (Line no. 178). Within that community of Japanese people, just as Rina had positioned herself within the context of her school in Japan, she again positioned herself as isolated, left out and 'othered', or what Iino (1996) referred to as 'gaijinized'.

Rina blamed the teachers at the Japanese Saturday school for not being very comforting (Line no. 183). However, she also made the point clear that it was not the _schoolwork_ at the Japanese Saturday school which bothered her, but it was her _feelings of isolation_ and lack of friends which was troublesome. However, while Rina constituted herself as having little control over being excluded by her Japanese peers, she presented another construction in which she pointed out that some of the people at the Japanese Saturday school had invited her to their homes and that acting through her own agency, she herself refused the offer, attributing the reason to time priorities. Her quickly added statement – that she was pleased with and happy with the local school (Line no. 190) – served to establish her self-positioning as a member of (an insider within) the community of the local American school rather than the Japanese Saturday school.

The following extract continues from the above, with the topic centering first on the school in America and next shifting to the Japanese Saturday school in America and then to Rina's school back in Japan.

(Extract 4.3) Rina's house (age 12): 'Bullied by the boys'

190	**L:**	did that really help you to speak English a lot too? were you speaking so well,
191	**R:**	yeah, yeah
192	**L:**	before you were there?
193	**R:**	I wasn't, I don't, I don't remember that much, but I don't think I was speaking
194		as much when I went in as when I came out, and I think that that helped me
195		improve my English but then since I didn't really take the *Nihonjin gakkou* (Japanese Saturday School in America)
196		so seriously,
197	**L:**	mmmmm
198	**R:**	my Japanese was very low
199	**L:**	it got worse? your speaking?
200	**R:**	yeah, and I came back and I had to, I could read still, but I, there were many words
201		that I'd forgotten, like someone would say one word and I'd suddenly think,
202		'oh, I've forgotten that word', kind of thing, but, um, I did have friends
203		in Japanese school, it's just I sometimes was bullied by boys, but, yeah,
204		I got through it
205	**L:**	but not by the girls?
206	**R:**	no, the girls were fine, kind of, yeah (laugh)

Rina uses the adjective 'low' (Line no. 198) to refer to her Japanese language attrition as a result of her 10-month residence in America. This description is interesting from a linguistics point of view where language proficiency or language loss is seldom described in terms of 'low', as one might describe the diminishing power of a battery which could potentially be re-charged and 'high' again. She attributed this temporary Japanese language attrition to not taking the Japanese Saturday school very seriously.

Rina was talking in some detail about her Japanese attrition (Line nos 200–202) when she suddenly shifted the topic as she began to reaffirm that she 'did have friends in Japanese school', as if to draw attention away from making a connection between her 'low' Japanese ability and her ability to make Japanese friends at Japanese school. While she stated that she 'did have friends in Japanese school', she introduced the topic of bullying in which she positioned herself as 'victim' with the boys as the agents of bullying (Line no. 203). When asked if she was bullied by the girls, Rina initially gave a negative response (Line no. 206), but she followed this with the qualifier 'kind of, yeah' and then laughed, implying the possibility of uneasiness at times also with the girls (see Extract 4.10, for more discussion of what 'girls say').

In the following extract below, Maya – during her first appearance in the dataset at the Hot Springs meeting – also related an experience where she had been constituted as *gaijin*, similar to Rina above.

In this and other data throughout the analysis chapters, when I could not decipher from tape recordings which girl was speaking or laughing I placed a question mark in the column for person's name [?], or [?s] in the case of two or more girls speaking or laughing at the same time. In the following extract and others, the participants' Japanese speech is transcribed in bold print. An English translation with the same numbering is transcribed in italic print (not bolded) below and denoted with an asterisk (e.g. Extract 4.4*). When participants are speaking in English, it is transcribed in regular print. (Refer to transcription conventions at the beginning of this book.)

(Extract 4.4) Hot Springs (age 13): '*Gaijin* sounds like *gaikotsu* (skeleton)'?

1248	?:	'gaijin' wa yameta hou ga
1249	M:	ahh, ano
1250	?:	'gaikoku no kata'
1251	M:	chichakatta toki kara mou, nanka doko aruku ni shitemo,
1252		'gaijin ya', 'gaijin ya' tte
1253	R:	sore, sore, sore demo, uchi, gaijin Kyoto ookunai?
1254		kirai ni natta

1255 M: ne, 'gaijin' to iu, nanka, koe, ano, hibikitte sa
1256 ?:   yeah
1257 M: nanka 'gaikotsu' mitai, 'gaikoku', 'gaikokujin' tte atte,
1258   'gaikotsujin' mitai ya
1259 N: (laugh)
1260 ?s: (laugh)
1261 ?:   so, so
1262 M: kimochi warui, nen
1263 R: sore de watashi joudan iwarete, sensei okorarehatta,
1264   sensei okorarehatta, sono hitotachi
1265 ?:   (laugh) gaikotsu

(Extract 4.4*) (translation)

1248 ?:   *it would be better not to use 'gaijin'*
1249 M: *ah, um*
1250 ?:   *'a person from a foreign country'*
1251 M: *every since I was small, well wherever I went people would say*
1252   *'[there's] a gaijin' '[there's] a gaijin'*
1253 R: *that, that, that's, but I, don't you think there are a lot of*
             foreigners in Kyoto?
1254   *[I have] come to not like [them being there]*
1255 M: *hey, saying 'gaijin', somehow, the voice, um, it has a*
             reverberation
1256 ?:   yeah
1257 M: *somehow it (gaijin) is like 'gaikotsu' (skeleton),*
1258   *saying 'gaikokujin' (foreign person) is somehow like 'gaikotsujin'*
             (skeleton-person)
1259 N: (laugh)
1260 ?s: (laugh)
1261 ?:   *right, right*
1262 M: *that's sickening*
1263 R: *about that [kind of thing], someone said a joke to me and*
             the teacher got angry,
1264   *the teacher got angry at those people*
1265 ?:   (laugh) *gaikotsu (skeleton)*

Maya told of how she had always felt herself to be 'gaijinized' or con-stituted in Japanese society as a *gaijin*. This passage is a continuation of Maya's narrative of how she associated the sound of the word *'gaijin'* or 'gaikokujin', since early childhood with another similar sounding word – gaikotsu – (meaning 'skeleton'), perhaps even before she really understood the meaning of gaijin/gaikokujin.

While the girls notice and comment on the improper use of the rough form of the word 'foreigner' as gaijin (Line no. 1248), and one girl suggests a much more respectful, but seldom-used term, gaikoku no kata (Line no. 1250), they nevertheless reject the positioning of themselves as foreigner, even in the polite form. Maya begins to tell a short narrative (Line no. 1251) of how when she was small, she was often constituted as gaijin. In Line no. 1253, Rina positioned gaijin as outsiders, by expressing her dislike of 'them' (foreigners), as they have come to increase in numbers in the community where she resides. She seems to have identified herself as insider where she could be positioning herself as 'Japanese' or also possibly as 'veteran/special-status foreigner'. She may feel that an increase in foreigners diminishes her unique status as non-Japanese.

In Line no. 1255, Maya, continuing her earlier narrative of when she was a child, recalled how the sound of people calling her 'gaijin' or 'gaikokujin' leaves a reverberation in her ear, sounding very similar to the sound of another word, 'gaikotsu' (skeleton). Gaikotsu can have a very scary and terrible connotation for a small child. She confirmed her horrible feelings about the nuance of this word with the expression 'kimochi warui', which I have translated colloquially as 'that's disgusting', but it also has the meaning of sickening, gross, or disagreeable. Although Maya's connection of the word gaikokujin with gaikotsu brought laughter from the other girls, she constructed her childhood association of this gaikokujin positioning with a 'sickly unpleasant' feeling.

In Line no. 1263, Rina returned to 'a discourse of gaijin otherness' in her telling of a narrative of being 'gaijinized' at school when someone cracked a joke about her (connected with the word gaijin), which was significant enough that a teacher stepped in and got angry about it. An ideological dilemma can be identified here, where, in contrast to Rina's earlier (Line nos 1253–1254) positioning of herself outside of the category of gaijin (where she expressed dislike of foreigners increasing), now Rina identified herself outside of the category of 'Japanese' as she took a stand of solidarity with the marginalized outsider. At the same time, along with the other girls, she contested and rejected the negative label of gaijin.

Later in the same Hot Springs meeting, the topic of standing out emerged as I showed the girls an illustration that had appeared in Time Asia magazine [see Appendix 2, (1)]. The following extract begins as I asked the girls if they had ever felt like the girl depicted in the drawing.

(Extract 4.5) Hot Springs (ages 13): 'Have you ever felt like this?'

3215	L:	OK, mouhitotsu misetai, kore shita, koiu, a,
3216		kimochi shitakoto arun desuka? anata,
3217		koiu, nihon no shakai no naka ni,
3218		koiu kimochi shitakoto arun desuka?
3219	M:	aaru
3220	L:	aru?
3221	R:	ARU
3222	N:	aru

[...]

3264	M:	demo doko ni iku ni shitemo, medatsu
3265	L:	to omou? jibun
3266	M:	mm, nanka, mou, shisen bakkari kanjiru

(Extract 4.5*) (translation)

3215*	L:	OK, there's one more thing I want to show you, this,
3216*		have you ever felt like this? you,
3217*		like this, within Japanese society,
3218*		have you ever felt like this?
3219*	M:	I have
3220*	L:	you have?
3221*	R:	I HAVE
3222*	N:	I have

[...]

3264*	M:	but anywhere I go I stand out
3265*	L:	you think so? yourself
3266*	M:	mm, somehow, I feel like I'm always in the public gaze

Maya, Rina and Naomi quickly and loudly blurted out positive affirmation to my question asking them if they had felt like the image depicted in the illustration. A few lines later, Maya constituted herself as standing out *anywhere* she goes and as always being in the public gaze, again making a point similar to that which she expressed earlier in the same meeting (see Extract 4.4). While she does not place a good or bad value on this 'standing-out' here, her apparent conspicuousness seems to be a phenomenon beyond her agency.

Constructing and Deconstructing Othering and Otherness

This section presents several extracts recorded early in the dataset during the Café meeting with Rina, Sara and Naomi who had just recently entered middle school (all aged 13). The girls talked about their earlier disempowering elementary school experiences and demonstrated through their discursive work how they had come to take up newly available alternative discourses in order to contest and mitigate racialized and ethnicized positionings. They narrated events of how they were learning to cope with ethnic slurs and name-calling as they became better at 'taking-control of' ethnic and gendered 'othering' within a wider range of discourses as they entered adolescence. Rina was annoyed that even though her mother is British, she and her mother were always being constituted as American by Japanese people (shown below).

(Extract 4.6) The Café (age 13): *'Amerikajin, Amerikajin'*

2276   **R:**   you could be anyone, but they say, always say
2277   **'amerikan, amerikan'**
2278   **L:**   uh-huh
2279   **S:**   **nande yarona?**
2280   **R:**   **soko atari chotto** narrow-minded **ya to omou kedo**
2281   **N:**   yeah

(Extract 4.6*) (translation)

2276   **R:**   you could be anyone, but they say, always say
2277*   *'American, American'*
2278*   **L:**   uh-huh
2279*   **S:**   *why do they do that?*
2280*   **R:**   *I think that is a bit narrow-minded*
2281*   **N:**   yeah

In this short passage, we can see Rina code-switching between English and Japanese several times. She seems to be making an effort to include Sara (who up to this point in the meeting had only used Japanese) while also addressing myself and Naomi who were using both languages, like herself. Rina contested being constituted by Japanese people as *'amerikan'* (American). After all, she is not American at all; she is British and Japanese. Sara's rhetorical question, 'Why do they do that?' further co-constructed a rejection of this positioning. Instead of letting herself be positioned by this construction, Rina asserted her agency and discursively turned the situation around in order to shift the marginality onto the name-callers, by positioning them as 'narrow-minded'.

In the following extract, Rina told a short narrative in which she was able to re-position herself away from a *bad* relationship with a boy at her school – who used to ethnically marginalize and bully her – to a relationship of *acceptance and friendship* with the same boy. The segment below begins directly following the above extract with Rina's answer to my question, 'does that really bother you?'

(Extract 4.7) The Café (age 13): 'The bully's actually a really nice guy'

2283	R:	it used to but once, um, my, um, parents wrote to the school, I mean
2284		well yeah, and the teacher had this, you know, whole class discussion
2285		kind of thing so it stopped, **demo** [*but*]
2286		I mean it was a really small school, so once you get used to it and
2287		you know each other
2288		well, it didn't really become a problem anymore
2289	L:	uh-huh
2290	R:	so, and then the guy that was actually a bully to me, became,
2291		we became, he's, we, we always had this major fight every year at
2292		school, and then suddenly at
2293		**go-nensei pitta to**
2293*		*in fifth grade, suddenly*
2294		it stopped, and you know, we went to the same **juku** [*cram school*]
2295		and we were really, you know, I saw his good side, and I thought (?),
2296		**'daijoubu', to omotte (?), nnde**
2296*		*I thought, 'oh, things are fine now', and,*
2297		he actually goes to the same school as Anna right now but, yeah
2298	L:	he'll probably end up marrying a **gaijin** [*foreigner*]
2299	R:	(laugh)
2300	L:	(laugh)
2301	R:	because, he's, he's actually a really nice guy, but, so it's a good thing

2302   that you know, you get to know your (laugh),
2303 **L:**   yeah
2304 **R:**   bullies

Again we see in Rina's speaking style occasional alternations into Japanese in the presence of me, Naomi and Sara. Rina started out in her first reference to *the bully* by naming 'the guy' as the agent of the bulling (Line no. 2290). Then immediately, she started to again name the agent 'he' (Line no. 2291). Then without pause, she rephrased herself, using 'we' (Line no. 2291) to now construct the fight in terms of *shared agency* between herself and the boy. Instead of constituting herself as weak and the boy as powerful, Rina rhetorically constructed a more balanced relationship (even though the relationship consisted of a yearly fight).

Rina not only re-positioned herself away from being marginally constituted by a name-calling bully at school, but she also re-positioned the boy in her school who used to tease her from 'bully' (Line no. 2290) to 'a really nice guy' (Line no. 2301). Through Rina's developing relationship with the boy in the shared goal of improving their chances of entering a better middle school by means of their attendance at a *juku* (after-school cram school), Rina came to reconstruct her ethnic and gendered identity *vis-à-vis* their changing perceptions and constructions of each other. Even though Rina and the boy at this point had both quit the cram school and had moved on to different middle schools, they remained in a similar social network, as Rina shared the information that the boy was presently attending the same school as Anna (Line no. 2297). In the above extract, I also helped to co-construct with Rina the idea of the boy's changing ethnic and gendered positioning, by jokingly remarking that 'he will probably end up marrying a *gaijin'* (Line no. 2298).

While Rina tried to play down the importance of this bullying event at her school, it was significant enough that her parents intervened by contacting the school, which resulted in the school staff having the entire class deal with the problem. Over time, this problem got resolved, perhaps due in part to the success of the 'whole class discussion kind of thing' (Line nos 2284–2285) and also to Rina's one-to-one confrontation with the boy who used to bully her.

In the following extract, Naomi also does not allow herself to be positioned by ethnic slurs of boys. Naomi rejected the racializing positioning of *'gaikokujin'* (foreigner) by Japanese and instead interpreted the taunts of 'big boys' as being their strategy of just 'using it as an excuse' to try to weaken her.

(Extract 4.8) The Café (age 13): 'They'll use it as an excuse'

2512	L:	and what about you Naomi, do you think there's racism in Japan?
2513	N:	umm, they just use it as an excuse (.) (laugh)
2514	L:	who's they?
2515	N:	uh, some people that, you know, big boys and stuff,
2516		they'll use it as an excuse
2517	L:	for?
2518	N:	for, um, if they're bullying me or something, they'll call me
2519		**'gaikokujin yakara', 'gaikokujin (?)' to ka**
2519*		*'that's because you're a foreigner', or 'because you're a foreigner (?)' and things like that*
2520	L:	oh, I see, they'll just, it would just be another form of bullying?
2521	N:	yeah
2522	L:	otherwise, if you weren't 'half', they'd find a different word
2523		to bully you, you mean?
2524	N:	yeah, and
2525	L:	oh, I see what you're saying
2526	N:	um,
2527	L:	just looking for a weak point, or something
2528	N:	yeah

In this extract, Naomi also code-switched, but she did so in the voicing of a Japanese-speaking bully. Throughout this passage, Naomi used the lexes of *bullying* numerous times. And again, similar to several of the above extracts, she identified these bullies as *boys*.

Naomi implied that 'big boys and stuff' (Line no. 2515) use racism as an excuse to marginalize her. She illustrated her point by giving an example in the voice of the boys, *'gaikokujin yakara'* (Line no. 2519), which translates as 'because you're a foreigner'. This phrase is generally used in two ways. One of the ways that it is used is to diminish giving credit to someone. For example, even if Naomi works very hard to learn to read in English, someone might say to her, 'you are good in English just because you are a foreigner', minimizing her invested efforts and setting her apart as already having an unfair advantage. The other usage, which is probably more what Naomi was referencing here, is a situation where, for example, she might have made a mistake, a slip-up, or come up short in some kind of skill (as everyone does from time to time). Then for someone to say, 'that's just like a foreigner [to be innately, genetically, racially at fault]' puts himself, as Japanese, superior to her, the foreigner, with her inbred foreign faults and weaknesses.

I took Naomi's meaning of 'they use it as an excuse', to indicate that 'big boys' marginalize her on the basis of her ethnicity as a means to try to get at her weak point – an excuse to 'hurt' her in a fight or argument – where if she were not of mixed-ethnicity, the boys would find a different way to offend her. When I suggested that this is what she meant, Naomi said 'yeah'. Reflexively, I acknowledge that this interpretation is based on my co-construction of this interaction as I tried to confirm her meaning by making several suggestions as to what she meant. Her responses of 'yeah' (Line nos 2521, 2524, 2528) to my suggestions, while potentially signifying acknowledgment, do not necessarily indicate strong agreement.

In brushing off the boys' use of racist statements as simply an excuse to try to get at a possible weak point, Naomi re-positioned herself as empowered against such an attack by already noticing the strategy ahead of time. In her rejection of being constituted as *gaikokujin* or *gaijin* in this manner, Naomi resisted a subject positioning, which marginalizes her and instead she was able to take up a more empowering position for herself.

Sara also began to tell a short narrative where a boy in her school similarly tried to constitute her as *gaijin* and described how it really bothered her. When I asked Sara a question similar to the one I asked Naomi above, 'is there racism in Japan', she first off said 'no', but then immediately remembered an incident when she had a fight with a boy from her class.

(Extract 4.9) The Café (age 13): 'That's just like a *gaijin*'

2327	S:	nai, aa, demo nanka, kenka, eto, kurasu no danshi to kenka shite,
2328		'gaijin no kuse ni'
2329		to iwareta toki ni kanari mukatsuita
2330	N:	uun, mukaTSUKU, sore
2331	R:	un, mukatsuku wa
2332	S:	dakara donai shiten, 'gaijin no kuse ni',
2333		'sonna koto iu na yo'
2334		toka ittenna (.), 'aho, mukatsuite' (.) sono ato wa
2335	L:	mmmm

(Extract 4.9*) (translation)

2327*	S:	*none, oh, yeah, well, a fight, um, I had a fight with a boy from my class*
2328*		*[he said to me] 'because you're a gaijin'*
2329*		*and when he said that, it really disgusted me [angered me]*

2330*	N:	*that's disGUSTING*
2331*	R:	*yeah, that's disgusting*
2332*	S:	*well, so what, he said, 'because you're a gaijin',*
2332*		*[I said] 'just shut up about saying [things like] you're just*
		like a gaijin'
2333		*'don't say that',*
2334*		*and stuff like (.), 'you're stupid, disgusting', (.) after that*
2335*	L:	mmmm

When it became Sara's turn to speak, she also positioned *boys* as the agent of racism toward her, although she referred to her interaction with them as *a fight* which implies more of a two-way agency than the one-directional implication of 'bullying'. In this extract, we can see in Sara's speech several intertextual voices that include both her male peers at school and also her own voice at the time of the encounter.

Although Sara first deferred my question as to whether or not she felt there was racism in Japan by answering in the negative, she quickly recalled a fight she had with a boy from her class. She quoted the boy, *'gaijin no kuse ni'* ('because you're a *gaijin'*) (Line no. 2328) and expressed how that had disgusted (or angered) her. This phrase itself is often used to marginalize other groups of people besides foreigners, where the word *gaijin* might be replaced with *girl*, for example, to disvalue girls. This structure is an abbreviation of something longer, where what comes after *kuse ni* is an action that is not usually bound to the category that comes before it. However, in this extract, nothing follows this expression. The implication with this phrase generally is that one is doing or being something that one should not do or be. In this context, it is clearly used to denigrate and disvalue foreigners. Naomi and Rina showed support and understanding by loudly positioning the boy's actions as 'disgusting', in which they implicitly switched the marginal positioning from themselves to the boy. Then Sara completed her narrative of how she had stood up to the boy's ethnic slur in front of him, by strongly telling him to 'shut up about it'. She positioned the boy's actions as 'stupid' and 'disgusting' as she turned the situation around to marginally position him, instead of allowing herself to be racially positioned by him.

The next extract follows directly from the above, when the discussion came to focus on what *girls* say to them.

(Extract 4.10) The Café (age 13): 'Girls say *haafu*?'

| 2340 | L: | soremo, ano, dansei desune, amari josei? |
| 2341 | S: | wa iwahen |

2342   R: un, onnanoko wa soiu no wa iwanai
2343   S: iwahen yo na
2344   R: un, onnanoko, onnanoko, kou, sakendari jyanakute, kou,
            'amerikajin?'
2345   toiu, kou, shitsumon toiu kanji de
2346   N: to iu kana?
2347   R: kimetsukenai no, kimetsukenai no ne
2348   S: nanka kou, 'gaijin?' toka toitte, soiu warui hou ni iun
            jyanakute,
2349   nanka, 'ha, haafu?' to katte
2350   N: 'haafu?'
2351   all: (laugh)
2352   S: 'haafu?' to kiitekite [*haafu* is spoken in a soft, sweet
            sounding tone]
2353   R: de, 'un' toka ttsuttara, 'ii naa' toka iware
2354   S: so, 'ii naa, ii naa' toka, 'kakkouii naa', toka
2355   N: un
2356   R: un
2357   N: are chotto uchi iya yanen kedona
2358   S: 'kakkouii naa' toiu hou ga ooi, uchi no baai
2359   R: un, 'kakkouii'
2360   N: sore iwaharu
2361   R: uchi 'ii naa' to iwareru (laughs)
2362   S: uso, uchi 'kakkouii'
2363   N: uchi wa 'eigo perapera, de, shabetemite',
2364   uzai 'yamete, chotto' (laugh)
2365   R: soko made ittara 'yamete', tte kanji de
2366   S: un, 'shabetemite' ga iya
2367   R: watashi mo
2368   N: watashi mo iya

(Extract 4.10*) (translation)

2340* L: *that also, um, that was boys, but girls don't?*
2341* S: *they don't say that*
2342* R: *um, girls don't say those kinds of things*
2343* S: *they don't say that, huh?*
2344* R: *yeah, girls, girls aren't so loud, and like '[are you] American?'*
2345*   *like, well, kind of like asking a question*
2346* N: *do they say that?*
2347* R: *they don't come right out with it, they don't come right out with it*

2348*	S:	it's like, well, they don't say really bad things like 'gaijin',
2349*		it's like 'ha–, half?'
2350*	N:	'half?'
2351*	all:	(laugh)
2352*	S:	they ask me '[are you] half' (spoken in a soft, sweet sounding tone)
2353*	R:	and like if I say, 'uh-huh', they say something like, 'wow, that's cool'
2354*	S:	yeah, 'great, great' or 'that's so cool', or something like that
2355*	N:	yeah
2356*	R:	yeah
2357*	N:	what, but I don't really like that [when people say that kind of thing]
2358*	S:	for me, I usually hear them saying 'that's so cool'
2359*	R:	yeah, 'cool'
2360*	N:	that has been said to me
2361*	R:	I always hear people saying, 'that's great' (laughs)
2362*	S:	really, for me [I hear] 'that's cool'
2363*	N:	for me, I'm always hearing, 'you're so fluent in English, let's hear you say something',
2364*		and I'm like, 'that's annoying, stop it, come on' (laugh)
2365*	R:	if they go that far, I feel like, 'stop it'
2366*	S:	yeah, I hate it when they say, 'let's hear you say something'
2367*	R:	me too
2368*	N:	I don't like it either

Up until now, the girls had been constituting *boys* as the agents of the bullying without any mention of how Japanese girls constitute them in their school and other communities. I introduced a new topic by asking if *girls* call them names like '*gaijin*'.

Throughout this extract, we again see the participants using many intertextual voices of what Japanese girls say to them in regard to their mixed-ethnicity, as well as depictions of their own voices in a hypothetical interaction. Sara refers to the girls' construction of them as 'not as bad' as the boys' who use the word '*gaijin*' (Line no. 2348).

Sara, who had been holding the floor as speaker, was the first to respond that girls do not call them that (Line no. 2343). Then Rina joined in to construct Japanese girls as more indirect, polite and subtle by framing talk about their mixed-ethnicity in terms of questions, 'Are you American?', rather than shouting pejoratives such as '*gaijin, gaijin*' as we witnessed in earlier extracts of their reports of what boys say. Here Naomi subtly challenged Rina's and Sara's constructions in Line no. 2346 and then a few turns later in Line no. 2350, but both times no one responded directly to Naomi.

Rina continued in her explanation that the girls 'don't come right out with it' (Line no. 2347), which may instead be indicative of an alternative covert type of aggression (Simmons, 2002) and marginalization, and which Naomi later more explicitly challenged (Line no. 2357). At this point in the talk, however, Sara continued the positive co-construction, mimicking a voice of the Japanese girls in a soft and sweet sounding manner, and ending with a rising intonation of a question, '*haafu*?' Rina further positioned the Japanese girls as kind and respectful in their acknowledgment of her mixed-ethnicity by their expressions of admiration, 'wow, that's cool' (Line no. 2353).

Here again Naomi entered the talk to take an opposing stance where she contested such behavior (of the Japanese girls) and constituted them as disagreeable (Line no. 2357). And here again, no one responded or reacted to her stance. The other two girls continued for several more turns to further *positively* describe the Japanese girls. Sara and Rina offered up expressions that they had often heard Japanese girls say in positive acknowledgment of their mixed-ethnicity using expressions that indicate modesty, respect and deference (Line nos 2353–2362).

Then Naomi took the floor again to illustrate an example of what she saw as a negative covert type of 'othering' when Japanese girls ask her to speak in English (Line no. 2363). Naomi voiced what she would like to say to these Japanese girls, 'that's annoying, stop it, come on' (Line no. 2364).

For Naomi, instead of positioning the Japanese girls as modest and respectful, she portrayed them as negatively condescending in their constitution of her. Following this, the two other girls end their *positive* constructions of what Japanese girls say to them and they come to co-construct the notion put forward by Naomi of the *disagreeableness* of being asked to say something in English.

This section has looked at 'othering' within the participants' schools in which both boys and girls were seen to be the agent of the bullying or other forms of marginalization. Where boys were the agents, often the bullying was seen to be more overt. While Japanese girls phrased themselves in a soft questioning tone, which sounded humble and admiring to Sara and Rina, it was seen by Naomi to be (covertly) marginalizing. The girls were often able to overcome ethnic marginalization by deconstructing the narrow discourse of homogeneity and by drawing on a wider range of available alternative discourses.

The next section continues to look at other examples of bullying and 'othering' in the context of peer-group dynamics within the communities of school and school groups, but mostly focuses on later data from the Hot Springs meeting when all six of the girls were present.

Hamideru: Avoiding Being 'The Nail that Sticks Out'

The Japanese word *hamideru*, and its various grammatical forms, was found occurring repeatedly in the talk of the girls, especially in the early data collection period, and was appropriated by them to serve various nuances such as *standing out, being left out, being yourself* and *being the odd one out*. Aside from the grammatical infinitive form of the verb *hamideru*, these girls also used some non-standard grammatical forms of this word, such as the slang infinitive verb *hamiru* (not found in standard dictionaries) having a meaning of 'to stand out' or 'to protrude', similar to *hamideru*. The slang noun *hamigo* was used to refer to the *kid left out* or the *kid who stands out*. Another slang form, *hamitteiru hito*, also appeared in the data, meaning a person *(hito)* who is standing out or is isolated out *(hammiteiru)*.[1]

Ethno-gendered positioning: Allowing yourself to stand out or restraining yourself

The extract below examines the intersection of ethnicity and gender. This extract was preceded by a discussion in which the girls responded to my prompt for them to imagine how their lives might be different if they had been born with two Japanese parents rather than just one. Following in a similar vein, I then proceeded to ask them to imagine how their lives might be different if they were born *a boy* instead of *a girl*, in order to stimulate discussion related to gender. Linguistically, as well as discursively, this passage is interesting in the unconventional interpretation that Naomi offered and that Rina accepted for the concept of *hamideru*. Rina began by constructing her imaginary 'boy' self, as being similar to her younger brother, Ren.

(Extract 4.11) The Café (age 13): 'Hamideru (being yourself)'

1483	R:	if I was a boy, I think I, I don't know,
		I think I'd be really similar
1484		to my brother, Ren
1485	L:	yeah, what's he like?

1486   **R:**   well, I mean, even if he is, I mean he is into Japanese society
                  and he seems
1487   more Japanese than me, but that's because boys are more
                  difficult to get out
1488   of this society than girls.
1489   **L:**   get OUT of the society?
1490   **R:**   well not get out,
1491   **douiuka, nantoiu kana, hamideru, hamideru**
1491*   *I mean, how do I say that? hamideru, hamideru*
1492   **N:**   ah, um, be yourself in the
1493   **R:**   yeah, be yourself in the society
1494   **L:**   in Japan?
1495   **R:**   yeah
1496   **L:**   do you think he's more, you said you think he's more
                  assimilated to Japanese
1497   than you
1498   **R:**   yeah, because, I mean if you're in, if you're girls they just
                  let you be,
1499   but if they're boys they might bully you
1500   **L:**   oh, I see
1501   **R:**   if you're, if you just try to be yourself and you'll stand
                  out from the crowd,
1502   so I think it would be much harder to just be yourself
1503   **L:**   uh-huh

Both Rina and Naomi, who are very proficient in English, were comfortable with an unusual English rendition of this concept of *hamideru*, which the dictionary defines as 'to protrude, to project, to jut out, to stand out'. When Rina began by saying in English 'boys are more difficult to get out of this society than girls' (Line nos 1487–1488), I asked her to clarify what she meant by 'get OUT'. She then switched into Japanese, introducing the notion of *hamideru*, but requested help in how to define it (Line no. 1491). To this, Naomi offered the English translation 'be yourself in the'. Rina accepted this nuance right away by completing Naomi's sentence, 'yeah, be yourself in the society' (Line no. 1493).

Their agreement on this translation is interesting, because, for them it implies that *being yourself* in society is equivalent to *standing out*. It implies that one has to hide one's true self (not be oneself) in order to not clumsily protrude and draw attention to oneself. In Japanese society *being yourself* is a quality that needs to be restrained. The concept of restraint or deference, referred to as *enryo* in Japanese, is a very highly valued traditional quality in Japan (LoCastro, 1990). Rina finally stated this explicitly, 'if you just try to be yourself and you'll stand out from the crowd' (Line no. 1501). Then Rina concluded by again making the point that she feels if one were a boy, 'it would be much harder to just be yourself' (Line no. 1502).

Rina constructed boys as being under more pressure to conform to the Japanese societal rules and norms or have to face bullying, while she constructed girls in Japanese society as being more secure (Line nos 1498–1499). Rina is here drawing on the gender differences discourse, which Sunderland points out 'is probably the most frequently invoked "popular" gendered discourse' (Sunderland, 2004: 52).

Rina identified her position of girl as allowing her a broader social boundary (Wenger, 1998) in which to assert and negotiate her identity. On the other hand, as an example of *boys*, Rina's brother is, according to Rina, 'more Japanese than me' (Line nos 1486–1487), and cannot be 'himself' in society as easily as girls can, in that as a boy he must subject himself to more social pressure. Rina does not need to be as 'Japanese' as her brother, on the basis of her gender, allowing her (as girl) to be more 'non-Japanese' or 'more ethnic'. Simultaneously drawing both on gender discourses ('gender differences discourse', 'discourse of female social flexibility') and ethnic discourses ('discourse of conformity', 'discourse of diversity'), Rina is discursively enacting what I refer to in this study as 'ethno-gendering' – taking up both ethnic and gendered subjectivity at the same time. This notion will be further explored in Chapter 7.

Being left out of groups

Trying to avoid 'being the nail that sticks up' is universally relevant in most peer-group school settings for adolescents in industrialized societies (Orenstein, 1994; Simmons, 2002). In particular, girls find themselves more concerned with 'alternative aggression' (Simmons, 2002: 9) among girl peers and girl groups. Alternative aggression of girls involves various forms of 'relational violence' (Simmons, 2002: 266) and covert aggression, in contrast to boys, who more often tend to use overt forms of aggression and bullying.

The next four extracts highlight the girls' narratives of themselves or others as the one who stands out or as the one who is isolated, often with their references to the formation and exclusion of groups at their schools. Here, they also often mentioned how they were bullied or teased particularly by boys, as was also shown to be the case in several extracts above. During the Hot Springs meeting when I introduced the topic of *groups at their schools*, Hanna was the first to take the floor to describe in a detailed humorous narrative, her dilemma of which of two groups at her school to join: *otaku* or *aho*. Hanna described *otaku* as someone who 'wears glasses' and 'takes books to the *loo*[2] with them'. Naomi clarified the English translation of *otaku* as 'nerds'. Hoffman defines *otaku* as, 'the generic term for individuals with a disproportionate interest in a socially marginal pastime' (Hoffman, 2005: 9). *Aho*, on the other hand, according to Hanna, are people who 'can only earn a score of 98 out of a total of five subjects [with a total possible score of 500]'. They are 'stupid people', according to Naomi. In her construction of the characters involved, Hanna implicitly positioned the people from both of the two groups in a negative manner. The following is a section of Hanna's narrative about these two groups.

(Extract 4.12) Hot Springs (age 13): Hanna: 'You'll really get bullied by the boys'

1924	H:	un, to ka, sochi shika erabahenkute,
1925		dochika ni hairahen katara, kurasu no danshi ni SUGOI ijimerareru
1926	?:	danshi ni ijemeru no?
1927	H:	mecha ijimerareru
1928	?:	so nan no
1929	M:	nande?
1930	H:	'hamigo' tte iwaretee, sore de mecha ijimerarete,
1931		watashi ni wa, saishou, toiuka, ko, saisho nyuugaku shita toki wa
1932		kekkou gocha gocha gocha to kanji yanka, de K. to iu hito ga itte,
1933		watashi wa sono hito to kekkou naka yoku shiteitara,
1934		sono hito ga 'otaku' yatta iu koto ni kizuite, batte to hanarette,
1935		saishou E. to iu hito, K. to iu hito to atashi, ga sannin de isshou ni itara,
1936		sono K. to iu hito ga 'otaku' yatte,
1937		yatte iu no ni kizuite, K. o kara hanarete,
1938		T. to iu hito to futari de itara,
1939		T. to iu hito ga chou 'aho' yatte kizuite,
1940		kouiu fuu ni natta watashi wa koko ni itte
1941	?s:	(laugh)
1942	?:	wakaru (laugh)
1943	H:	dochini, dochini haireba iinka wakarahenkute,
1944		de ima kekkyoku kochi ni haiteiru kedo,

1945 **R:** **e, kochitte? otaku?**
1946 **H:** **otaku jyanai, aho**
1947 **R:** **aho?** (laugh)

(Extract 4.12*) (translation)

1924* **H:** *um, you can only choose between those,*
1925* *if you don't join one of those two, you'll REALLY be bullied by the boys in the class*
1926* **?:** *bullied by the boys?*
1927* **H:** *really get bullied*
1928* **?:** *is that right?*
1929* **M:** *why?*
1930* **H:** *they call you 'hamigo', and then you really get bullied,*
1931* *I, at first, that is, like, when I first entered the school,*
1932* *I felt that it was really a confused mess and there was this girl named K.,*
1933* *when I began to become friends with her,*
1934* *I finally realized that she was 'otaku', and then I tried to get away from her quickly*
1935* *at first a girl named E. and K. and I became a group of three,*
1936* *and then I realized that K. was 'otaku',*
1937* *when I realized this, I split away from K.,*
1938* *and a girl named T. and I became a twosome,*
1939* *and then I realized that T. was a complete 'aho',*
1940* *this is how things have been happening to me as I came here*
1941* **?s:** (laugh)
1942* **?:** *I know what you mean* (laugh)
1943* **H:** *which one, I don't know which one I should join,*
1944* *and now I have finally decided to join this one,*
1945* **R:** *huh, this one? otaku?*
1946* **H:** *no, not otaku, aho*
1947* **R:** *aho?* (laugh)

In this extract, Hanna told of how she was placed in a position of having to choose between one of two undesirable groups at school or risk 'REALLY being bullied by boys in the class'. Hanna used the lexis *'ijimerareru'* (be bullied), modified with the word *sugoi* (super, extremely). Hanna was referring to being severely bullied by boys for not joining one of the two groups. When one of the girls expressed interest in the form of a question (Line no. 1926), Hanna used another similar adjective, *mecha*, a slang term with *ijimerareru* to signifying unreasonable or extreme bullying (Line no. 1927). As seen above in other extracts, Hanna again designated 'boys' as the agents of the bullying here. Hanna made the point here (and also in Extract 4.13) that this action by the boys is not just teasing or jostling, but is the more severe bullying.

Several other girls expressed interest in Hanna's story and when one of them asked 'why', Hanna went into a long, uninterrupted narrative drawing on the discourse of conformity (Line nos 1930–1940). She used the word *hamigo* (Line no. 1930) to refer to the marginalization by boys who bully and marginalize others who stand out or who do not conform to one of two undesirable groups at school. *Hamigo* is a slang noun form of *hamideru* or *hamiru* (to stand out), in this case to refer to 'a kid who stands out' or 'is isolated out'.

Hanna detailed how she shifted from one group to another, trying to avoid those from the 'wrong' group. She discursively told of her own work to marginalize others whom she considered to be in the wrong group, although it is clear that Hanna herself struggled with which group was the 'in group' to be associated with. She showed how the formation of groups with others at school was important and hard work for her. Another girl expressed sympathy and understanding of the situation (Line no. 1942). When Hanna stated that she had been having trouble deciding which group to join, but had finally decided to enter 'this one' (Line nos 1943–1944), Rina assumed Hanna meant the *otaku* group. However, when Hanna said that she has joined the *aho* group, it brought laughter from the girls.

This next extract follows a few lines after the above. Now Hanna and I are speaking in English.

(Extract 4.13) Hot Springs (age 13): Hanna: 'Not just teasing, bullying'

2016 **L:** there's only those two choices?
2017 **H:** yeah, otherwise, the boys really, really (.)
2018 **L:** tease you?
2019 **H:** not just teasing, bullying
2020 **L:** bully you?
2021 **H:** uh-huh
2022 **L:** why?
2023 **H:** I don't know but

Here again Hanna explicitly stated that this 'bullying' at her school is not just teasing; it is much more severe and serious. Hanna continued to constitute *boys* as the agent of the bullying. For Hanna, it was important to join one of only two groups at her school, both of which she constituted negatively, but gave important consideration to, in order to avoid censure and bullying by boys. It was not only her ethnic identity that she had to work to position positively, but she also had other identity concerns within the context of her school, such as her gendered identity and her social status within groups. While not an issue limited to *ethnic* 'othering', in Hanna's narrative of groups and bullying at her school, she was *unable* to resist the 'othering' by boys who used their power (upon threat of bullying) to force her to have to join one of two undesirable groups at her school.

The following extract further examines another occurrence of *hamideru* in the dataset. In a discussion about groups and bullying at school, Maya talked about a Japanese girl who stands out as 'different' because of the unusual way she pronounces words, similar to a lisp.

(Extract 4.14) Hot Springs (age 13): Maya: 'She really stood out as hamigo'

2080	M:	nanka na, nanka, nanka mecha ijime uketehatte,
2081		nanka shaberikatta to ka, ano, nanka chigau nenka,
		de sore de,
2082	?:	(laugh)
2083	M:	de hamigo ni nattehan nen, futsuu wa yen kedo kou,
2084		chotto, kou, 'sha-shi-su-se-so' mitai ni naru,
2085		'sa-shi-su-se-so' ga ie henkute,
2086		'sha, shi, shu, se, so', mitai ni naru mitai na

[...]

2107	M:	mou, o, nanka okamainaku nandemo suru guruupu to,
		hon demo ato
2108		hitori kou, onnanoko, ni wakarete, hamitteru hito toka de,
2109		demo zenzen chigau nenka guruupu ga (?)

(Extract 4.14*) (translation)

2080*	M:	*like, like, like, she was bullied really a lot,*
2081*		*there was something about the way she talks, something is different, it's*
2082*	?:	(laugh)
2083*	M:	*she really stood out as a 'hamigo' [protruding kid], ordinarily it should be like,*

2084*   *a bit like, 'sa-shi-su-se-so' [it should] be like that*
2085*   *the way she said 'sa-shi-su-se-so' was strange*
2086*   *she sounded like 'sha-shi-shu- se- so', like that*

[...]

2107* **M:**   *also, like, there are groups where anything-is-alright, and, then,*
2108*   *all by oneself, a girl, separated, like hamitteiru hito [the one left*
                out, standing out],
2109*   *but it's completely different, [those] groups (?)*

Maya used the lexis of *ijime* (bullying) and *hamigo*, a variation of *hamideru*, denoting a kid who protrudes or does not fit in – isolated and marginalized. Maya started out explaining that a girl at her school was bullied because of something 'about the way she talks' (Line no. 2081) that was different. Maya used two terms that set this girl apart in a negative manner – *chigau* (different) (Line no. 2081) and *hen* (strange) (Line no. 2085). As a consequence of her slight speech lisp, Maya described this girl as being constituted (by her peers at school) as *hamigo* (Line no. 2083) or 'the kid who stands out'. Later (Line no. 2108), Maya talked about other groups such as an 'anything-is-alright group'. Then she used yet another form of 'standing out' – *hamitteiru hito* (the one left out, the person standing out) – to refer to girls who are isolated and constituted as different due to their inability to conform to the group norms. Within the context of schools, this 'standing out' could extend to not only behavior and idiosyncrasies, but also to physical or speech differences.

The following extract presents another example of this use of 'standing out', this time presented by Rina as she also talked about Japanese groups at her school. Rina switched codes between Japanese and English several times in this extract. The English translation is indicated by an asterisk (*) and appears directly below the line of Japanese and is written in italics. The actual spoken Japanese is indicated in bold print and the actual spoken English is indicated in regular print.

(Extract 4.15) Hot Springs (age 13): Rina: 'Hamiru' (with English translation*)

2350   **R:**   and they're just,
2351   **nantoiuno, minna nanka hamiru, hamirutte wakaru?**
2351*   *how do I say that, everyone, like hamiru, do you understand*
                hamiru?
2352   it's like someone
2353   **hamiru tte nantoiu?**

2353*		*how do I say hamiru*
2354	N:	aah, left out
2355	R:	someone
2356	L:	aah aah,
2357	R:	like once in a week, someone is definitely left out,
2358	L:	oh really
2359	R:	**kanarazu**
2359*		*absolutely*
2360	L:	uh-huh
2361	R:	and **sore ga dare ga, jibun ni atarun jyanai katte,**
2362		**sono gurupu no ko wa sugoku, itsumo kowagattete**
2361*		*and that is someone, so that you aren't the one whose turn is next,*
2362*		*the kids in that group are extremely, always afraid*

Whereas in Extract 4.11, *hamideru* is represented as 'being yourself' and in Extract 4.14, *hamigo* is 'the kid standing out', in this section above, the verb *hamiru* is used to mean 'left out' or 'the odd one out'. Again (as in Extract 4.11), Rina, who is highly proficient in English, switched into Japanese in her dilemma in how to express the meaning of *hamiru* in English. And again, Naomi stepped in to help translate this word, but differently here, than before. In place of the earlier 'be yourself' usage of the term (Extract 4.11, Line no. 1492), now Naomi suggested the nuance of 'left out' (Line no. 2354), which Rina accepted in her explanation of how 'once in a week someone is definitely left out' (Line no. 2357). Rina depicted a scary world at school in which (especially girls) have to work hard to try to avoid being the one isolated and left out. Rina portrayed the inevitability of being eventually left out in a rotational situation that comes around to everyone: 'the one whose turn is next' (Line no. 2361).

As exemplified in the proverb, 'the nail that sticks up gets hammered down', again it was shown how this very dominant discourse of Japanese conformity binds social behavior and the constitution of identity for these six adolescent girls at their schools, in terms of social status and gender as well as ethnicity. As with school groups in Western societies such as in America and UK, there are various similar groups within Japanese schools. In the dataset, besides Hanna's reference to *otaku* and *aho* groups, and Maya's reference above to *okamainaku nandemo suru guruupu* (anything-goes group) (Line no. 2107), Naomi, elsewhere in the dataset in talking about groups that she witnessed during her short residences in American school, also made mention of 'normal people' groups and groups of people as *chou moteru* (having extreme 'cool style' or great looks/appeal).

Negotiating Identities and Change Over Time[3]

The follow three segments of one continuous extract came from the final meeting with all six girls. Compared with the ways in which the girls had expressed themselves in earlier data, changes can be seen, which have occurred over time in how they come to negotiate their identities and come to position themselves in terms of isolation. The girls and I were talking about feelings of being constituted as 'half' in their past, and how they felt about it presently (given below). Following is the first segment.

(Extract 4.16a) Last Reunion (ages 14 and 15): 'I hated *haafu*; Now I'm happy'

361	H:	iya yatta haafu yattan na
362	?:	chiisai toki wa iyayatta
363	?:	(?) mukashi wa
364	?:	chiisai toki wa yatta kedo
365	L:	ima wa?
366	?:	ima wa zenzen ureshii
367	?:	mmmm
368	?:	mmmm
369	L:	Sara wa?
370	S:	shougakkou no toki toka mecha iya, yakedo
371	H:	watashi mo meccha iyayatta
372	?:	unnn
373	S:	kedo, ima wa, nanka, minna ii na, toka ippai iitte kurerushi
374		jibun demo ii to omoihajimeta
375	L:	nnnhonto
376	S:	sou mitai
377	L:	yokattane, minna
378	?:	yokatta

(Extract 4.16a*) (translation)

361*	H:	*I hated being half*
362*	?:	*I hated it when I was little*
363*	?:	*(?) a long time ago*
364*	?:	*I did when I was little*
365*	L:	*and now?*
366*	?:	*now I am totally happy*
367*	?:	*yeah*

368* ?:   *yeah*
369* L: *how about you, Sara?*
370* S: *I really hated it when I was in elementary school, though*
371* H: *I also really hated it*
372* ?:   *yeah*
373* S: *but now, somehow, everyone thinks it's good, and a lot of people tell me that*
374*   *it's good, and now even I am beginning to think that*
375* L: *mmm, really*
376* S: *it does seem like that*
377* L: *you're glad [about that], right, all of you*
378* ?:   *I'm glad [about it]*

The girls expressed their 'hatred' of being constituted as *haafu* (half) at an earlier time when they were little (Line nos 361–364) using the Japanese word *iya*, which indicates strong dislike of something. This contrasts with how some of them state they are now totally happy to be half (Line nos 366–368). When I prod Sara to respond, she reflected on how, as an elementary school pupil, she hated the way that she had been constituted (Line no. 370), to which Hanna and another girl offered agreement (Line nos 371–372). While in this extract, I was not able to determine the speaker in many places, it seems that most, if not all, of the girls had a part in co-constructing the negative, disagreeable experience of being positioned as 'half' when they were little. (In the following segment, Hanna, Anna and Naomi also expressed similar feelings, each using the same Japanese word: *iya*.)

Then Sara positioned herself in terms of an 'ascribed identity' (see Day, 1998; Ivanic, 1998) based on how others have constituted her (Line nos 373–374, 376). She came to place value on the cultural capital of her halfness/doubleness, which was recognized and esteemed highly by others. Over time, Sara can be seen as coming to access more enhancing alternative discourses of diversity enabling her to emerge from earlier, less empowering positions within limiting dominant discourses of homogeneity. Now, into her third year of middle school, she presently identified her ethnicity as 'good' and positive. The talk continued when I asked Anna the same question:

(Extract 4.16b) Last Reunion

382 A: **yapa, chiichai toki iyayatta nanka shuugou shashin tokane,**
383   **jibun dake nanka kao ga chigau kara, nanka iyana to omotteta kedo, ima wa**

384 L: **yokatta?**
385 A: **ii kana mitaina** (laugh)
386 L: **hai, Hanna wa?**
387 H: **mmm, issho, shougakkou gurai no toki wa mecha tsurakatta**
388 L: **mmmm**
389 H: **nanka, nihonjin ni naritai to omottetashi**
390 ?:   **wakaru**
391 ?:   **meccha omou**
392 ?:   **minna (?) narou, narou to**
393 ?:   **kaminoke kurokushitai to omoteittamon**
394 L: **assonano?**
395 ?:   **kaminoke dake ureshikatta, kao wa iyayatta** (laugh)
396 N: **watashi mo kaminoke motto kurokatta kara na**
397 ?:   **itsumo (?)**
398 L: **mmmm**
399 R: **kinpatsu yatte shuugou shashin mitai (?) hitori dake na kin,**
400   **kinpatsu ni kagayaiten na**
401 ?:   **kakkoi**
402 L: **ahontou? Naomi wa soiuno nakatta?**
403 N: **ah, meccha iyayatta**
404 L: **un**
405 N: **nanka, meccha chicchai gakkou yakara, sugu naretakedo,**
         sai-, nanka,
406   **meccha, mukatsuku hito toka ga, sore o riyuu nishite**
         'anata haafu yakara', dounokouno haafu (?)

(Extract 4.16b*) (translation)

382* A: *yeah, I hated it when I was little, somehow the school trip photo*
            and stuff,
383*   *only MY face was somehow different, so I somehow felt like*
            I hated that, and now
384* L: *do you like it?*
385* A: *it's like it's good, I guess* (laugh)
386* L: *yes, and you Hanna?*
387* H: *mmm, same with me, it was really hard to bear just during*
            elementary school
388* L: *uh-huh*
389* H: *I felt like I wanted to be Japanese and stuff*
390* ?:   *I know what you mean*
391* ?:   *I totally know [what you mean]*

392*	?:	*everyone becomes (?), tries to become*
393*	?:	*I felt like I wanted to darken my hair*
394*	L:	*oh really?*
395*	?:	*the only thing I was happy about was my hair, I hated my face*
		(laugh)
396*	N:	*me too, because my hair was darker then, than now*
397*	?:	*always (?)*
398*	L:	*uh-huh*
399*	R:	*I was blonde, in my school trip photo (?), I was the only one*
		with blond,
400*		*sparkling blonde hair*
401*	?:	*that's cool*
402*	L:	*oh really? didn't that kind of thing happen to you Naomi?*
403*	N:	*ah, I totally hated it*
404*	L:	*uh-huh*
405*	N:	*somehow, because my school was extremely small, I got used*
		to it soon but,
406*		*somehow, there were totally disgusting people, using the reason,*
		'because you're half', you're like this or that because you're half (?)

Here again the word '*iya*' is used by Anna (Line nos 382, 383), Naomi (Line no. 403) and another girl (Line no. 395) to indicate their strong dislike of being constituted as 'half' when they were little. Hanna also expressed strong negative feelings using the lexis *tsurai* (hard to bear, trying) (Line no. 387) to describe her feelings during elementary school.

In this segment of the extract, in their telling of their elementary school experiences, the girls can be seen co-constructing the notion of conformity and enacting Japaneseness by positioning themselves as wanting to conform to something that they were not: dark haired and Japanese looking. Anna expressed her hatred of having only *her* face appear as 'different' in the school-trip photo (Line nos 382–383). One of the girls stated, 'I felt like I wanted to be Japanese and stuff' (Line no. 389). Another girl said, 'I felt like I wanted to darken my hair' (Line no. 393). This was followed by another girl, 'I hated my face' (Line no. 395). While I was unable to determine which girl was speaking in several places here, it seems that most or all of them expressed having wanted to look more Japanese. Repeatedly, the girls resisted and contested having been constituted in such a powerless manner and having taken up these positions within dominant discourses.

While revealing traces of a discourse of homogeneity in their expressions of their feelings of shame based on their mixed-ethnic features, they also worked to deconstruct this discourse. Rina in describing herself as conspicuously standing out in her school photo with her 'blond, sparkling blonde hair' (Line nos 399–400), appears to have used an ironic 'double-voice' (Bakhtin, 1986). While she may have intended to nuance 'difference' as marginal, at the same time this construction calls up a 'white-Western female beauty' discourse (see Sunderland, 2004). The more positive positioning was supported and co-constructed by one of the girls who stated, 'that's cool' (Line no. 401). Now having other alternative discourses available to her, Naomi also expressed a contesting voice (Line no. 403), 'I totally hated it'. She positioned herself as being in control over the situation, 'I got used to it soon' (Line no. 405) and took the empowering role of positioning those who constituted her as 'totally disgusting people' (Line no. 406). Naomi contested being constituted in a discriminatory manner by others solely on the basis of her *ethnic* appearance.

Naomi voiced her peers at school, saying, '*anata haafu yakara*' ('because you're half') (Line no. 407), similar to the way we examined her using this construction earlier (Extract 4.8, Line no. 2519). Here she refers to people at her school who racially and ethnically marginalize her as being (or maintaining) a certain (undesirable) condition because she is 'half'.

The topic of discussion shifted in the next segment of the same extract, which follows directly after this, to the introduction of being constituted as *gaijin* (foreigner).

(Extract 4.16c) Last Reunion

407	?:	'haafu, haafu' to iwaretara ii kedo betsuni,
408		'gaijin' toka iwaretara
409	?:	'gaijin' toka iwaretara mou owari dayone
410	?:	owari
411	?:	zenzen chigau mirarekata
412	?:	kenka no toki toka ni na, 'kishoinen' toka ittara,
413		'gaijin no kuse ni' toka ittekite
414	?:	ah, wakaru, meccha mukatsuku
415	?:	meccha mukatsuiten
416	?:	'gaijin'
417	?:	kuyashi namida yashina
418	N:	nanimo iehen na, sore o iwaretara
419	H:	demo na, tomodachi ga soko de
420		'gaijin chau de' toka iutte kuretara kandoushita
421	N:	kandou?
422	H:	'gaijin chau de, haafu yade'
423	?:	(laugh)

424   N: **dochimo issho yanke mitaina, nanka dojji bouru shiteru**
            noni sa,
425   **mukou ga mukatsukareta 'gaijin ya' to itte,**
426   **a kankeinaiyo, mitaina** (laugh)
427   **'gaijin nigeyou' to**
428   ?:   (laugh)

(Extract 4.16c*) (translation)

407*   ?:   *it was alright being called 'half, half',*
408*   *but being called 'gaijin' or something*
409*   ?:   *it was like all over if they said something like 'gaijin'*
410*   ?:   *all over*
411*   ?:   *a completely different way of seeing things*
412*   ?:   *like in a fight or something, if I say to someone 'you're gross',*
413*   *they would say 'because you're a gaijin'*
414*   ?:   *oh, I know what you mean, that's totally disgusting*
415*   ?:   *that's totally disgusting*
416*   ?:   *'gaijin'*
417*   ?:   *it's enough to make you weep*
418*   N: *I can't say anything, if someone says that to me*
419*   H: *but, when my friend said at such a time [in my defense]*
420*   *'she's not a gaijin', I was moved*
421*   N: *[you were] moved?*
422*   H: *'she's not a gaijin, she's half'*
423*   ?:   (laugh)
424*   N: *they're both, like, the same, like when I was just playing dodge ball,*
425*   *they disgustingly said 'gaijin',*
426*   *it was like not related [to anything] at all* (laugh)
427*   *they said 'gaijin dodge the ball'*
428*   ?:   (laugh)

Up to this point, the girls had been co-constructing their disgust and dislike of being constituted as '*half*' when they were younger and realigned their present subjectivities by positioning themselves within a 'discourse of diversity' in which 'halfness' is self-enhancing and positive. 'Halfness' is a category that they took up in their self-identification by deconstructing the negative, outsider aspect of 'halfness' into a positive category. However, these girls did not take up the category of *gaijin* (foreigner) at all, even in a deconstructed manner. Discursively, their contestation of being positioned as *gaijin* took on a much stronger tone.

In Line nos 407–418, the girls used various adjectives to describe their contestation and rejection of being positioned in the category of *gaijin*, 'it was like all over if they said *gaijin*' (Line no. 409). 'that's totally disgusting' (Line nos 414, 415), 'it's enough to make you weep'[4] (Line no. 417). In Line no. 413, one of the girls used the racialized expression *gaijin no kuse ni* (because you're a *gaijin*) similar to how Sara used the same expression earlier (Extract 4.9, Line no. 2328) in voicing the ridicule of bullies meant to disvalue foreigners. All the girls join in this co-construction by narrating their experiences and offering support and solidarity in words of acknowledgment and understanding (Line no. 414).

A shift in topic occurs in Line no. 419 when Hanna began to tell a narrative where a Japanese friend stood by her side. In the telling of this event, Hanna aligned herself as Japanese in a rejection of the categorization of herself as *gaijin* in her statement 'when my friend said at that time "she's not a *gaijin*", I was moved' (Line nos 419–420). Hanna *felt moved* that her (Japanese) friend (on behalf of her), in effect *contested* (in the presence of other Japanese peers) the positioning and categorization of her as *gaijin*. Then in Line no. 421, Naomi subtly raised doubt by asking '(you were) moved?', as if to challenge the significance of the event.

Hanna continued to elaborate further in the voice of her friend (Line no. 422), 'she's not a *gaijin*; she's half'. In Hanna's celebration of her friend's defense of her, she took up the self-categorization of *haafu* and at the same time rejected the categorization of *gaijin*.

But then, in Line no. 424, Naomi again subtly contested Hanna's separation of *haafu* and *gaijin* into two separate categories with the words, 'they're both, like, the same'. The use of the hedge *mitai na* (like) softens Naomi's rebuttal somewhat; however, Naomi can be seen as contesting the constitution of herself as either *gaijin* or *haafu*, as both to her signify forms of *othering*. Hanna felt moved by her friend's support because to deny Hanna's *gaijin*ness is to *Japanize* her as insider, a positioning and categorization that Hanna chose to assume in the context of her Japanese school peers.

In contrast, Naomi contested being racialized as either *gaijin* or *haafu*. Throughout the dataset, Naomi is seen repeatedly challenging the positioning of *gaijin* or *haafu*. Instead she is seen to position herself as *unmarked* (*haafu/daburu*) within a discourse of diversity (which does not need to be pointed out) (see Extract 5.3) and as *privileged/special* (*haafu/daburu*) (see Extract 6.11).

Finally, above Naomi offered her own example of being 'disgustingly' positioned as *gaijin* at school during a game of dodge-ball. Naomi narrated an event where a classmate positioned her in terms of an ethnic slur which, 'was like not related [to anything] at all' (Line no. 426), when someone yelled to her, '*gaijin*, dodge the ball'. Naomi was upset that she had allowed herself to be *interpellated* in this hailing (Althusser, 1971) when she recognized it as such. At this point, she was able to assert her agency to resist being hailed and racialized as a *gaijin* and instead called upon an alternative discourse of diversity to subjectively position herself in a more empowering manner.

This section has highlighted the notion of *change over time*. We have seen how the girls talked about their change from being *gaijinized* and racialized as 'half' or '*gaijin*' when they were in elementary school to more empowering subjectivities of their ethnicities by middle school. They expressed having wanted to change their hair color or their face in order to comply with the embodied conformity of Japaneseness. But in their telling of their 'hated' past experiences, we explored how they worked to deconstruct the limited discourses available to them at the time. While they deconstructed the negative 'outsider' aspect of the referent *haafu* and turned it into a positive category, they totally rejected the referent of *gaijin*. Over time, it was shown how they came to be better discursively able to take control of this disagreeable positioning. They instead asserted agency to resist it and in place called upon alternative discourses of diversity and interculturalism to position them in a more empowering manner.

Throughout this chapter, we have been examining the theme of how the girls *negotiate their identities*. We can see evidence here of changes the girls went through in their ability to better negotiate and articulate their ethnic identities over time. In the earlier meetings with the girls, while expressing well their feelings of isolation and exclusion, they were not able to clearly articulate their own personal positioning. In the Café meeting and the Hot Springs meetings, when the girls were in their first year of middle school, we saw how they were able to deconstruct othering and turn the situation around to position the bullies as marginal instead of allowing themselves to be negatively positioned. But it was not until their third year of middle school at the Last Reunion meeting that we see the girls really taking affirmative stances in clearly negotiating their identities by asserting their own agency to position themselves in an empowering manner.

Summary

This chapter has addressed the first central question exploring the tensions and dilemmas in the ways mixed-ethnic girls in Japan identify themselves and their ethnicities. Here I have focused on how the girl participants negotiate their 'othered' identities, in terms of isolation and exclusion at school. This included exploration of both isolation as a result of middle school group dynamics as well as racialization and ethnicism due to their ethnic differences.

Even as an elementary school student, Rina at 12 years old was observed drawing upon her intercultural experiences and knowledge to overcome feelings of isolation and exclusion at her various school associations. Rina related how within the more narrow range of discourses that she had to draw on in her past, she was disempowered and marginalized. However, later as Rina gained experiences, which exposed her to a greater range of available alternative ethnic and gendered discourses upon which to draw, she was able to empower herself and become free of limited racializing discourses. Within a discourse of interculturalism, Rina came to position herself and other mixed-ethnic girls as more mature, sophisticated and worldly than the Japanese girls who do not have access to the uncommon kinds of experiences that she had already had.

Most of the girls expressed the theme of 'standing out' *(hamideru)* and its occurrence in their schools, but with varying nuances attached to this concept. Rina and Naomi equated 'standing out' with 'being yourself in the society' implying that you must work hard to mask or hide your 'true' self so that you do not stand out. Here Rina took up an 'ethno-gendered' positioning for herself as she positioned boys (like her brother who is 'more Japanese' than her) as having to be more constrained in terms of not standing out or being themselves. Through this positioning, she implied that she can be 'less Japanese' (or more blatantly ethnic or mixed-ethnic) (than her brother) without having to suffer being the 'nail' that stands out from the crowd and being a target of bullying.

Almost all of the girls mentioned other situations at their schools where standing out was associated with bullying, with *boys* as the agent. Besides defining the concept of *hamideru* as 'being yourself' and 'standing out from the crowd', the girls also described it as 'the one who stands out' *(hamigo, hamitteiru hito)* and 'left out' *(hamiru)* as they talked about 'othering' and exclusion on the basis of *difference* at their schools. As well as the 'work' these girls did to insure that they were not 'othered' or excluded from groups at their schools, they had the added challenge of trying to avoid standing out on the basis of their ethnic obtrusiveness. Over time, instead of allowing themselves to be marginally positioned, they were shown to use various rhetorical techniques and discursive tools to turn around the situation to where they re-positioned the bullies as marginal. In some cases, they positioned the bully as a person who was 'sick' or 'disgusting'. A boy, who used to bully Rina, but was seen by Rina to have later changed, was subsequently re-positioned by Rina as a 'really nice guy'. The girls came to question and confront such marginal positioning by rejecting and deconstructing the negative discourses.

We also saw how Sara and Rina started out constituting their Japanese *girl* peers as humble and respectful in their expressions of admiration of their mixed-ethnicity. Sara and Rina constructed the Japanese girls' references to their ethnicity as starkly differing from the overtly 'racist' ways in which *boys* racialized and marginalized them, by calling out *'gaijin, gaijin'*. However, Naomi contested the notion of Japanese girls' use of softly spoken questions (*haafu?*) as being respectful, and instead implicitly constituted Japanese girls as agents of (covert) marginalization.

The following chapter specifically examines how the girls position themselves as 'different' in a *good* meaning, as they work to deconstruct difference as *bad*.

Notes

1. While a full-scale analysis of bullying (*ijime*) in Japan is beyond the scope of this study, it is important to note here that there is a close linking of 'othering' with bullying in the Japanese context. A common form of bullying prominently occurring in Japanese schools involves the actions of members of a group or network of friends who consciously work to exclude an individual on the basis of their inability to conform to the groups' norms by 'othering' them as an outsider.
2. Loo is British slang for 'toilet'.
3. Part of this section in Extracts 4.16a–c and earlier versions of the analysis have been previously published (Kamada, 2006a), and have been reproduced here with permission from the Bilingualism SIG of JALT.
4. See *kuyashi namida* (it is enough to make you weep) in the Glossary.

Chapter 5

Claiming Good Difference; Rejecting Bad Difference

Introduction: Good Difference; Bad Difference

This chapter looks at how the six girls discursively construct themselves in their account giving and self-representations concerning their ethnicities. Here I continue to address the first central question by asking what tensions and dilemmas underlie the ethnic subjectivities of these girls. In particular, in this chapter, I highlight how they negotiate their ethnic identities within the contrasting notions of 'good difference' and 'bad difference', which emerged throughout the data, based on the two discourses of 'diversity' and 'homogeneity' as outlined in Chapter 2.

In the section 'Doing difference' [p. 39], I introduced West and Fenstermaker's (1995) notion of 'doing difference', which showed how the accomplishment of race creates differences among people who are seen to belong to certain racial categories. Within this conceptualization, the exploration of how people are simultaneously gendered, raced and classed can explain how inequality works in interaction with others in society. In this chapter, how the girls 'do difference' or how they accomplish their difference is examined in terms of both claiming and rejecting difference.

Within discourses of homogeneity and conformity, *difference* is constituted negatively, where being 'the nail that sticks up' will surely get you hammered down, according to the Japanese proverb. While socialized in Japanese mores and customs, and attending Japanese schools, these girls did not want to stand out and be constituted as different within the frame of *bad difference*. However, at other times, for some of the girls in particular, the constitution of difference as *good* was a very important aspect of their identity, which they constructed and performed for themselves.

During certain moments some of the girls foregrounded their Japanese-ness as they minimized their non-Japanese ethnic attributes in their subject positioning. At other times (and for others of them), they proudly proclaimed their ethnic diversity and differences and constituted them-selves within a worldview of diversity, interculturality and ethnic embodi-ment. How these girls constantly maneuvered and negotiated their identities within these conflicting subject positions is explored, as they worked to constitute their memberships when confronted with the ques-tion 'who am I?' asked of themselves and 'who are you?' asked by others.

The following section looks at how some of the girls deconstructed ethnic social 'othering' through a privileging of themselves.

Deconstructing 'Othering' and Privileging Self

This section looks at how, in the process of deconstructing marginaliz-ing discourses, the girls used alternative empowering discourses and rhetorical devices in order to privilege themselves. I show extracts from the data where the girls positioned themselves as 'different', but in the context of 'good difference'.

Mature self and 'low level' other

In the extract below, collected during the first interview when Rina was at the end of elementary school (age 12), she can be seen creating *good difference* for herself. Here she positions herself as privileged and elevated in terms of her 'mental maturity' in comparison with her Japanese peers. However, when it comes to the question of 'physical maturity', a dilemma arose for her (see Extract 5.2).

It was Rina herself who first introduced the topic of 'maturity' when we were discussing a previous topic. I asked her if she thought there was a difference (in 'result') between mixed-ethnic children with English-speaking mothers compared to those with English-speaking fathers. While I had meant to probe Rina's view about the level of *English profi-ciency* of the child, Rina took my meaning to be not only about their English-speaking ability, but also about their level of *maturity* when she answered that girls with English-speaking *mothers* seemed to be more mature. Since she herself had brought up this new topic of *maturity*, I took the opportunity to then ask her to consider the maturity of herself and her fellow mixed-ethnic girlfriends in comparison with her Japanese girlfriends. In the following extract, Rina answers this question.

(Extract 5.1) Rina's house (age 12): 'Mental maturity'

427   **L:**   do you find that all of you are more mature than the Japanese girls your age?
428   **R:**   oh, well, yeah, in a way, yes, yes
429   **L:**   in what way, would you say?
430   **R:**   mentally
431   **L:**   mentally? what does it mean, mental maturity, though?
432   **R:**   well like, um, like in what we do, like they prefer, um,
433   to play outside you know, play outside and uh in the snow,
434   when it snows and stuff,
435   while we would rather, um, on cold days like that, go indoors,
436   you know, all the teenage girls' stuff (laugh)
437   **L:**   yeah
438   **R:**   but, um, yeah they seem to be kind of more outdoor,
439   you know and you know walking dogs and all that kind of thing
440   and also that our conversations a year ago,
441   our conversations didn't seem to match,
442   they'd be talking about more kind of low level stuff,
443   we'd be talking about more, you know like music and that kind of stuff,
444   but this year I feel like they are all catching up,
445   so it's much more, easy to play with them,
446   because we all seem to share the same interests,
447   well basically the same interests
448   **L:**   I see
449   **R:**   yeah

As mentioned above, it was Rina who initially introduced the topic of 'maturity' into the talk. I then took the chance to expand on this topic. Interestingly, here Rina appears to categorize this 'maturity' into types by making a specific reference to *mental* maturity to talk about and compare her mixed-ethnic self (and her other mixed-ethnic friends) with her Japanese peers. Rina referred to the Japanese girls' talk and play as being 'low level stuff' (Line no. 442) using the examples of outdoor play such as playing in the snow or walking dogs (Line nos 432–434, 438–439), while the more 'mature' mixed-ethnic girls play indoors, talk and listen to music (Line nos 435–436, 443).

Rina aligned the mixed-ethnic girls and herself as insider 'we', while she constructed her Japanese friends as 'the other' and referred to them as 'they'. Even though still in elementary school and still pre-teen at 12, Rina positioned herself and her mixed-ethnic friends as more mentally mature using the lexis of 'teenagers' when describing what they do together (Line no. 436), even while still in elementary school.

While Rina positioned her Japanese peers as being less mature and their talk as consisting of 'low level stuff', she also acknowledged her Japanese peers as 'catching up' in terms of maturity (Line nos 444–447). Here Rina positioned her Japanese peers as now coming to share in the maturity, which the mixed-ethnic girls had already been enjoying.

Rina's introduction of this specific *mental* maturity seemed to imply the existence of another type of maturity – its antithesis (physical maturity). Thus, I decided to take this idea further and ask her about differences regarding the *physical* maturity of the two groups of friends. The following extract follows directly after the above.

(Extract 5.2) Rina's house (age 12): 'Physical maturity'

450	L:	what about PHYSICAL maturity?
451	R:	well, none of us bilingual girls have gotten our periods yet and all,
452		most of my school girlfriends have periods
453	L:	oh really
454	R:	yeah because we thought we were very kind of mature, but,
455	L:	yeah
456	R:	mentally (laugh) yeah
457	L:	interesting
458	R:	yeah, yeah, very interesting

[. . .]

475	L:	that really surprised me that they, that they had their periods before,
476	R:	yeah
477	L:	yeah
478	R:	because I thought that we'd have them way before them, but
479	L:	yeah
480	R:	none of us have gotten

While it was actually I who introduced the notion of 'physical maturity', Rina had implied, by specifying 'mental' as a category of maturity, that at least one other category also existed. Rina's prompt response to my question and her statement 'we thought we were kind of mature' (Line no. 454) shows that she had already thought about and had perhaps discussed this question with her other mixed-ethnic girlfriends of the comparison of 'physical' maturity between themselves and Japanese girls.

While *mental* maturity is something that is very difficult to measure or to factually account for, the *physical* event of a girl having started her menstrual period is an undisputable 'reality' with producible evidence that Rina had to concede to her Japanese friends, even though she did so with some reluctance and feelings of surprise.

The start of a girl's menstrual cycle is a very important turning point in a young girl's life, signifying the beginning of pubescence. In contrast to findings of both Lovering (1995) and Coates (1999), in which menstruation was discussed by girls in terms of discourses that positioned them undesirably and unempoweringly,[1] Rina used a discourse of 'menstruation heralding maturity', which *positively* values 'the start of menstruation' as a manifestation of maturity. While Rina positioned herself (along with her other mixed-ethnic girlfriends) as more mentally mature than their Japanese counterparts, she had no explanation as to her (and her mixed-ethnic friends') tardiness of their 'physical maturity' in comparison to the already-menstruating Japanese girls.

While the above section looked at how Rina created *good difference* for herself in terms of 'mental maturity' in comparison with her Japanese peers, the following section looks at how Naomi rejected being constituted as different in a negative manner.

Contesting 'the marked other' positioning

In this section, Naomi is shown deconstructing a discourse that constituted her as the 'marked other' solely on the basis of her physical difference and she instead reconstituted herself as the 'privileged' insider.

The extract that follows occurred in the context of Naomi comparing how she was differently constituted in the USA and in Japan. Naomi's construction of her life in the USA was very positive 'yeah, um, well, if I go to school there, I'll make friends there, I'm really quick at making friends there'. When I then asked her, 'how do you think that you are perceived over there? [in America ...] how different from here?', she answered by making a reference to people she meets for the first time 'here' in Japan.

(Extract 5.3) The Café (age 13): 'Just shut up about it'

1258   **N:**   here, if they're people I meet for the first time, they're like 'oh my gosh',
1259   she's not Japanese', it's like

1260 **L:** yeah
1261 **N:** 'just shut up about it'

Naomi employed a sarcastic voice to represent Japanese people around her in Japan who try to 'gaijinize' (Iino, 1996) her: 'oh my gosh, she's not Japanese'. She then presented an ironic voice of how she would hypothetically like to respond to them (Line no. 1261), but in words that she would probably not really use in an actual situation.

Naomi was contesting being positioned within a *discourse of homogeneity* in which everyone is expected to be Japanese in Japan and those who are not become 'the other'. She rejected being constituted by strangers she meets for the first time who turn her into 'the other' based only on her physical appearance. She further rejected this positioning as *the marked other* in her statement 'just shut up about it', implying that it does not need to be pointed out as a marked difference; although, as will be shown below in this chapter, Naomi also later claimed *good difference* for herself (see Extract 5.6). Above, she deconstructed the positioning of *bad difference* by implying an alternate ideology of diversity. Naomi seems to have internalized and observed a greater tolerance to difference/diversity during her short-term experiences in American schools where her mixed-ethnicity is not specifically marked (or named) and is not seen as *strange* or outside of the norm, as in Japan.

Linguistic traces can also be seen of Naomi rejecting and deconstructing a discourse of conformity as epitomized in the Japanese proverb 'the nail that sticks up will be hammered down' and instead she implied a competing discourse: 'Everyone's different, and everyone's okay'. Within a discourse of diversity, Naomi was also implying, 'why can't they just "shut up about it" and accept me as I am'. Also drawing on a discourse of interculturalism, Naomi constructed a comparison with another culture beyond Japan with which she had familiarity. Her ability to draw on her 'outside of Japan' knowledge and experience ascribes to her empowerment and self-confidence in her deconstruction of ethnic 'othering' within Japan.

Privileging difference/diversity

In this section, Naomi, similar to Rina, also positioned herself as 'different' from her Japanese peers, in a positive meaning. In the following extract, Naomi expressed how the boundaries of her rural community were too restrictive for her – particularly within her small school with a total population of only 11 pupils. Below, Naomi is responding to my question as to whether she has friends at her school or not.

(Extract 5.4) The Café (age 13): 'I don't like my friends at school'

2837 **N:** but, ummm, I don't really like my friends at school, I don't
2838 **L:** oh, OK, you don't have much choice do you?
2839 **N:** no
2840 **L:** you're going to a small school
2841 **N:** so I'm not going to school for my, I'm not going to school
          for my
2842   (laugh, caused by a distraction of a fly)
2843   for my, for my friends, I just go to school for what they
          teach me
2844 **L:** oh
2845 **N:** and I think that's really sad, but

Similar to Rina's construction of viewing her Japanese peers' talk as 'low level stuff' (Extract 5.1, Line no. 442), Naomi, above, also produced a construction that placed herself apart from her peers, 'I don't really like my friends at school' (Line no. 2837). Also parallel to Rina's construction, treated earlier that the problems of isolation and name-calling that she was having at school were not *academically grounded* (Extract 4.2, Line nos 183–184), similarly, Naomi implied that the *academic* aspect of school was not problematic for her and was, in fact, her main motivation for attending school (Line no. 2843). In contrast to this, both Rina and Naomi constructed the problems at school as having to do with *social relationship* issues between themselves and their 'friends' at school.

There is No Difference

While it was shown above how the girls often worked to claim *good* difference for themselves while rejecting *bad* difference, there were times when the distinction of *ethnic difference* in itself took on importance, regardless of how that difference was valued. This became particularly evident in discussion about a photo from *Time Asia* magazine that I showed the girls, which featured a newly released 'multiethnic' Barbie Doll [see Appendix 2, (4)]. The following extract takes place during the Hot Springs meeting as I showed the girls the magazine photo.

(Extract 5.5) Hot Springs (ages 13): 'A multiethnic Barbie doll'

3165 **L:** **kore o mita koto aru? baabi dooru aru deshou?**
3166 **H:** **kawaii**
3167 **L:** **baabi dooru ga suu nen kan mae ni kokujin no** Barbie doll **ga**

3168		dettan desukedo, kore wa saikin detano wa, ano
3169	N:	ajiajin to yooroppa
3170	?:	China
3171	L:	what do they call it? um, multi-ethnic, I think, yeah, multi-ethnic
3172		no 'ningyou mo detemashita'
3173	H:	misete, kawaii, de konna,
3174	L:	'kaira' to iu namae
3175	H:	konnan kanpeki kokeejyon yan na
3176	S:	nande tsume tsuiteiruno?
3177	?:	na?
3178	H:	to iu ka kampeki kokeejyon
3179	L:	kokeejyon jyanai yo
3180	H:	e, mikake zettai konna ko orude
3181	N:	'mixed looks Caucasian' is what they're all saying
3182	L:	oh, she LOOKS Caucasian?
3183	H:	zenzen ajiantte kanji shiihin na
3184	L:	kanji nai? tabun ajia to iu no wa Indian, India
3185	N:	a, indo kei na yatsu
3186		a, nanka indojinppoi toko mo arukedo, fukosou
3187	S:	ima made no baabi to issho yan
3188	M:	issho, kawarinai to omou
3189	A:	iro dake
3190	R:	kaminoke no iro dake ka
3191	N:	kaminoke yori hada no iro kawaranai
3192	R:	kawaranai ka
3193	L:	her hair is straight
3194	N:	fuku to, kaminoke no iro to nanyaro, so no hou
3195	?:	kao toka
3196	N:	to iu ka sa, me aokunai?
3197	?:	midorika?
3198	?:	midori

(Extract 5.5*) (translation)

3165*	L:	*have you seen this? you know Barbie dolls, right?*
3166*	H:	*[the doll] is cute*
3167*	L:	*several years ago Barbie doll came out with a Black Barbie doll,*
3168*		*but this one just came out*
3169*	N:	*an Asian and European*
3170	?:	*China*

3171	L:	what do they call it? um, multi-ethnic, I think, yeah, multi-ethnic
3172		'a multi-ethnic doll has also come out'
3173*	H:	*let me see, it's cute, this*
3174*	L:	*the [doll's] name is 'Kyla'*
3175*	H:	*this is totally Caucasian*
3176*	S:	*why does [the doll] have finger nails?*
3177*	?:	*huh?*
3178*	H:	*that is to say, [the doll is] completely Caucasian*
3179*	L:	*[the doll is] not Caucasian*
3180*	H:	*hey, there are [Caucasian] kids who look [just] like this*
3181*	N:	'mixed looks Caucasian' is what they're all saying
3182*	L:	oh, she LOOKS Caucasian?
3183*	H:	*[the doll] doesn't seem anything like an Asian person*
3184*	L:	*you don't think so? maybe by Asian, [the doll] is Indian, India*
3185*	N:	*ah, an Indian person*
3186*		*ah, [the doll] has some Indian like things about [it/her], the clothes*
3187*	S:	*[the doll] is just like all the other Barbie's up to now*
3188*	M:	*it's the same, I think there's no difference*
3189*	A:	*only the color*
3190*	R:	*only the color of the hair*
3191*	N:	*rather than the hair color, the skin color is no different*
3192*	R:	*it's no different*
3193	L:	her hair is straight
3194*	N:	*the clothes, the hair color and what is it, just those things*
3195*	?:	*the face and*
3196*	N:	*speaking of that, aren't the eyes blue?*
3197*	?:	*[are they] green?*
3198*	?:	*[yes, they're] green*

The discussion was mostly conducted in Japanese with a few switches into English by Naomi and me. In Japanese, the subject of a sentence is often left unstated and although the listener is usually able to imply the subject, sometimes it is left ambiguous without being problematic. In this text, when the girls and I used Japanese, we did not explicitly state the implied subject – the Barbie doll. In translation, the subject could be thought of as *the doll, her* or *it*. In the transcript, I indicated this by using brackets: [the doll]. In contrast, in the English switches, looking at my own discourse, in referring to the doll, I used feminine pronouns twice: 'she' (Line no. 3182) and 'her' (Line no. 3193). These differences between

Japanese and English in a text that includes code-switching reveal both the difficulties of translation, but at the same time open up interesting means to examine situated language usage.

While the purpose of this study was to get the girls together to talk about their ethnicities, this was the first time that any of the girls actually used the lexis of 'Caucasian' to talk about ethnicity. However, in this context, they were not talking about themselves, but about a doll. Hanna began by twice describing the doll as 'cute' (Line nos 3166, 3173). But then upon closer scrutiny of the photo, Hanna changed her stance as she introduced this descriptive adjective 'Caucasian' (Line no. 3175) into the talk to contest the commercial promotion of the doll as 'multiethnic'. While this rendition of the word 'Caucasian' into Japanese pronunciation does appear occasionally in Japanese spoken or written texts, the context in which Hanna used it would not likely be used by her Japanese peers. Most Japanese people would much more likely use the Japanese word *hakujin* (literally, a 'White person'). Hanna's uncommon usage here is indicative of the context under which this interaction took place among mixed-ethnic girls who know and use such language regularly. The other girls present also co-constructed other implied references to the doll as 'Caucasian/ White' in terms of the doll's face as well as the skin, hair and eye color.

In Line no. 3178, Hanna challenged the manufacturer's claim of the doll as being multiethnic by stating that 'it's completely Caucasian'. When I then remarked that it is not Caucasian, Hanna continued by saying that there are people that look like this. She was probably implying that there are *Caucasian* people who appear like the doll who have somewhat ambiguous coloring, but who are not actually 'mixed'.

Then in Line no. 3181, Naomi switched into English, taking on the role of translator/mediator for my benefit in clarifying Hanna's meaning that the new doll looks (totally) Caucasian (even though it was intended to look Asian as well). Then in Line no. 3183, Hanna explicitly stated that the doll does not look Asian at all, as the manufacturers claim. In Line no. 3184, I suggested to the girls that the term 'Asian' probably referred to the Indian people of India. Most Japanese think of the notion of 'Asian' as referring to themselves and other 'Far-East Asian' ethnicities such as Chinese, Korean and Mongolian, rather than people from more central Asian regions such as India and Pakistan whose facial features and coloring differ greatly from them.

Naomi's response '*a, indo kei na yatsu*' (Line no. 3185) indicated a recognition and likely acceptance of my explanation. Her response is interesting here in that she used the informal noun *yatsu* (chap/guy/gal) which is masculinely gendered in that it is generally used by men or boys and generally refers to males. It is seldom used by women or girls in most contexts. Her usage may indicate a derisive attitude about the doll being manufactured to represent Indian mixed-ethnicity rather than their Far-East-Asian mixed-ethnicity. Then she acknowledged that the doll did have 'some Indian things (about it), the clothes' (Line no. 3186).

From here, the other girls joined in to co-construct the notion that there was no difference between this 'new' doll and all other (Caucasian) Barbie dolls before. Naomi mentioned (Line no. 3191) that the skin color was no different and Rina agreed. According to the girls, there was nothing particularly multiethnic or Asian about the doll as commercially promoted, other than superficial aspects such as clothing and dark hair color (Line no. 3194).

Then, Naomi drew attention to the eye color as blue, an eye color generally associated with Caucasian people. Another girl suggested that they might be green, also an eye color associated with Caucasians. Finally, another girl took the floor to co-construct this 'Caucasian' feature by confirming the eyes to be green.

What the girls were trying to express and what annoyed them about the new 'mixed-ethnic Barbie' was that it was *not different enough.* They were unhappy with the commercial promotion that this doll was supposed to represent a mixed-ethnicity; but to them it was really just the same Caucasian Barbie mold, but fitted with a slightly darker skin and dressed in an Indian sari – an artificial identity that even a Caucasian girl could easily assume. Here it was of less significance to the girls as to whether there was a *good difference* or a *bad difference* portrayed in the doll, but rather the problem for them was that there was *insignificant difference* represented. The girls were 'doing difference' in their contestation of this *lack of difference,* which they took as a denial of a different/separate/distinct ethnic identity of mixed-ethnicity.

The next section looks at how the girls took up a good meaning of difference as they positioned themselves as privileged in terms of their difference.

Constituting Difference and Privileging Self

This section further investigates Naomi's discursive construction of 'difference' as she performed her non-conformity. The extract below occurred nearly a half year after Naomi had already positioned her Japanese peers at school as 'really sad' (see Extract 5.4). Once again, the topic returned to Naomi's relationship with her friends at school where she produced a similar construction, but now she articulated herself even more explicitly. In the following extract, we were discussing friends and groups at school.

(Extract 5.6) Hot Springs (age 13): 'I'm different; They're below me'

2288	L:	do you have, I mean, do you have like a best friend or a friend
2289		that you hang around with there?
2290	N:	no
2291	L:	no? not at all?
2292	N:	they're, they're disgusting, they're so isolated, they're so, the way they think is
2293	L:	really, that must be hard, to not have a friend there then
2294	N:	yeah, I can, like
2295	L:	'they're so disgusting', I mean, to feel that, it must be hard
2296	N:	(laugh) uh, it's OK to play with them and everything
2297		but I can't really talk to them, at all
2298	L:	yeah, uh-huh, yeah
2299	N:	and they are like, 'well you're kind of different, so',
2300	L:	yeah, do they think that you're really cool? I mean do they want to be friends
2301		with you or do they,
2302	N:	no, no
2303	L:	they don't?
2304	N:	no, I'm like really different from everyone
2305	L:	so they, they have their groups and you're not in it?
2306	N:	um, everyone has their own group, kinda, and
2307	L:	how are you different from them?
2308	N:	I TRY to be different from them
2309	L:	so you don't have a problem with being different? you like to be different?
2310	N:	no, I don't mind (L: uh-huh.) but, I don't know, I'm, I'm like it's OK, I have
2311		other friends (L: uh-huh) in other places (L: right, hu-huh), and, yeah, I don't
2312		really kind of think that they're, it's funny, but I think they're below me
2313		(L: uh-huh) kind of (L: uh-huh) because I, I see a lot, a lot more of the world
2314		(L: uh-huh, yeah) than they do (L: uh-huh) so, there is maybe one girl that has a
2315		larger perpe-, perspective and
2316		stuff, but, yeah, anyway

Several important things are going on in this passage. Naomi again used strong rhetoric to position her Japanese peers at her school as 'disgusting' and 'isolated' (Line no. 2292). In this context, similar to Rina's compensatory representation of her Japanese 'friends' that 'they're all catching up' (Extract 5.1, Line no. 444), Naomi also used a similar compensatory and contrasting construction here: 'It's OK to play with them and everything' (Line no. 2296) contrasted with, 'but I can't really talk to them, at all' (Line no. 2297). Here again, similar to Rina's earlier construction, Naomi associates 'playing' with immaturity and 'talking' with greater maturity. This might be interpreted as a signal of change both in terms of Naomi (as well as of Rina above) moving out of childhood into adolescence and also a change in positioning by means of Naomi confronting the actors in her school who relegated her to a marginal position. Naomi positioned herself as not only being distinct and different from them, but also as superior.

Naomi used an intertextual voice of her classmates 'othering' her with: 'well, you're kind of different' (Line no. 2299). She rejected my suggested construction of her as popular when I asked her if her friends at school think she is 'cool' and if 'they want to be friends' with her (Line nos 2300–2301). To this, Naomi empathically answered in the negative 'no, no' and then, positioned herself also as 'really different from everyone' (Line no. 2304), claiming *good difference* for herself, in her deconstruction of *bad difference*, from the viewpoint of her Japanese peers at school.

At the same time, Naomi also clearly affirmed her control over her other separate group memberships by emphasizing her outside-of-school affiliations and friendships (Line nos 2310–2311). Naomi used the disclaimer 'it's funny but' to soften the impact of her positioning of her Japanese peers as 'below' herself (Line no. 2312). While positioning herself as separate and different on the one hand, Naomi also positioned herself within a discourse of interculturalism by implying her greater worldliness and sophistication based on her having 'other friends, in other places', which (she assumed) her Japanese friends did not possess. She was able to make her differentness an asset through her positive self-positioning, 'I TRY to be different' (Line no. 2308), 'because I, I see a lot, a lot more of the world … than they do' (Line nos 2313–2314).

Eckert (1993) found, in her study, girls (in their talk about boys) expressing two themes of wanting to be popular in school and also wanting to express their independence by, for example, not idolizing boys or choosing a non-mainstream boyfriend. Eckert's themes of popularity and independence can also be applied to Naomi's situation. Naomi discursively positions herself as peripheral within the context of her school community in which popularity had become inaccessible to her due to her constituted 'differentness', but at the same time, popularity at school also becomes undesirable to her as a consequence of her 'differentness', which she appropriates as her independence.

While Naomi's *contestation* of being positioned by others as 'different' was discussed above (Extract 5.3), paradoxically, Naomi also explicitly constituted her own differentness, but in a reconstituted *good* meaning. This action of Naomi occurs repeatedly in other instances throughout the data-set. Following are other examples of Naomi constituting this difference.

The extract below looks at the girls' responses to my question of how their own personal choice of style (such as hair style, accessories, clothing, etc.) might resemble or be different from that of their Japanese peers. Differences between some of the girls can be seen in the varying ways that they positioned themselves here.

(Extract 5.7a) Birthday (ages 13 and 14): 'I'm different; I'm the same'

1184   N: tomodachi to chigau
1185   S: tomodachi to issho

(Extract 5.7a*) (translation)

1184*   N   *I am different from my friends*
1185*   S   *I am just like my friends*

While Naomi claimed differentness for herself in terms of style, Sara chose to align herself with her Japanese friends. In answer to another related question regarding their *choice of fashion styles*, the girls provided a range of answers, but it was particularly Naomi who constituted non-conformity for herself as she explicitly proclaimed her difference. In contrast to this, in the extract below, several of the other girls again positioned themselves as Japanese or as preferring Japanese style, discursively downplaying the notion of 'good' difference, which Naomi had claimed for herself, as their talk continued. Linguistic traces of a discourse of conformity can be seen as Maya, Anna and Hanna performed Japaneseness in their self-positioning. I asked the girls if they thought their own personal styles (including hair style, dress, accessories, etc.) were more similar to their Japanese friends or if they thought these had a foreign influence. The girls responded in English as follows.

(Extract 5.7b) Birthday

1195   M: umm, Japanese style
1196   L: Japanese style, OK, **ii you** [*that's fine*] and Hanna?

1197   **H:**   hundred percent Japanese style
1198   **L:**   OK, hundred percent Japanese, and Anna?
1199   **A:**   Japanese

Differences between the girls can be seen again, as we compare Naomi's celebration of difference for herself earlier and Maya, Hanna and Anna's 'doing being Japanese' above. Moments later, in the same Birthday meeting, in a discussion about the styles of their houses, I asked the girls how they thought their non-Japanese parent might have had an influence on the style of their houses. In spite of the fact that Naomi's house is probably the most traditional of any of their houses in that it is an older Japanese-style country home, she nevertheless took the opportunity to construct difference again. She was the first one to speak up, stating 'my house is really different'. She then stated that the 'one' different thing about it is that the *shouji* (indoor sliding paper doors) do not *slide* open, but *open out* as a regular Western door.

The following section further looks at dilemmas of ethnic identification that these girls faced. While Naomi continued to constitute her difference, this next section, in particular, looks at how the girls discursively categorized themselves in terms of their self-constituted multimemberships comprising their multi-identities.

Categorizing Ethnic Selves: Multimemberships

The three extracts presented below in this final section further examine the girls' dilemmas of negotiating their ethnic identities. Here they constituted themselves within multimemberships as they struggled to categorize their various identities in maneuvering the paradox of 'what kind of person' they are.

The first extract below is from the first interview with Rina. She was responding to my question as to whether she thought she looked Japanese or Western.

(Extract 5.8) Rina's house (age 12): 'Do you look Japanese or Western?'

110   **L:**   do you think that you look Japanese or Western?
111   **R:**   you mean the way I look?
112   **L:**   the way you look
113   **R:**   well, yeah, yeah
114   **L:**   what do you think?

115	**R:**	well, I do think that I look more Western, well, yeah, because Japanese think
116		I'm *gaijin* and when I go over to The States and things,
117		they don't think I'm half Japanese
118	**L:**	oh, I see (laugh)
119	**R:**	but, I think I look more Western
120	**L:**	um-hum, yeah, you feel that you are too? you just,
121	**R:**	well ...
122	**L:**	your (?) identity – you feel that you are more?
123	**R:**	actually identity, I feel more of a Japanese citizen because Japan is where
124		I have lived most, well ALL of my life and, but in some ways, like how I feel,
125		how I think, I feel as if I'm more Western, I don't like the Japanese,
126		how they do whatever so and so,
127	**L:**	what kind of so-and-so?
128	**R:**	well, like how they like, kind of, um, uh many feelings like, well, for an easy example,
129		like how they eat (laugh), like they slurp their noodles, and Mom always says,
130		quotes my manners, but, um, I feel that that's like kind of gross
131		and in those kind of ways I feel I'm more Western although Mum thinks
132		Gramma would faint if she saw my manners
[...]		
141	**R:**	but, I do think that some manners in Japan are kind of gross and like the way
142		they kind of spit, spit in the drains whenever and stuff, and stuff like that,
143		but also things like, like how they kind of, like, if, like Mum always says um, that
144		um, you know

In answer to my question asking if she 'looks' more Japanese or more Western, Rina constituted her physicality as more Western. She accounted for this self-assessment on the basis that Japanese people think she's *gaijin*. Rina used the un-translated word *gaijin* in an intertextual Japanese voice, giving it a pejorative nuance (Line nos 115–116). She continued in the same turn to compare this with how she felt she was perceived by Americans, who do *not* constitute her as 'half-Japanese'. She implied here that her ethnicity is 'unmarked' by Americans (Line nos 116–117), similar to Naomi's construction in Extract 5.3.

However, when I asked Rina about her 'identity', she initially represented her *identity* in terms of citizenship, to which she more closely identified herself as Japanese (citizen) – even though she also holds British nationality/citizenship. Her reason was that Japan is where she has lived *most* of her life. But she quickly corrected herself here to emphasize that she has lived 'ALL' of her life in Japan. This repair is based on the fact that she had actually spent 10 months of her life attending a school in America. This word/concept 'identity' does not exist in Japanese and it has only recently come into Japanese as an English loan-word. While most Japanese people have trouble conceptualizing what this word means and how to describe their individual identities, Rina understood the meaning right away, as revealed in her quick response.

While Rina identified herself as a Japanese citizen, she also discursively distanced herself from 'Japaneseness' in the way that she 'feels' and 'thinks' (Line nos 124–125). In a rejection of this Japaneseness, she constituted 'Japanese' as 'the other' in her use of the pronoun 'they' (instead of 'us') to refer to Japanese people (Line nos 125–126). In contrast, she positioned herself as 'Western' (Line no. 125), within a discourse of interculturalism in which she constructed Western people as more sophisticated and well mannered. When asked to give examples of what she does not like about Japanese people, Rina went on to cite several examples of Japanese mannerisms that particularly annoyed her such as eating and grooming habits of slurping noodles and spitting in sink drains. She positioned 'Japanese' as 'gross' and unmannered, which she set against the 'Western' standards of her British mother and grandmother.

The next section also looks at dilemmas of multimemberships, this time as Naomi tried to articulate what it was she liked about going to America. I asked her 'what do you enjoy about it? English, or?' as this extract begins.

(Extract 5.9) The Café (age 13): 'I'm not myself; I'm two people'

1162	L:	what's the most (?)
1163	N:	the (?) I get a break from Japan
1164	L:	oh
1165	N:	yeah, like that, (laugh), and, and, I don't really realize it,
1166		but I really change when I'm in America or when I'm in Japan
1167	L:	how do you change?

1168	**N:**	I, I, I don't know, but I'm not myself when I'm (.) well, that's funny (. .)
1169		I'm two people and I'm one of them in Japan, the other one in America
1170	**L:**	can you describe it a little bit? (.) are you freer, do you think, or are you
1171	**N:**	that's what will be easier in that
1172		**kankyou, soko ni atta hito ni naru** (laugh)
1173		**sono basho ni atta hito ni naru**
1172*		*environment, I become the people that I meet there* (laugh)
1173*		*I become like the people in that place*
1174	**L:**	so you like yourself better in The States?
1175	**N:**	not better or anything like that, it's, I'm just different
1176	**L:**	it's just different and it's nice to get a change?
1177	**N:**	yeah
1178	**L:**	and then you're, about that time you're ready to come back and
1179		change back to, to your life here?
1180	**N:**	yeah

Naomi started out explaining what it was that she liked about going to America by saying she gets 'a break from Japan'. But then she meta-linguistically framed herself as *not really realizing* that she 'really changes when [she] is in America or when [she's] in Japan' (Line nos 1165–1166). Her use of lexis to self-position herself is interesting when I asked her *how* she changes. She began by saying 'I'm not myself when I'm' (Line no. 1168), but then after a short pause, she again meta-linguistically amused herself by her own revelation, 'well, that's funny'. She followed this with a longer pause before she constituted herself as being 'two people . . .', 'I'm one of them in Japan, the other one in America' (Line no. 1169).

I asked her to elaborate. Then following a pause, I asked her if she feels freer (during the time that she is in America). But Naomi rejected this construction of her feelings. In trying to articulate herself, she momentarily switched into Japanese in stating, 'I become the people that I meet there, I become like the people in that place' (Line nos 1172–1173) revealing a kind of chameleon nature. Again I joined in to suggest that perhaps she likes herself better in The States, and again Naomi rejected this construction of her with, 'not better or anything like that, it's, I'm different' (Line no. 1175). When I again tried to surmise Naomi's feelings as being ready then to return to Japan and change back to her life here (Line nos 1178–1179), this time Naomi responded with 'yeah', which can be interpreted as agreement.

The following extract continues to examine the question of multi-memberships and how the girls constitute themselves in terms of their ethnicities. The following extract is unique in the data selected for analysis in this book in that it does not come out of discussions with me present (see also Extract 7.1). Rather, this extract comes from a recording made privately by two of the girls talking among themselves, in my absence, which they recorded at a sleepover at one of their homes (see the sections 'Hanna and Anna meeting' and 'Audio-tapes made by the girls'). While I had asked them to make a tape for me, I did not specify the contents of their talk or prompt them in any way. The girls were talking late at night in bed.

(Extract 5.10) Hanna/Anna (age 13): 'We'd have to have cosmetic surgery'

527	**A:**	**iyayana otona no tachibatte doko ittatte 'gaijin' yan**
528	**H:**	**honma iyana, sore iyada**
529	**A:**	**kokuseki sa, nijussai ni natte na, kimatta to shitemo,**
530		**kao wa kawarahen yan, seikei shini ikanto**
531	**H:**	**docchi ni naritai no?**
532	**A:**	**mada wakarahen kedo, tabun nihonjin ni naru, wakarahen**
533	**H:**	**demo chau kao yatte**
534	**A:**	**a, kao?**
535	**H:**	**daburu no kao ga iya nano?**
536	**A:**	**datte dokkara mitatte 'gaijin' yankedo,**
537		**amerika toka ittara, kekkou gaijin atsukai sarehen de,**
538		**nihon dake yanen shimaguni konjou dena 'gaijin gaijin ya'**
539	**H:**	**ima wa sonna koto naiyo daburutte meccha urayamashigarareru**
540	**A:**	**uuun seyakedo tonikaku 'e, daburu?' tte kanji yan**

(Extract 5.10*) (translation)

527*	**A:**	*I don't like it, as adults, wherever you go it's 'gaijin'*
528*	**H:**	*really, I hate that, that's awful*
529*	**A:**	*your nationality, when you turn twenty, even if you decide [which to choose: Japanese or your other nationality],*
530*		*your face won't change, we'd have to have cosmetic surgery*
531*	**H:**	*which one [nationality] do you want to be?*
532*	**A:**	*I am not sure yet, but I will probably be Japanese, I don't know*
533*	**H:**	*but your [our] face is different*

534* A: *ah, my [our] face?*
535* H: *do you hate having a double's face?*
536* A: *it's like, where ever you look, it's 'gaijin', but if you go to places*
537* *like America, you are not really treated as a 'gaijin' [foreigner],*
538* *only Japan has this island disposition, 'gaijin, gaijin'*
539* H: *now there is no more of that kind of thing, double is very envied*
540* A: *yeah, that's right but anyway, it's like the feeling of 'hey [are you]*
double?'

In this extract, Hanna seems to take on the role of interviewer with her leading the topic and asking several questions. Thus in this extract, Anna's views are centrally expressed in her responses to the questions. While the girls turned on a tape recorder because I asked them to and focused their talk on issues of ethnicity for my purposes, it seems that they were expressing how they really felt.

It is interesting that much of what Anna said here is very similar to what Rina and Naomi had also stated in previous meetings when Hanna and Anna were not present. Anna voiced her Japanese peers who racialize her as *'gaijin'* (Line nos 527, 536–538), resembling Rina above (Extract 5.8, Line nos 115–116). Also Anna (Line nos 536–538) made the same point as Naomi had earlier (Extract 5.3) that in Japan they are ethnicized and othered as *'gaijin'* whereas in America (or Australia) they are not treated as 'foreigners', implying that they are unmarked.

In Line no. 529, Anna made a reference to the making of a decision after turning 20. She is referring to a law in Japan currently in place, where children of Japanese international marriages are permitted to hold dual citizenship until the age of 22 when they must choose one nationality and abandon the other. Anna made the point that even if one did choose Japanese nationality, their faces would still be seen as 'foreigners'. She was using humor and sarcasm in saying that they would have to have cosmetic surgery in order to look Japanese.

While in this short extract, the girls used the word *gaijin* five times, they also used the non-standard lexis *daburu* (double) three times to refer to themselves. In Line no. 535, Hanna asked Anna if she hated having a 'doubles' face. In Line no. #539, Hanna positioned herself and Anna in an empowering discourse of diversity in her use again of the alternative term in saying that 'double is very envied'. While agreeing with Hanna to some extent, Anna also again used a hypothetical sarcastic voice of Japanese people marginalizing her, 'hey [are you] double?' (Line no. 540). While she mimicked a Japanese voice, in reality, it is highly unlikely that a Japanese person would actually be heard using the word 'double' (*daburu*) instead of 'half' (*haafu*) to refer to Anna's ethnicity, as the word has not come into common usage in most Japanese circles. Both Anna and Hanna use the word *daburu* instead of *haafu* in their common talk with each other as a means of accomplishing empowerment and solidarity.

In Line no. #538, Anna used the Japanese term *shimaguni konjou* to say that 'only Japan has this island disposition'. Anna is making a reference to the commonly held notion of Japan as having a very insular worldview based on its geographic feature as an island country.[2]

Much later, in the final meeting again, the dilemma of multimembership arose when Rina asked the question to all of the girls, 'what kind of person do you consider yourself to be?' The following extract is the girls' responses to Rina's question.

(Extract 5.11) Last Reunion (ages 14 and 15): 'What kind of person do you consider yourself?'

861	**L:**	OK, start with Maya
862	**M:**	heeee, (..) futsuu ni amerika to nihon, (?) ni kangaekata ni
863	**L:**	Hanna
864	**H:**	nihonjin
865	**L:**	nihonjin, Anna?
866	**A:**	watashi mo nihonjin
867	**L:**	Sara
868	**S:**	he, nihonjin demonai, amerikajin demonai (?)
869	**L:**	ryouhou demonai?
870	**S:**	aaa
871	**L:**	de nani?
872	**S:**	ryouhou
873	**L:**	ryouhou, OK, Naomi wa?
874	**N:**	mmmm, jibun no, basho ni yottari
875	**M:**	atashi mo basho ni yotte chigau
876	**N:**	na, basho ni yottari
877	**M:**	basho ni yotte kibun ga chigau na
878	**?:**	nnn, wakaru
879	**N:**	jibun no seikaku no, kono bubun wa nihonjin,
880		kono bubun ga suGGOI amerikajin to iu toko ga aru
881	**?:**	seyana
882	**?:**	nnnn
883	**L:**	naruhodo
884	**N:**	so, nanijin te kimetsukerarehen to omou
885	**L:**	uh-huh

886	R:	**nanka, nanka (?)**
887	L:	**uh-huh, uh-huh, Rina?**
888	R:	**mixed**
889	L:	**mixed, OK.**
890	R:	**jibun mo amerikajin to omou toki ga aru**
891	L:	**assone, anata amerikajin denai no ni, naruhodo**

(Extract 5.11*) (translation)

861*	L:	OK, start with Maya
862*	M:	*ahh, (. .) usually my thinking is America and Japan (?)*
863*	L:	*Hanna*
864*	H:	*Japanese*
865*	L:	*Japanese, Anna?*
866*	A:	*I am also Japanese*
867*	L:	*Sara*
868*	S:	*ah, not Japanese, and not American (?)*
869*	L:	*you are neither of them?*
870*	S:	*yeah*
871*	L:	*so what are you?*
872*	S:	*both*
873*	L:	*both, OK, what about you, Naomi?*
874*	N:	*mmmm, for me, it depends on the place*
875*	M:	*for me too, it differs depending on the place*
876*	N:	*right, depending on the place*
877*	M:	*depending on the place, my feeling is different*
878*	?:	*yeah, I know what you mean*
879*	N:	*my own personality, there is this part that is Japanese,*
880*		*and there is this part that is REALLY American*
881*	?:	*that's right*
882*	?:	*yeah*
883*	L:	*I see*
884*	N:	*so, I think it can't be decided which kind of person [race, nationality] I am*
885*	L:	*uh-huh*
886*	R:	*somehow, somehow (?)*
887*	L:	*uh-huh, uh-huh, Rina?*
888*	R:	*mixed*
889*	L:	*mixed, OK.*
890*	R:	*sometimes I think I am American*
891*	L:	*yeah right, even though you aren't an American, I see*

Rina's question, 'what kind of person do you consider yourself to be?' again brought a range of answers from the six girls. Maya began by saying her thinking is American *and* Japanese. Hanna and Anna both positioned themselves as Japanese. Sara rejected the notion of being either 'Japanese' or 'American' (Line no. 868), and after a few turns constituted herself as 'both' (*ryouhou*) (Line no. 872). Naomi could not quickly answer what kind of person she was, as the other four girls had done. For Naomi, 'it differs depending on the place'. She positioned herself as having a part of her personality which is Japanese, but she even more emphatically stated, 'and there is this part that is REALLY American' (Line no. 880) to which a few of the girls responded in agreement. In the end, Naomi stated that she could not decide how to categorize herself (Line no. 884). As she tried to articulate which kind of person she is, Rina stepped up to take the floor (Line no. 886). When I designated Rina to take her turn (Line no. 887), she positioned herself as 'mixed', switching into English. She also added that sometimes she thinks she is American even though neither of her parents is American.

These girls could not always easily categorize themselves in terms of their ethnicity. They hold more than one membership, foregrounding one or the other depending on the situated context. For some of the girls, this dilemma could not be easily solved as the range of subject positions that they take up is unfixed and fluctuates according to their interactions with others. Some of the factors affecting negotiations of their ethnic identities had to do with how they were constituted by others around them, including their school peers and family members as well as the change in the surrounding environment.

Differences between the Girls: Unevenness of the Data

As mentioned in Chapter 3, some of the girls' voices appeared more than others creating a degree of unevenness in the representation of the participants. This is not intentional, but as an analyst, I have attempted to select 'rich data', which best reveals clues to the themes that I have raised in my original research questions.

Already evident in these first two analysis chapters, the data have shown that there are quite remarkable differences among the six girls, which partly contribute to the degree to which they appear in the data. While this book mainly focuses on examining the similarities apparent in the shared mixed-ethnicities of the participants, in this section, I highlight their differences. Following, I summarize some of my observations concerning differences between the girls and specific characteristics of each participant as shown up to this point. In later chapters, I continue to examine each girl individually (see explanation of their self-portraits in the section 'The self-portraits' [p. 199]).

The girls articulate their identities and take up subject positions in various ways. Naomi is often seen in the data positioning herself within a 'critical' view of the world and is not afraid to oppose incongruities that she notices around her. She freely speaks out and shares her feelings with others within our group, but she does so in a non-threatening manner in collaborative interaction with the others. Like Naomi, Rina is also a very articulate informant who expresses her feelings well. She is often seen in the data using kind words and showing support to encourage others among us. Hanna often appears in the data sharing humorous narratives of events in her life, revealing a rich sense of humor and a talent for dramatic presentation. Sara comes across in the data as somewhat reticent, but openly offers her honest opinion when asked. Maya is enthusiastic and also does not hold back in sharing her feelings, but she appears in the dataset less than any of the other girls. This is due, in part, to her attendance at only three of the meetings and also to her somewhat quiet nature in comparison to some of the other girls. Anna's voice also appears in the dataset less than most of the other girls, even when they are all assembled together.

Anna, Maya and Sara especially have soft voices and I had difficulty on many occasions telling them apart in the audio recordings. Thus these voices often appeared as question marks in the participant column of the extracts. Anna and Hanna seemed more to identify with aspects of their Japaneseness and a desire to want to fit in with their Japanese peers than did Naomi or Rina who seemed more anxious to explore their non-Japanese identities. Maya and Sara seemed to be more in-between.

As far as language use is concerned, Rina and Naomi seemed to prefer to use English when speaking to me and perhaps it may be partly due to their high proficiency in English that they appear more frequently in the dataset. Hanna also is very proficient in English, but she often identifies with her Japaneseness and when speaking to the entire group she usually used Japanese. Maya seemed to want to use English if given the chance to express herself to a sympathetic audience where English errors are not only allowed, but also comprehended. While preferring to use Japanese, Sara and Anna understand English quite well and use it when they need to. Chapter 6 further examines this differential in linguistic capital among the girls.

The following section discusses changes that the girls underwent, especially in the transition over the summer vacation during the second year of middle school when they were 13 or 14 years old.

Changes over Time

While all of the girls claimed good difference in referring to themselves and rejected bad difference at various times during the meetings, it was particularly Naomi who most strongly positioned herself on this theme of 'difference'. However, it can be seen that Naomi's positioning changed and became more articulate, even over a relatively short period or time of just four or five months from the Café meeting (Extracts 5.3 and 5.4) until the Hot Springs meeting (Extract 5.6). In Extract 5.3, Naomi expressed her disgust at being positioned as different and in Extract 5.4, she created difference between herself and her school peers in order to claim her independence. However, it was not until the final meeting that Naomi was able to very powerfully articulate herself by proudly claiming her difference: 'I TRY to be different from them' (Extract 5.6).

Other significant changes were seen in all of the girls in a relatively short span of time. At the Birthday meeting, half way through their second year of middle school, summer had just ended with all of the girls having returned from an overseas experience, except for Maya who instead traveled within Japan with her mother. During the summer, they all had clearly taken more control of their attempts to use and improve their English, mostly aided by their travel experiences. Anna went with Hanna to Australia to study English for a few weeks. Naomi and Rina both spent one to two months in the USA, meeting up for summer camp together. Sara spent three weeks in the USA, but this time did not long to return to Japan after the first week, as she had so voiced in a previous meeting.

The girls all came into this meeting with *school* as a central focus of their lives and with a clearer idea of which high school they might want to go to in a few years' time. Some of them even had a vision of their future job. Most of the girls had become more body conscious: Sara had gotten a straightening permanent for her hair and appeared to be wearing make-up. Anna and Hanna expressed that they liked being girls because they were able to be more feminine in style, dress and make-up. These changes coincided with their increasing ability to draw on a wider range of more empowering alternative discourses of ethnicity and gender.

The importance to the girls of my arranged meetings with them appeared to grow and take more centrality in their lives. Before this study, the six girls had almost never all gotten together at one time. However, during the Birthday meeting, I heard them discussing a plan for all six of them to get together for a sleepover. Although I had arranged for them to all get together for our group interviews, this was the first time they had orchestrated a meeting on their own to all get together.

By the final meeting, when Rina asked the girls what kind of person they considered themselves to be (Extract 5.11), although it was not an easy question for them to answer and there was some ambivalence in the responses of most of the girls, over time, they came to be able to more clearly define themselves: as *Japanese* (Hanna and Anna), as *both* (Sara), as *mixed* (Rina) and as *depending on the place* (Naomi). This is in contrast to their earlier accounts of themselves where, for example, their *difference* was more defined by the positionings of others around them: 'well, I do think that I look more Western ... because Japanese think I'm *gaijin* ...' (Rina: Extract 5.8; Line nos 115–116). In Extract 5.9, through the process of her articulation, Naomi reflected upon her own thought processes: 'I'm not myself when I'm, well, that's funny ... I'm two people ...' (Extract 5.9, Line nos 1168–1169). Later, there was no ambivalence in Naomi in her confidently claiming that her identity cannot be decided (Extract 5.11, Line no. 884). During her second year of middle school, in speaking about which identity/nationality Anna would want to assume in her future, she answered with some uncertainty: 'I'm not sure yet, but I will probably be Japanese, I don't know' (Extract 5.10, Line nos 532–533). However, by her third year of middle school, there was no longer any uncertainty in Anna's response to Rina's question when she clearly identified herself as Japanese. Nonetheless, it is important, even here, to view these newer positionings as still unfixed and potentially changeable.

Summary

In this chapter, I have continued to explore the first central question of how the girls represented themselves based on the tensions and dilemmas of their mixed-ethnic subjectivities. Dilemmas of how these girls were ethnically marginalized and how they negotiated their ethnic identities, often by reconstituting *bad difference* to *good difference*, was examined in their speech.

I have shown how, for many of the girls, the deconstruction of 'othering' often took the form of privileging and placing themselves in an elevated position and constituting themselves as insider, while constituting 'the Japanese' as the outsider and as *the other*. Naomi was shown to position herself as peripheral and different within the context of her small school. While her 'differentness' prevented her from becoming popular, at the same time, she rejected the positioning of 'popularity' for herself at school in lieu of her self-constituted differentness, which she took up as her independence within a discourse of interculturalism. Her world of friends – outside of and larger than the small community of her school – allowed her to take up this difference as positive, self-enhancing cultural capital.

In this chapter, I have explored dilemmas faced by the girls in trying to categorize themselves within various and often conflicting memberships. Naomi exemplified this with her statement of self-realization that she is two people. Some of the girls did not constitute their difference to the extreme that Naomi did and instead positioned themselves within discourses of greater conformity of Japaneseness. Naomi was shown to have particular trouble in articulating her ethnicity, while Hanna and Anna proclaimed Japaneseness for themselves; and Maya, Sara and Rina claimed neither one nor the other, but *both* for themselves.

In the following chapter, I further look at how the girls constitute themselves, but I focus specifically on positive negotiations of their identities through their discursive construction and celebration of various forms of cultural capital.

Notes

1. In a study on adolescent talk on menstruation, Lovering (1995) showed, using PDA, how girls' subjectivity is constructed by the discourses and practices available to them in a *disempowering* manner. Lovering focused on the problem of negative 'taboo' attitudes of adolescents toward menarche and their general ignorance about it. She found that 'For girls, menstruation brought undesirable attention and male oppression, and an undesired "bleeding" associated with pains, injuries and accidents' (Lovering, 1995: 26). Similarly, Coates (1999), using discourse analysis to examine adolescent girls' talk about their periods, found them using three dominant discourses: a medical discourse, a self-disclosure discourse and a repressive (patriarch) discourse.

2. Historians have explained Japan's insular worldview as resulting from Japan's *Sakoku* (Locked-up Country) Policy. During the Edo Period, Japan closed its doors off to the rest of the world, not allowing foreigners to come in or Japanese to go out. This policy continued for nearly two-and-a-half centuries (1633–1868), a feat that only an island country would have been able to maintain for that long.

Chapter 6
Celebration of Cultural, Symbolic, Linguistic and Social Capital

Introduction

As shown in the preceding chapters, the participant girls of this study work very hard to positively maneuver and negotiate their identities into positions of control over marginalizing discourses, which ethnicize and gaijinize them as 'the other' within Japanese society. However, while these girls are sometimes negatively disempowered as ethnic minorities, paradoxically, they also at other times enjoy an elevated social status of a *double dominance*. As briefly mentioned in Chapter 1, I use this term 'double dominance' to refer to two forms of dominance that these girls enjoy by means of their *doubleness* (see the section 'Central Questions' [p. 11]). On the one hand, the girls stake claim to their Japaneseness in terms of both nationality and heritage; Japanese is their majority language (and their first or *one* of their first languages) and is the medium of instruction in their schools. On the other hand, they also have access to the high-status foreign language, English – one of the three main subjects required in secondary school along with Mathematics and Japanese. The linguistic capital of biliguality, which they discursively create on the basis of their *access* to English, allows these girls to lay claim to connections with a foreign, but politically and economically dominant, white-Western culture – a *dominance* to which most of their Japanese peers generally do not have access.

This chapter attends to the second central question posed in Chapter 1, restated again here:

> How, if at all, do children (adolescent girls) of Japanese and 'white' mixed-parentage in Japan *celebrate* their ethnicity? How, if at all, do they construct ethnic (and gendered) cultural, symbolic, linguistic and social capital for themselves on the basis of their hybrid identities?

This question is addressed by drawing on Bourdieu's (1977) theory of cultural capital. Bourdieu (1977) uses the notion of linguistic capital interrelatedly with cultural (and other forms of) capital to refer to the class-related asset of language acquired within the home, which is transformed during the process of education. Regarding use of language, Bourdieu's (1991) linguistic capital theory predicts that the ability to use the dominant language of a country provides a transferable resource (linguistic capital) helpful in gaining access to the economic goods, services and connections of that society. Smits and Gunduz-Hosgor (2003) found Bourdieu's (1991) theory to aptly apply to non-Turkish speaking people in Turkey, who faced a linguistic 'barrier' in regard to their *inability* to gain such access. Their incapacity to use the dominant language of Turkey resulted in them receiving fewer years of education, being less employed in regular jobs, and having lower family incomes and economic status.

For the participant girls of this study, it is the other side of the coin. They not only have the ability to use the dominant language of Japan (Japanese), but they also have access to another high-status and educationally well-placed *minority* (home) language: English. This chapter examines how linguistic, and other forms of capital resources available to these girls, are discursively constructed as valuable assets for them as a result of their hybrid identities.

This chapter shows how these girls construct and celebrate the notion of 'cultural capital' (cultural goods, services, educational credentials), symbolic capital (legitimation), 'linguistic capital' (language proficiency) and 'social capital' (acquaintances, networks) through their discursive work and self-positioning within the various discourses available to them. They do this by means of their access to greater choices, information, connections, intercultural savvy, overseas relatives and experiences, and mixed-ethnic girl friendships outside of their schools. Bourdieu (1977, 1991, 1993, 1999), Bourdieu and Passeron (1977), and Passeron (2000) theorized that these resources of capital (including other forms of capital such as 'economic capital' [money, property]) can be accumulated, invested, exchanged and exercised, as well as converted into other forms (Swartz, 1997).

I draw on Phillips and Jorgensen's (2002) notion of multiperspectivism in order to 'translate' or 'import' Bourdieu and Passeron's (1977) theory of cultural and symbolic capital into a discourse analytic approach. Multiperspectivism includes the combination of not only different discourse analytic approaches, but also allows for different discourse analytic approaches to be combined with *non-discourse* analytical approaches (Phillips & Jorgensen, 2002).

Here I examine how the participants themselves construct various forms of symbolic, linguistic, social and cultural capital. I explore the interactions of these girls among themselves and with me in their taking up of subject positions and their use of rhetorical devices to explore, reject, confront, contest and alter constituted subject positions.

Discursive Construction of Cultural, Symbolic, Linguistic and Social Capital

Bourdieu and Passeron hypothesized that the outcome of education (pedagogy) can be measured by the gap between the practical mother language learned in the home and the 'scholarly mastery of scholarly language' (Bourdieu & Passeron, 1977: 72). They used the term *linguistic capital* interrelatedly with *cultural capital* to denote this scholastic capital that changes its form through the process of education. Linguistic capital is class-related in that those people of the lower and middle classes must go through a more stringent selection process in terms of linguistic competence in order to be selected to higher education at each step along the way (Bourdieu, 1991, 1999; Bourdieu & Passeron, 1977).

Ethnic identity and language as linguistic capital

For the participants of this study who have access to two languages in the home, the influence of language on their ethnic identity becomes a question of relevant importance. Studies have revealed how identities or subject positions in multilingual contexts are negotiated and re-negotiated in linguistic practices inseparably from political relations of power and ideologies (e.g. Blackledge, 2002; Blackledge & Pavlenko, 2001; Norton, 1997, 2000; Pavlenko & Blackledge, 2004). Makoni and Pennycook (2007) argued for the need to imagine and rethink the role of languages and their historical 'invention' and from there to 'disinvent' and 'reconstruct' languages. Pennycook (2007) problematized the 'myth' of English as an international language in which he established that languages are produced and performed through acts of identity. What is important is 'the multiple investments people bring to their acts, desires and performances in "English"' (Pennycook, 2007: 110–111). Similar to the notion of 'gendering' as a verb, Pennycook (2007: 111) further points out that the activity of using English also could be best conceived of as a verb, by drawing on Joseph's (2002: 4) term 'Englishing'. Pennycook emphasized the importance of revealing how language is materialized through discourse:

> English is not so much a language as a discursive field: English *is* neoliberalism, English *is* globalisation, English *is* human capital ... the

question [becomes] ... what kind of mobilizations underlie acts of English use or learning. (Pennycook, 2007: 112)

This _human capital_ that Pennycook speaks of above draws on Bourdieu's (1977) theory of cultural capital. _Human capital_ may be seen as a resource that can be converted into a fundamental linguistic or cultural capital contributing to an individual's personal worth in the social world.

Cultural capital and adolescent girls

How mixed-ethnic adolescent girls in Japan create and use cultural, social, linguistic and symbolic capital in order to positively position themselves and accomplish various functions was one of the central focuses of this study. This section presents several studies drawing on Bourdieu's (1977) notion of cultural capital that explained the ways in which adolescents create and celebrate various forms of cultural and symbolic capital.

Eckert (1993, 2000) showed how high-school girls increase their competitive power through their 'girl talk' as they build up their symbolic capital. Traditional gender roles – women in the domestic realm and men in the work place – are often still resistant to change in terms of the norms of society and interactions between people (Eckert, 1993). Drawing on Bourdieu (1977), Eckert examined the importance of social networks as symbolic capital for women who create their status on the basis of their social relationships and their character, in contrast to men who 'can justify and define their status on the basis of their accomplishments, possessions, or institutional status' (Eckert, 1993: 34). Eckert gave the example of _popularity_ in high school as being contingent on the symbolic capital of 'an individual's good personhood' (Eckert, 1993: 36). In order to achieve a status of popularity, girls must not only be 'likable', but they must also be visible within the school community by virtue of their activities based on competition. Girls must be concerned with status and whom they choose to associate with. Eckert found evidence in her data of high-school 'girl talk' of simultaneously occurring themes of popularity (association with mainstream and popular boys) and independence ('emphasizing the importance of not idolizing popular boys ... [and] endorsement of their involvement with non-mainstream boys' [Eckert, 1993: 41]).

In her study of teenage girls and how they represent their embodiment, Bloustien (2001) applied Bourdieu's (1984) and Schilling's (1993) notion of the significance of the body as symbolic capital. Using the notion of _physical bodily praxis_, Bloustien showed how her girl participants used this 'capital' to accomplish various functions such as to 'compete with the boys in terms of space, language and an assertive sexuality' (Bloustien, 2001: 105) or in other instances, to appropriate 'a particular exaggerated, extreme representation of femininity' (Bloustien, 2001: 105).

Also drawing on Bourdieu, Bucholtz (1999) showed how teenage 'nerd' girls use language as a social practice to contribute to the display of intelligence or knowledge as their main symbolic capital. According to Bucholtz, nerds make a conscious attempt through their language and social practices to reject both 'Jockness' '(overachieving students who oriented to middle-class values)' (Bucholtz, 1999: 211) and 'Burnoutness' '(underachieving students who were bound for work, rather than college, at the end of their high-school careers)' (Bucholtz, 1999: 211).

In this study, I selected extracts from the data in order to demonstrate how the teenage girl participants discursively construct various forms of cultural capital for themselves through their positioning within their talk. The following types of capital resources taken up here are bilingualism, biliteracy, friendships, femininity, interculturalism and access to choice. Later, the cultural capital of ethnic embodiment is explored in Chapter 7 (see the section 'Celebrating Ethnic Embodiment as Privileged Cultural Capital' [p. 188]). First, how these girls construct the cultural and linguistic capital of bilingualism is presented below.

Linguistic Capital of Bilingualism

Emerging from a position as both a former colonial power and as a post-occupied state, the place of English in present-day Japanese society can be described as a discursively constructed realm (see Pennycook, 2007; Ramanathan, 2005). In this study, the position of English as a well-placed foreign language in Japan is illustrated by examining how the girl participants perform their identities through co-constructed acts of 'Englishing' (Joseph, 2002).

The following two extracts are examples of how two of the girls, Sara and Maya (with the other girls and me 'co-constructing'), discursively created for themselves the cultural and linguistic capital of bilinguality. The six girls almost exclusively use Japanese when conversing among themselves when I or other native English speakers are not present. While I started out our Café meeting using Japanese with the three girls present, two of them who are highly proficient in English – Naomi and Rina – began responding in English to my (mostly Japanese) questioning, while Sara used Japanese. Throughout this meeting, I had been using Japanese to address Sara, and I (along with the other two girls) worked to keep her included in the talk as much as possible whenever it switched into English.

But then late into our session, when I inadvertently addressed Sara in English instead of Japanese, she suddenly and unexpectedly entered the conversation using English for the first time that day. We were discussing dating among girls and boys at their schools.

(Extract 6.1) The Café (age 13): Sara's bilinguality[1]

1	**L:**	how about your school?
2	**S:**	yeah, lots
3	**L:**	mmm
4	**S:**	(?) together and (.)
5	**L:**	a lot?
6	**S:**	yeah, and always together (.)
7	**L:**	really, a lot in your school?
8	**S:**	umm
9	**R:**	there are some people that are really sick,
10		like they go to the cafeteria together like, oh
11		(gestures like a couple are brazenly holding hands)
12	**all:**	(laugh)
13	**R:**	then all these people try to um,
14	**L:**	(laugh)
15	**R:**	'sorry, excuse me, I'm on my way to the (?)'
16	**all:**	(laugh)
17	**R:**	**sore wa omoshiroi**
17*		*that's funny*
18	**all:**	(laugh)
19	**L:**	so they date, they go dating and stuff
20	**R:**	sorry, excuse me, I'm on my way to the (?)
21	**all:**	(laugh)

After I addressed Sara in English (Line no. 1), she began to give very short replies in English for several turns (Line nos 2–8), followed by pauses. In Line no. #9, Rina entered the talk, but instead of following Sara's turn in *Japanese* as she had previously been doing, she now followed Sara in *English*, in what might have been a discursive gesture to relieve tension and to acknowledge Sara's English proficiency. After a few turns continued with Rina and I speaking in English, Rina switched into Japanese (Line no. 17), perhaps to try to keep Sara in the talk, but even that failed to get any further response from Sara.

This behavior from Sara was unexpected by all of us present and I felt a twinge of astonishment among us around our lunch table when she suddenly broke into English for the first time that day. This sense of the unanticipated was confirmed directly after the lunch meeting when the three girls and their mothers and I assembled at Rina's house for tea to discuss my project. Rina's mother mentioned to me that while we were all shuffling into the house, in response to her question to Rina, 'How did the lunch meeting go?' Rina, right away, mentioned Sara's sudden use of English.

I felt that this exchange was significant in that Sara was not only displaying her ability to use English (albeit, a very limited demonstration), but it also served the purpose of demonstrating her trust in the supportive context of her mixed-ethnic peers in a potentially risk-taking situation by her venturing to use her only-partially proficient minority language among highly proficient peers. Rina's and my discursive work to try to support and keep Sara in the talk, while not totally effective, helped to constitute and position Sara as 'owner' of the cultural capital of bilinguality. Significantly, we were all left with the 'big news' at the end of the day of Sara's spontaneous use of English.

The high value of the cultural capital of bilingualism was also discursively demonstrated when it became Maya's turn to speak during the Hot Springs meeting at her first appearance in the study.

(Extract 6.2) Hot Springs interview (age 13): Maya can speak English

1	L:	OK, chotto matomete, English
2	N:	um
3	R:	Ma, Maya shaberareru no ne
4	L:	ah, Maya, ja Maya
5	R:	Maya, du yua besuto
6	L:	OK, do your best
7	M:	iyaa
8	R:	gambaru
9	L:	OK, gambaru
10		just sort of say a little bit
11	M:	um, there's a girl
12	L:	uh-huh
13	M:	she's not a bad girl, but everybody thinks that she's so different

(Extract 6.2*) (translation)

1*	L:	*can someone summarize that, English*
2	N:	um
3*	R:	*Ma, Maya can speak English*

4* L: *Maya, well then, Maya*
5* R: *do your best*
6   L: OK, do your best
7* M: *yuk*
8* R: *try hard*
9* L: OK, *try hard*
10   just sort of say a little bit
11 M: um, there's a girl
12 L: uh-huh
13 M: she's not a bad girl, but everybody thinks that she's so different

Maya had been telling a narrative in Japanese when I asked if someone could summarize in English what she had said. Naomi and Rina had served this function at other instances in the meeting. In Line no. 2, Naomi responded with 'um', a filler that reserves the turn, but significantly at this point in the sequence it is an English filler which denotes that she is self-selecting to fulfill my request for translation. However, before she could do so, Rina announced that Maya can speak English (Line no. 3), positioning Maya as bilingual and implicitly selecting her as the one to perform the translation. It took several turns of encouragement (Line nos 4–10) between me and Rina to finally get Maya to speak in English. Rina started off in Japanese (Line no. 3). Then I also addressed Maya in Japanese (Line no. 4) and followed Rina's lead by affirming the selection of Maya to take the floor and summarize her story in English. Next, Rina lent further encouragement to Maya (Line no. 5) by use of a phrase, appropriated in Japanese as a Japanese-English phrase (*du yua besuto*), but also very clearly an English phrase, 'Do your best'. I mimicked Rina's words, but in English using the English pronunciation (Line no. 6) to further encourage Maya. She faltered at first (Line no. 7), but in the end, Maya began to speak in English (Line nos 11, 13), taking up for herself the position of Japanese/English bilingual.

The importance of this exchange was that when given the opportunity, Maya took up the chance to demonstrate her English proficiency. Similar to Sara above, Maya (along with the other co-constructing girls) discursively placed value on binguality. Through this action, she 'performed English' through her identity work (Pennycook, 2007).

The following extract of Anna reveals her understanding of the personal importance to her of English. This extract was preceded by my asking Anna what language her bilingual Australian father uses with her in the home.

(Extract 6.3a) Birthday (ages 13 and 14): Anna: 'Recently I asked dad to speak English with me'

A: kore made wa zutto nihongo datta, demo saikin, 'eigo tsukau you ni shite' tte tanonde

(Extract 6.3a*) (translation)

A: *up until now it was totally Japanese, but recently I have requested [of him] 'use English [with me]'*

Anna related to me how her mother had been asking her father to use English with her since she was little. However, being that they lived in Japan, and being that Anna's father was fluent in Japanese, Anna stated that it was more natural for him to speak Japanese, 'and [because of that] he purposely didn't bother to speak English' (*de, wazawaza eigo shaberanakatta*). However, recently, within the last year, Anna herself had approached her father, asking him to speak English with her, as shown in the extract above. Moments later, Anna explicitly displayed her knowledge of the value of the linguistic capital of English speaking, as shown in the following extract.

(Extract 6.3b) Birthday (ages 13 and 14): Anna's valuing of English

A: ikan to isshou shaberahen ka na to omotte
I thought that it would be bad if I couldn't speak [English] my whole life

Here again Anna placed value on the linguistic capital of speaking English. Her reason for suddenly wanting to put efforts forward to learn English more diligently is that she came to realize that *not* being able to speak English for her entire life would be a shameful waste of opportunity. She revealed her understanding of the linguistic capital which she could gain by utilizing the resource available to her in her home.

A half year after the Hot Springs meeting, we assembled together again for the Birthday meeting. This meeting took place just after the summer vacation had ended, during which time Hanna and Anna had gone together to Australia to enter a language school to improve their English. During the Birthday meeting, Hanna elected to use English with me much of the time, occasionally switching into Japanese. After returning from Australia, at the start of the Birthday meeting before the others showed up, when only Hanna, Anna and I were present, Hanna told how she hated the tourist villages that she had been taken to that were designed to cater to Japanese-speaking tourists. She alternated several times between English and Japanese to express her understanding of the value that English linguistic capital can afford her.

(Extract 6.4) Birthday (ages 13 and 14) Hanna: 'We really wanted to speak English'

135	H:	they just really, really stupid, little, um,
136		**dou ittara iiyan, un, um omiyage**
136*		*how can I say that, um, um, souvenir*
137		shop, they just go in, I was sitting down and look at, looking at those,
138		thinking like, 'who's going to buy that?', and they buy it
149	L/A:	(laugh)
140	H:	they buy, they few bunch of it, and they
141		**'umm, naka naka oshare, ne'** (in an affected voice)
141*		*'umm, this is really quite smart looking, isn't it'* (in an affected voice)
142	all:	(laugh)
[…]		
152	H:	yeah, so there's lots and lots of people like them that don't understand
153		English, so I think it's good for them, and but it wasn't good for us
154		because we really wanted to speak English

Hanna presented a colorful and humorous narrative depicting the situation of Japanese tourists shopping at a souvenir shop in a tourist village in Australia. Hanna started out in English, but then in Line no. 136, when she could not recall the English word for *omiyage* (souvenir), briefly broke into Japanese asking for clarification, and then embedded the word *omiyage* in the English sentence. Without losing her tempo, she continued to complete her thoughts now back in English. She continued to speak in English, except for a brief switch into Japanese (Line no. 141) when she used an affected and sarcastic voice to mimic a Japanese tourist, 'umm, this is really quite smart looking, isn't it'. This skillful Japanese voicing brought laughter from Anna and me, as Hanna very humorously depicted Japanese tourists in Australia. At the same time, she clearly positioned the tourists (most likely of her parent's generation) as 'the other'. She identified herself and Anna, *apart from* such Japanese tourists who foolishly shop for over-priced, low-quality souvenirs, and who do not make efforts to understand English (Line nos 3152–3153). Hanna instead constructed herself and Anna as people who really want to speak English. Here she demonstrated her knowledge of the value of the linguistic capital of English.

Accumulation of linguistic capital over time

By the time of our last meeting together, a year-and-a-half later, the girls had even more so come to understand the value of linguistic and bilingual capital to which they had access by means of their two ethnicities. During the Last Reunion meeting, in answer to Hanna's question, 'what is special or good about being *double*', Sara more confidently positioned herself as owner of the cultural capital of English proficiency.

(Extract 6.5) Last Reunion (age 14): Sara: 'I can get good in English'

S: okaasan toka wa chicchai toki toka mo eigo shabetteiru kara, kiku no toka narateiru kara, eigo ga umakunaru, nantoka

(Extract 6.5*) (translation)

S: *because my mother and others have been speaking English since I was little, I am used to hearing it, and I can get good in English, somehow*

Here, Sara positioned herself as having become proficient in English based on the influence of her native-English-speaking mother's presence in the home as well as others in her world, most likely a reference to her mother's circle of friends and relatives. Sara implied that her family situation exposing her to English was special in the context of Japan and it allowed her to become accomplished in English, particularly in contrast to her Japanese peers. While Sara was seen creating positive linguistic capital for herself in Extract 6.1, it seems that in the extract above – which occurred a year-and-a-half later – a change has occurred in Sara's self-positioning. She seems to have more confidently taken ownership of this privileged linguistic capital of English on the basis of her unique home environment over time.

Also during the final meeting, the girls revealed further 'acts of Englishing' (Pennycook, 2007) in their future-oriented high-school choices. All of the girls wanted to pursue entry to schools, which would allow them greater educational chances to create bilingual and linguistic capital as a means to survive in a globalized world of their generation. During the last meeting, we were talking about their move in the coming year from middle to high school. I had asked them what kind of high school they might want to enter. All six of the girls stated that their choice of high school was connected with the school's ability to offer opportunities to increase their English proficiency. Sara had mentioned that she would like to go to a particular Japanese high school which would allow her to do an exchange in an American school for a year. Anna said that she was interested in a particular school because it concentrated on English. When I further asked her if she would like to go overseas for a year like Sara, she answered first in the negative, 'no, not just one year', and then continued '*more* than just one year', putting value on English. In taking up this positioning, she was creating linguistic capital for herself.

Capital Resources of English Language Literacy and Possession of English Books

While some mixed-ethnic children who attend Japanese public schools in Japan become (nearly) balanced bilingual speakers of two languages, a much smaller percentage reach a level of (near) native-like *literacy* proficiency in their minority language (Kamada, 1995a, 1995b, 1997; Noguchi, 1996; Yamamoto, 1995, 2001a, 2001b). Rina and Naomi are among exceptional examples of mixed-ethnic children attending Japanese schools who have been able to reach very high levels of English reading and writing proficiency, allowing them to become biliterate. Both of these girls discursively prided themselves not only in their possession of many English books as a form of symbolic and economic capital, but they also vigorously created for themselves the cultural and linguistic capital of biliteracy as they boosted their self-esteem in their ability to read such English literature. This was expressed by Rina below.

(Extract 6.6)[2] Rina's house (age 12): Rina: 'I much prefer English books'

1 **L:** but you do read? do you pick up English books sometimes and read them?
2 **R:** not SOMETIMES, I much prefer English books
3 **L:** do you?
4 **R:** to Japanese books
5 **L:** really? why?
6 **R:** somehow the Japanese books are very hard to get stuck into
7 **L:** just the, why? because of the content you mean?
8 **R:** content and how they have written the first page kind of counts too, it's not that,

9   **L:**   literature, you can get a hold of better things, you think for young kids?

10 **R:**   yeah, yeah because most of my books upstairs, I've got are English

11 **L:**   kind of, what are some of your favorite things that you've read, that are English?

12 **R:**   recently I've read a very interesting, I wouldn't say it's my favorite, but it's not

13   meant to be a favorite, but it's called, it's a book called, um, 'The Giver' by Lois

14   Lowry, Lowr, Lowry, I like her books

15 **L:**   what's it about?

16 **R:**   oh, it's very complex, but it's about, it's in the future, and, in this, and its,

17   there is this community and they are made all equal and um, they go through

18   school until twelve and then, after twelve, they're assigned their jobs or work,

19   they still go to school, but they go in their recreation time and free hours and to

20   um, the jobs to um, be taught, how to do,

21 **L:**   that sounds interesting, is that a new, is it recent?

22 **R:**   I don't know if it's a new or very old book, but it's very difficult,

23   and it's very long, it's not LONG, but it's very complex and,

24 **L:**   uh-huh

When I asked Rina if she sometimes reads in English, she replied by strongly emphasizing a negation of the limited notion of *sometimes* (Line no. 2) and stating that she much *prefers* to read in English over Japanese. Rina assigned literature of her minority language (English) superior to her majority language (Japanese). This may be interpreted as a linguistic trace of Rina drawing on an alternative discourse of diversity as she highlighted her ability to choose from more than one option – a choice that is not readily available to her Japanese peers. In the process, she has created linguistic capital of English literacy (or biliteracy).

Drawing on the tools of DP to analyze this extract, Rina can be seen accomplishing various actions through language and building fact and interest in the ways that she constructed her accounts (see Horton-Salway, 2001). She discursively demonstrated her knowledge and pride in her highly proficient English literacy. The reality that she constructed not only signified her *possession* of English books as symbolic and economic capital, 'because most of my books upstairs, I've got are English' (Line no. 10), but she also exalted her arduously learned *ability to read them*. Rina produced several descriptive adjectives regarding a book that she had recently finished reading, 'interesting' (Line no. 12), 'complex' (Line nos 16, 23), 'difficult' (Line no. 22), 'long' (Line no. 23). These constructions function to position her as not only having acquired the highly valued cultural and linguistic capital of *biliteracy*, but also of having acquired the ability to concentrate and persevere (complex, long) and the intellectual capacity to comprehend profundity (difficult, complex) through the means of her learned ability to read in English.

Here Rina used exaggeration to build up a colorful and rich version of reality, which she then retreated from (Line no. 23), 'and it's very long, it's not LONG . . .' While her initial exaggeration accomplished the function of embellishment, Rina's immediate retraction helped to maintain her reliability and also to emphasize the more challenging aspect of *complexity* over *length*.

Linguistic traces could be seen in this extract in Rina's discursive work to draw on a discourse of interculturalism, which values a globalizing worldview larger than Japan. She put emphasis on her preference to read in English over Japanese, even while being schooled in a Japanese medium of instruction. Rina's reason given for her preference to read in English was the superior complexity and depth of books available in English.

In several other instances, Rina suggested that possession of English books is highly valued and is sometimes related to maturity. The next extract is Rina's reply to my question as to whether or not she uses English when she speaks with Naomi.

(Extract 6.7a) Rina's house (age 12): Biliteracy and books

R: no, we speak Japanese, but sometimes we speak in English because we all have, we both have about the same amount of English books as well

This extract is interesting here because on the surface, Rina applied an 'odd' logic in assigning the *possession* of English books as the reason or cause of the girls' use of English with each other. She here discursively attached value to biliteracy for herself and her friend as she drew a connection between the symbolic and economic capital of owning books and the cultural capital of being able to speak English. Rina furthermore implied that these owners of English books also possess the ability to read them and to speak about them in the language in which they were written. While Rina said, 'sometimes we speak in English', she implied, 'some of us speak in English, some of the time', as expressed by her backtracking from 'we all have' to 'we both have', referring (at this point) to just one other of the girls, instead of to all of them.

Rina, later in the same conversation, elaborated on this point, but now she included several other friends:

(Extract 6.7b) Rina's house (age 12): Biliteracy and maturity

431   **R:**   I don't know why, but I feel that, Naomi and my friend and I feel more mature
432   than the others and also we feel more fluent in English and we have many more
433   English books, but, um Hanna, whose father's American, she seems to be fluent
434   enough to understand what we're talking about and she speaks English and she
435   can write cursive and stuff, but she has many English books too

Rina discursively linked the possession of English books and fluency in English, this time, with maturity. She took up the position for herself, while also positioning several of her mixed-ethnic friends, as 'more mature' (symbolic capital). This is based on English fluency and the ability to understand English (cultural and linguistic capital), to write it (cultural and linguistic capital), and the possession of English books (symbolic and economic capital).

Rina's repeated emphasis on the possession of English books and the skills of literacy (such as being able to read books and appreciate them and the ability to write in cursive – a writing skill generally introduced at a somewhat more advanced stage) served the function of positioning herself, and other biliterate mixed-ethnic girls who possess this resource, as privileged or superior (more 'mature' [Line no. 431], more 'fluent' [Line no. 433]) than those without this resource.

Similar to Rina, Naomi also placed a high value on English literacy proficiency and emphasized her preference for English literacy, as follows:

(Extract 6.7c) The Café (age 13): Naomi's biliteracy and books

N: I don't find a lot of Japanese books interesting

(Extract 6.7d) Birthday (age 14): Naomi's biliteracy and writing

N: I would rather, um, write in English

In these two extracts, similar to Rina, Naomi also placed her majority language, Japanese, inferior to her minority language, English. Like Rina, linguistic traces can also be seen of Naomi drawing on a privileging globalizing discourse of interculturalism. She celebrates her English literacy capital, which has become available to her through her intercultural environment at home and through her access to a world beyond Japan. This is linguistic capital to which her Japanese peers cannot generally claim access.

As mentioned above, this construction of English as cultural and linguistic capital is legitimized by the historically situated place of English today in a former-colonial-power, post-occupied, modern-globalized Japan. The 'Englishing' (Joseph, 2002) that these girls accomplish occurs within a background of discourses, which allow these girls to perform and celebrate: English as globalization; English as human capital; English as linguistic capital (Pennycook, 2007).

As can be seen in this section, it was particularly Rina and Naomi who accomplished this 'Englishing', especially in terms of their biliteracy. If it can be said that Rina and Naomi had more of this linguistic capital than the other girls, perhaps it could also be said that this gave them more power in certain interactions with some of the other girls, particularly in the presence of English speakers, such as myself. I have considered this linguistic/power differential in how it shaped the interactions and in the overall resulting volume of each participant's voice appearing in the data. I have tried to balance this differential by also highlighting the voices of more silent girls as much as possible (see the sections 'The Unevenness of the Data Collected and Selected' [p. 74] and 'Differences Between the Girls: Unevenness of the Data' [p. 142]).

While this section examined the cultural and linguistic capital of bilingualism and biliteracy, the next section looks at another form of capital. Here the girls discursively create the social capital of mixed-ethnic girl friendships.

Mixed-Ethnic Girl Friendships

This section looks at how the participants discursively created the social capital of mixed-ethnic girl friendships. They revealed how their relationships with each other were extremely valuable to them, next in importance only to their families.

Rina's narratives of being left out and 'othered' at elementary school was presented in Chapter 4 where we examined descriptions of her feelings of alienation over being called *gaijin* by her school peers. In the extract below, during the same meeting, Rina talked about how the trusting relationships and feelings of solidarity with her 'bilingual' friends helped to comfort her in times of distress like this.

(Extract 6.8) Rina's house (age 12): Bilingual girl friendships

1	R:	they are honest and we can trust each other, and they've all been through similar
2		experiences so they know how we feel about being bullied and so they can give you
3		advice, and we, I give them advice, we give each other advice, and you know when
4		we are in similar situations or situations, like, when someone talks about,
5		we know how to handle them and it is VERY comforting or it's very good to ha', I think it's
6		very good to have very close friends like that
7	L:	yeah
8	R:	who know how you feel and everything

Rina expressed the importance of her trusting relationship with her other 'bilingual'[3] girlfriends who have had similar experiences of bullying. In this short narrative, Rina started out using the impersonal third person pronoun, *they*, and then switched to the use of the first person pronoun, *we*, shifting from a more distancing reference to her friends to a more personal stance which includes herself. Next, she employed the first person singular pronoun, *I*: 'I give them advice'. But then she made another repair using the plural form, 'We give each other advice'. At the end, she used the second person pronoun, *you*: 'who know how you feel'. Rina's narrative depicts her involvement in supportive, reciprocal relationships in solidarity of mixed-ethnic girl membership. She positioned herself and her mixed-ethnic friends as mutually interacting in this nurturing network, implicitly placing value on interculturality.

As mentioned earlier, at the beginning of the Rina interview, Rina cooperated in writing a short essay for me on the topic of 'Why my Life is Special' (which she selected out of three choices) (see Appendix 1). Similar to the extract above, in this essay, Rina attributed her 'specialness' to her having relationships with at least five other very close 'bilingual' girlfriends – the other participants of this study whom, at that time, I was yet to meet. In this essay, as in the extract above, Rina created the social capital of mixed-ethnic girl friendships by placing value on the intercultural supportive relationships with these outside-of-school friendships.

Naomi, as well, constructed her mixed-ethnic girlfriend relationships as cultural and social capital in the development of her hybrid identity. For her, it was based on her feeling of separation and her 'differentness' (examined in Chapter 5) and its effect in stimulating her to extend her world beyond the confines of her small, closed community of sameness (see Extract 6.11).

Mixed-ethnic girl friendships as highly valued

Even though these girls all attend different schools and were only able to get together on occasions, they all recounted during the Birthday meeting how they valued their relationships with one another more than their relationships with their friends at their schools. All six girls noted this point individually in a written exercise where I had asked them to diagram the significant relationships in their worlds by representing their more important connections by drawing them in larger circles. I asked the girls not to look at their neighbors' papers while they worked on this task. When we later discussed what they had written, it was revealed that all of them had placed their families first, in the largest circle. As well, all of them had designated their mixed-ethnic girlfriends (each other) in considerably larger circles (as more important to them) than their school friends (see the section 'Birthday meeting' [p. 72]). Below, I examine explanations of the diagrams made by Anna and Hanna, starting with Anna.

(Extract 6.9a) Birthday (age 13): Anna's important affiliations

566	A:	tto, ichiban taisetsu nano ga, kazoku (L: hai), tsugi wa (L: hai),
577		nihon no shinseki (?) itoko toka (L: hai),
578		tsugi wa daboru no tomodai
579	L:	daboru no tomodachi?
580		daboru no tomodachi wa kono hitotachi igai ni mo imasuka?
581	A:	inai (L: inai, OK, hai), sore de, Asutoraria no shinseki (L: hai),
582		amari awanaikara
583	L:	gaikgoku ni itta toki dake, ne
584	A:	so, de saigo wa gakkou no tomodachi

(Extract 6.9a*) (translation)

566*   **A:**   *um, the number one important thing is my family* (L: *uh-huh*), *next*
         is (L: *uh-huh*),
577*   *my Japanese relatives* (?), *my cousins and stuff* (L: *uh-huh*),
578*   *next are my double friends*
579*   **L:**   *your double friends?*
580*   *do you have double friends other than these here?*
581*   **A:**   *no* (L: *no, OK, fine*), *and then, my Australian relatives* (L: *uh-huh*),
582*   *because I don't meet them very much*
563*   **L:**   *only when you go overseas, right?*
564*   **A:**   *yes, and the last is my school friends*

In explaining her diagram to me, Anna was very articulate about stating the order of priority of her affiliations and relationships with others in her world as illustrated in her diagram. She put her nuclear family first, and then her Japanese relatives. Her 'double' friends came next, even before her Australian relatives who she does not meet very often. The 'double' friends were also markedly placed before her Japanese school friends who she put last. Anna also answered that she did not have any other 'double' friends aside from the six participants of this study. Clearly for Anna, her 'double' friends who do not attend the same school as her and who live a considerable distance from her are placed high in importance, even before her Australian relatives. In the following extract, Hanna also placed her 'double' friends in a high priority.

(Extract 6.9b) Birthday (age 13): Hanna's important affiliations

595   **L:**   OK, **kazoku** is one, **niban wa tomodachi, gakkou no
         tomodachi desune?**
596   **H:**   no, **gakkou gai**
597   **L:**   **gai?**
598   **H:**   these

(Extract 6.9b*) (translation)

595*   **L:**   *OK, your family is one, number two is your friends, your school
         friends, right?*
596*   **H:**   *no, outside of school*
597*   **L:**   *outside of?*
598*   **H:**   *these*

Here I was peering at Hanna's diagram and attempting to interpret it for her while asking for confirmation. Like Anna, Hanna clarified that following her nuclear family as first in priority, her 'friends' placed in the 'number two' spot were not those from school, but 'these' mixed-ethnic friends who were sitting around the table. She placed her school friends in the smallest circle.

It was not only Hanna and Anna, but all of the girls indicated that they valued their mixed-ethnic friendships (with each other) as more important than their Japanese school friends. And in some cases, as with Anna above, their mixed-ethnic friends were more important than some of their relatives who they rarely meet. The extracts above of Rina, Anna and Hanna, in this section, show how these girls create and celebrate their social capital of mixed-ethnic girl friendships in their valuing of their special relationships within the context of Japan.

Intercultural Savvy

The following extract was preceded by a long narrative in which Rina went into quite a bit of detail in trying to recall the sequence of a television commercial for a language school, which all of the girls and I had seen numerous times. Rina said, 'there is a Japanese person speaking Italian ... and an Italian person speaking Japanese ... then the screen goes black again ... a French-speaking Kansai[4] person ... and then they say "well, a middle-aged man like me" ... that's *Kansai-ben*'.[5] Here, drawing on discourses of diversity and interculturalism, issues dealt with in this commercial are not limited to *ethnicity* and *foreign languages*, but also include 'interculturality' of *age* (middle-aged man), *regional locality* (Kansai) and *regional dialect* (Kansai dialect). Rina continued:

(Extract 6.10) Hot Springs (age 13): 'Well, ain't that intercultural'

1	R:	**de kansaiben o hanasu uchuujin tsutte, 'ma, ibunka chuuno kana?'**
1*		*and then the Kansai Dialect-speaking spaceman says, 'well, ain't that intercultural?'*
2	?s:	(laugh)
3	R:	**nanka** (laugh)
3*		*somehow* (laugh)
4	L:	you think it's good?
5	R:	yeah, I think it's good
6	N:	yeah, I like that one

7	R:	and it says
8		**'hito wa mikake to chigaimasse' to, sore ga yokatta to omou**
8*		*'people are different than they appear'* (in Kansai Dialect) *and I thought that was great*
9	L:	uh-huh, uh-huh, uh-huh, why do you think it's good?
10	R:	well because it, I don't know, I just felt kind of funny
11	?:	**omoroi na**
11*		*it's interesting*
12	R:	it's funny and it's
13	N:	yeah, you kind of feel happier when you (laugh)
14	R:	yeah
15	L:	uh-huh, uh-huh
16	R:	**'hito wa mikake to chigaimasse' toiuno wa, yappari**
16*		*'people have different appearances' is, you know*
17	?:	**ii koto yane**
17*		*a good thing*
18	R:	**densha de, kou, niramareru, watashi toshite wa sugoi soiuno ga ureshii**
18*		*in the train, like, I am scowled at, so I am really happy about that kind of thing* [the commercial]

In applauding the promotion of a globalizing discourse of interculturalism produced in a language school commercial on television, Rina positioned herself within this discourse and put value on interculturality. Rina and the other girls expressed their approval of this mass-media commercial (Line nos 5, 6, 8, 10–13, 17, 18) in that it helps to promote the social consciousness of this discourse throughout society. Switching into Japanese, Rina intertextually voiced several discourses/repertoires from the commercial: 'people are different than they appear' (Line no. 8) and 'people have different appearances' (Line no. 16). In Line no. 18, Rina offered a real-life example (of being scowled at in the train for looking different) to illustrate how the promotion of a discourse of interculturalism, via the means of this mass-media TV commercial, might help to disseminate an alternative discourse to counter the overarching discourse of homogeneity (where everyone is expected to look the same). Rina applauded the distribution of this alternative discourse as having the potential to raise the consciousness of people who act to marginalize her on a daily basis in Japanese society.

In the following extract, Naomi again put value on the cultural capital of having a broad worldview as she discursively displayed her intercultural savvy *vis-à-vis* her Japanese peers who lack this capital resource.

(Extract 6.11) The Café (age 13): Naomi's interculturality

N: yeah, and I think it's really that no, um, a lot of people in my neighborhood don't go to take lessons for what they're interested in, they'll just stay at home and do whatever, they won't get together with their friends and go somewhere, even if they have a boyfriend, they don't go anywhere

L: hum

N: and stuff like that

L: really?

N: yeah, I think it's really sick

Here Naomi positioned herself as interculturally savvy in relation to the Japanese 'others' at her school and in her neighborhood as she created cultural capital for herself. In speaking of her Japanese peers, Naomi made a reference to what might be thought of as a signal of an elevated status – that of girls 'having a boyfriend'. However, Naomi here positioned Japanese girls, even with this elevated status of having a boyfriend, as less interculturally savvy than her. Even as a 13-year-old, Naomi rides the local train for over an hour into town by herself several times per week to take dance and other types of lessons and to meet her (mixed-ethnic) friends who attend other schools. Naomi further positioned such people as 'really sick' who 'don't get out' for their lack of intercultural savvy.

In the following extract, Sara also displayed her valuing of intercultural and linguistic capital. She was talking about her goal to enter a high school that can provide her with maximum overseas exchange-student experiences while still maintaining her same-grade-level status with her Japanese high school peers.

(Extract 6.12) Last Reunion (age 14): Sara's linguistic/intercultural capital

374   S: ka, nanka haittara, ichinenkan ryuugaku de kite,
375   demo betsu no chuuki ryuugaku suru kedo,
376   betsu ni nendai wa sono mama susunde iku kara

(Extract 6.12*) (translation)

374*   S: *if I can enter [the school], and if I can go overseas as a foreign student for one year,*
375*   *but do another short term study overseas, because,*
376*   *even if I do that I can stay in the same grade level [in Japan]*

Sara was talking about her first-choice hope for high-school entry for the coming school year. She described her strategy of making use of exchange programs within the Japanese school system. Her goal was to benefit from access to two worlds (overseas and Japan) in a program efficiently compacted within a regular three-year high-school span of time. She told of how her first-choice school would allow her to enter a Japanese high school but spend a considerable amount of time overseas on two separate programs (one for an entire year overseas, and another shorter-term trip) without having to be held back a year in her Japanese school. Sara could be seen here placing value on intercultural and linguistic capital in her plans to continue to nurture her foreign language proficiency and intercultural experiences. Sara constructs this 'ideal' scenario for herself of getting the best of both worlds, but she does so clearly within the context of her Japanese school, and thus Japanese society.

Access to Choice and Job Opportunity

Another form of cultural and symbolic capital that these girls constructed for themselves was the notion of having more *choices* and *employment opportunities* available to them than their Japanese peers by virtue of their mixed-ethnicity. Their foreign parents frequently provided them with a greater access to information and connections beyond the borders of Japan. These girls discursively articulated their sense of self-worth in their intrinsic possession of this available cultural and symbolic resource, allowing them potential access to choice and employment opportunity in which to expand their experiences. The option to 'exercise' or 'convert' this resource into economic or symbolic capital, such as jobs, at a later point in their future was left open for them. Below, in the Rina's house meeting, the topic of employment choices came up.

(Extract 6.13) Rina's house (age 12): 'Somewhere like Australia'

1   L: when you become an adult which society do you think you would want to

2   probably live in? have you thought about that?

3   R: not much, I, I thought, I am kind of thinking that it's gonna be very difficult

4   for me to, uh, decide which society to be in, to be in Japan or to be in England,

5   I was thinking I might move to a country totally different, somewhere like,

6   Australia, or something that would kind of, well, that's like
          being Western, but,
7   L: uh-huh
8   R: yeah, the thing is in Japan there are MORE jobs that I could do,
          well I suppose
9   in Australia there are a lot of Japanese that, uh, job-wise, I think
10   L: yeah
11   R: there is more jobs to do like translating and stuff and
12   L: yeah
13   R: in Japan more than anywhere else
14   L: right, it is nice that in a sense that you have a lot of choices
15   R: yeah, very nice
16   L: that other Japanese kids don't have
17   R: many choices (laugh)
18   L: do you feel privileged? you chose that, that topic, 'why I'm
          special', right?
19   R: yeah
20   L: uh-huh
21   R: I feel that, yeah, I have many choices for my future and
          bilingualism kind of um,
22   expands my future, I think, and

When I asked Rina what country she was likely to live in as an adult, rather than stating one of the more obvious countries of her two nationalities, she suggested a third country, Australia, positioning herself as privileged in her access to a diversity of choices. Rina placed a high value on employment opportunity and choice in her discussion of the broader selection of jobs for her. She stated that 'in Japan there are MORE jobs' that she could do (Line no. 8). Here she was probably making a comparison between her more-marketable bilingual-self in Japan compared with Japanese people without bilingual skills. She then stated that in Australia also there were a lot of jobs available for her (Line no. 9). In co-constructing this notion of more job opportunities available, I introduced the idea of abundant *choices* available to her (Line no. 14). Rina then further co-constructed the notion of *choice* in her self-positioning (Line no. 17). In Line no. 18, I made reference to the essay (mentioned above) that Rina had written for me, earlier in the same session, on the topic 'Why I am Special' (see Appendix 1). Finally, Rina summarized how her bilingualism has expanded her chances for greater job opportunities and choice (Line nos 21–22).

At the end of the Last Reunion meeting, the other girls also constructed the cultural capital of choice when I asked them to *take on the role of the interviewer* by having them each present a question for everyone to answer. The following extract is a discussion of Hanna's question to everyone (including herself), 'what is special or good about being *double*'?

(Extract 6.14) Last Reunion (ages 14 and 15): 'Choice of two nationalities'

1	A:	hajime kara, kimatteiru janakute, futatsu kokuseki ga aru kara,
2:		nanijin (?)nareruka eraberukara, sentakushi ga atte,
3:		toku yatto omou
4	L:	OK, good, Hanna
5	H:	etto, nanka Anna to issho de, nn, sono gaijin nareruka,
6:		[(?) nihonjin] eraberu no mo arushi,
7:		ato, etto, mm, nanka ironna, nanka daburu de,
8:		chicchai toki wa daburu de nanka,
9:		iya ya toiuno shika nakatta kedo, nanka, shourai no koto kangaete,
10:		ippai chansu ga aru
11	L:	uh-huh
12	R:	chansu aru yan
13	H:	futsuu no hito yori wa
14	?:	sore meccha
15	H:	zettai ni chansu ga arushi, toku yato omou, soiu men de

(Extract 6.14*) (translation)

1*	A:	*from the beginning, it's not already decided, because you have two nationalities,*
2*		*because which nationality (?) you want to become you can choose, you have a choice,*
3*		*I think it's a benefit*
4*	L:	*OK, good, Hanna*
5*	H:	*um, like, the same as what Anna said, um, you can choose to be a gaijin,*
6*		*you also have the choice [(?) of being Japanese]*
7*		*and also um, mm, like, somehow various, like if you're double,*
8*		*when I was little, being double,*
9*		*the only thing I thought was that I hated it, but, like, if you think about the future,*
10*		*you have a lot of opportunities*

11*   **L:**   uh-huh
12*   **R:**   *you do have a lot of opportunities*
13*   **H:**   *more than the average person*
14*   **?:**   *a lot more*
15*   **H:**   *you definitely have a lot more opportunity, I think it's advantageous,*
             in that sense

In Line nos 1–3, Anna positioned herself and the other girls as privileged in having access to greater choices as a result of their mixed-ethnicity. Drawing on a discourse of interculturalism, she stated that they have a choice of two nationalities to choose from, implying the contrasting situation of their Japanese peers who are simply Japanese with no other options available. Anna created the notion of there being more fluidity to their lives, 'it's not already decided' (Line no. 1). She also drew upon an intersecting discourse of diversity in the sense that this difference is 'a benefit' for them. Through this positioning, Anna constructed, for herself and the other girl participants, the value of *choice* and a greater space for the development of a multitude of identities. Something as basic as Japaneseness to the Japanese people is not something that Anna has to accept straight out, like her Japanese peers, although that too is one option open to her, if she so desired to act upon that choice. But the symbolic and cultural capital of 'choice' is a form of capital which she can 'cash in' if she so desires – a privileged resource that her Japanese peers do not have access to.

In Line nos 5–10, Hanna helped to co-construct Anna's notion of choice with her opening, 'um, the same as what Anna said', but instead of positioning herself precisely as Anna did in terms of nationality, Hanna constructed this notion of *choice* within the situated context of '*gaijin* in Japan'. In stating 'you can choose to be a *gaijin*' (Line no. 5), Hanna used the pejorative '*gaijin*' in order to 'reclaim' this 'otherness': which she nuanced as neutral and which she took up within a 'discourse of *gaijin* otherness'. The option, or choice of constituting herself as 'foreigner', is one that is open to her as a mixed-ethnic girl in Japan, while being closed to her Japanese peers. Hanna then twice shifted to the use of the word *daburu* (double) as another category of self-identification (Line nos 7–8). She could have used the much more standard word *haafu* (half) here, but instead, her selection of *daburu* serves to deconstruct the deficit connotation of *haafu* in her rejection of a discourse of (hybrid) 'halfness' and to empower herself and other mixed-ethnic people.

Nonetheless, Hanna was unable to totally throw off the positioning of herself as 'marginalized' within a discourse of homogeneity. Framed within the past, when she was little, Hanna constructed her 'double' ethnicity as being something she hated. However, framed in terms of 'the future', Hanna positioned herself and other mixed-ethnic girls as having 'a lot of opportunities' within a discourse of interculturalism and diversity, similar to Anna above. Thus Hanna does not have to allow herself to only be positioned powerlessly within a single discourse of homogeneity; she is able to exercise *agency* to 'multiply position' (Baxter, 2003) herself positively within more empowering alternate discourses. In Line nos 12–15, the other girls, by virtue of their ethnicity, also joined in to further co-construct this notion of the advantages that opportunity affords them as ethnic cultural capital. Naomi also constructed the notion of job opportunity later in the same interview by saying, '*shigoto to ka mitsuke yasukunaru jyanai*' ('it would make it easier to find jobs, wouldn't it').

Femininity and Feminism Capital

This section looks at two important interrelated aspects of girlhood: celebrating *femininity* and taking a *feminist* stance. In the section 'Constituting femininity capital', I analyze an extract where Rina constructs the positive value which femininity provides for women. Then in the section 'What kind of guy do you want to marry?', I examine how the girls position themselves in terms of their imagined marriage partner where they unconsciously position themselves within a feminist stance. Below, I examine how Rina created femininity capital for herself.

Constituting femininity capital

In Chapter 4, we examined Rina, at age 12, expressing how it is much harder for boys than girls to 'just try to be yourself' in Japanese society (Extract 4.11). Rina discursively positioned boys as having to be more concerned than girls about getting bullied for allowing themselves to stand out from the crowd (to be different or diverse). She aligned herself within a 'discourse of female social flexibility' and a 'discourse of advantaged femininity', in contrast to boys who she positioned as having to be more socially constrained.

Eight months later, in the following extract, Rina again constructed the cultural capital of 'advantaged femininity'. Here, Rina brought up a discussion between herself and her mother over an article that her mother had read. The article was about a movie based on the book, *Lord of the Flies*. The article discussed how femininity can proffer a greater potential for survival than masculinity. Here, in her re-telling of her mother's talk about the article, Rina positioned women and girls as being advantaged based on their femininity. She was responding to my question of how her life might be different if she were to have been born a boy instead of a girl.

(Extract 6.15) The Café (age 13): Femininity capital

79   **R:**   but, yeah, this question reminds me of an article that my mom read about,

80   you know, the movie called 'Lord of the Flies',

81   **L:**   mmm

82   **R:**   that, how different they'd react if they were all girls or women, you know, in the,

83   because in, um, in that movie, 'Lord of the Flies', they all try to be boss

84   and they bully all the other kids and if they're a woman, they'd probably

85   go around and make sure that everyone has shelter, make sure that everyone

86   has enough to eat, and you know they wouldn't divide into tribes or anything.

87   **L:**   oh, that's interesting, so in that movie, they're all boys?

88   **R:**   yeah, I mean 'Lord of the Flies' they're all boys, but the article is about, you know

89   **L:**   oh, I see

90   **R:**   yeah, how, how, yeah

91   **L:**   that's interesting, how would it be different if they were all girls

92   **R:**   yeah, yeah, exactly, and I thought that was very interesting to think about

In Rina's re-telling of the article, she implied that if the characters marooned on an isolated island, as in the movie *Lord of the Flies*, were all girls or women instead of boys or men, that instead of becoming violent and warring, they would be nurturing and helpful to one another, advantaging femininity over masculinity in terms of survival. Drawing on 'a discourse of gender differences' and 'a discourse of advantaged femininity' (see Sunderland, 2004), Rina put value on femininity in her self-positioning as she created the cultural capital of (positive) femininity.

Rina's narrative also brings to light how use of these gendered discourses were at least partly used and co-constructed at home through her relationship with her mother. It also shows the influence on Rina of her mother's 'outside-of-Japan' education, where the social implication of *Lord of the Flies* is studied in British schools. Very few, if any, of Rina's Japanese peers have even ever heard of the story and four of the Japan-educated girl participants present at our meeting also had never heard of it. This was evidenced at the Birthday meeting when I showed the girls a written copy of the above transcript and all of them, except for Naomi and Rina, had thought that I had mistakenly meant to write *Lord of the Rings* instead of *Lord of the Flies*, as they had never heard of the latter story.

The following section looks at how the girls position themselves in terms of femininity and feminism in their talk about what kind of guy they want to marry in their future.

What kind of guy do you want to marry?

Maya asked the group what kind of person each of them would want to marry. While Japanese sentence structure leaves open a certain vagueness with the term *nanijin* (literally, what person?), Maya's question implied such aspects as nationality, ethnicity, race, or languages. After I selected Naomi to answer first (not shown here), her immediate response was that she had no intention of getting married. She repeated it emphatically several times after the other girls brushed off her statement. Several lines later, Naomi emphatically responded '*zettai shiihin kara*' ('I definitely won't'). When I pressed her to respond in terms of a possible boyfriend (instead of a marriage partner), she stated that the person would be a Latino. Next, Rina stated that she would want to marry an American or a British person. Then she clarified that the best person would have a British nationality, but a Middle Eastern ethnicity and face. She concluded in English, 'I want them to be a very firm, confident kind of person, but I would like them to come from this exotic place, exotic blood'.

Sara stated that she would want to marry a person who was half Japanese and half American, and then concluded by saying the person should 'seem' American, but be Japanese-like. Anna spoke next saying that she would want to marry someone who could *speak* English. This segment is examined in detail below (Extract 6.16). Similar to both Anna's and Sara's response, Hanna also stated that she would like to marry someone who could speak English, but who was Japanese-like, preferably 'half'. Finally, Maya answered her own question by saying that she would like to marry an American or a European person, possibly an Italian. Maya emphasized that the person be fun loving, interesting, and happy.

When it became Anna's turn to respond, an interesting discussion ensued where issues of nationality/ethnicity became interconnected with questions of feminist positionings and marriage roles. The following extract begins with Anna answering the question posed by Maya: *kekkon suru hito wa nanijin ga ii?* (What kind of person do you want the person to be who you marry?)

(Extract 6.16) Last Reunion (ages 14 and 15): 'Who do you want to marry?'

1356	A:	mmmm, mmmm, eigo shaberu
1357	L:	nihonjin demo?
1358	A:	aaa, demo, nihonjin wa iya kamo, shirahen
1359	L:	iya desuka
1360	A:	nihonjin wa chotto, na
1361	S:	baribari nihonjin wa iya yano
1362	A:	iya na
1363	S:	nn
1364	?:	nn
1365	A:	ttte ka 'teishu kanpaku' na hito ga iya
1366	L:	mmmm,
1367	N:	hu-hu-hu (laugh)
1368	?:	iya
1369	?:	iya
1370	?s:	(laugh)
1371	H:	komakai na
1372	M/S?:	'teshu kampaku' tte?
1373	H:	he, nanka, otto ga ue mitai na
1374	?:	unn
1375	?:	'sampo ushiro ni aruite koi' toka
1376	?:	'goshujinsama' mitaina
1377	R:	'biiru, biiru motte koyoi' to iu yatsu yaro
1378	A:	so, so
1379	N:	shinbun zutto yonderu hito
1380	A:	sore wa zettai iya
1381	H:	aa, wakaru
1382	N:	to iuka, Nihonjin toka soiu hito ga ooi sou nan ya kedo
1383	A:	dakara, iya da na yan
1384	L:	uh-huh, uh-huh, **naruhodo, demo, so,**
1385		so denai nihonjin mo iru jyanai?
1386	?:	mmm, iru

(Extract 6.16*) (translation)

1356*	A:	mmmm, mmmm, he can speak English
1357*	L:	even a Japanese person?
1358*	A:	aaa, but, I might not like a Japanese person, I don't know
1359*	L:	you wouldn't like that
1360*	A:	Japanese are a bit, yeah
1361*	S:	I wouldn't like a typical Japanese [person]
1362*	A:	that wouldn't be good huh
1363*	S:	yeah
1364*	?:	yeah
1365*	A:	that is, I don't like a 'teishu kanpaku' [patriarchical husband] person
1366*	L:	mmmm,
1367*	N:	(laugh)
1368*	?:	I hate that
1369*	?:	I hate that
1370*	?s:	(laugh)
1371*	H:	[someone who is] picky/trivial
1372*	S/M?:	what do you mean 'teshu kanpaku'?
1373*	H:	huh, you know, a husband who acts like he's superior
1374*	?:	yeah
1375*	?:	like, 'walk three steps behind me'
1376*	?:	like the 'respected husband, Sir'
1377*	R:	like the kind of guy who says, 'beer, beer, get it'
1378*	A:	yeah, yeah
1379*	N:	a person who just reads the newspaper all the time
1380*	A:	I definitely hate that
1381*	H:	ah, I know what you mean
1382*	N:	that is, there are many Japanese and such like that
1383*	A:	and so, [that's why] I don't like that
1384*	L:	uh-huh, uh-huh, I see, but, so,
1385*		there are Japanese people who aren't like that, aren't there?
1386*	?:	umm, there are

When Anna began by saying that she would like to marry someone who could speak English, I asked her if an English-speaking Japanese person would also qualify. Her response that she might *not* want to marry a Japanese person opened up a discussion of the girls' rejection of traditional, patriarchal Japanese husbands. Here, using the word *iya* seven times throughout this extract, the girls co-constructed their strong dislike of such authoritarian-type Japanese men.

In Line no. 1361, Sara stated that she disliked the typical Japanese person (*baribari nihonjin*). It is interesting that she made a specific reference to a 'Japanese person' instead of a reference to a more general prospective husband. She was constructing a common stereotypical husband, which has been portrayed both in the West and in Japan. While in transcribing the extract, I was often not able to determine the speaker; it seems that all of the girls co-constructed their dislike of this traditional stereotypical Japanese authoritarian male figure as a potential husband (Line nos 1362–1383).

Then in Line no. 1365, Anna brought into the discussion the term *teishu kanpaku*, which could be translated as 'husband as the ruler of the home' (see Glossary). While this type of authoritarian husband has a long history in Japan, this particular expression came into common usage in Japan during Japan's Bubble Economy (1986–1990) to refer to the stereotypical 'salary-man' husband who comes home late after work, sits down and orders his wife to bring him a drink, make his bath, fix his bed and so on. Such a husband yields total authoritarian power in the home with the wife doing all of the house work and child care.

Several of the girls co-constructed their strong dislike of such a marriage partner, with Hanna offering another example of a stereotypical disagreeable Japanese trait of being *komakai* or overly picky or trivial. Then in Line no. 1372, one of the girls – I could not determine if the speaker was Sara or Maya – asked for clarification of the meaning of *teishu kanpaku*. For women of these girls' mother's generation when this term was first popularized, its usage was widespread and the meaning was broadly known, especially among a highly educated population. This girl's unfamiliarity with this expression is perhaps indicative to some extent of how the present-day prototypical male figure has shifted to some extent from the authoritarian 'male chauvinist' (*teishu kampaku*) figure to a somewhat more feminized sensitive male in Japan.

Following this, for several turns, the girls construct various sayings and coinages that negatively construct this authoritarian figure: 'a husband who acts like he's superior' (Line no. 1373), 'like the respected husband, Sir' (Line no. 1376), 'beer, beer, get it' (Line no. 1377), 'a person who just reads the newspaper all the time' (Line no. 1379). Also in Line no. 1375, one of the girls produced a traditional saying '*sampo ushiro ni aruite koi*' (walk three steps behind me). This is an abbreviated form of a traditional Japanese saying which says that the wife/woman should stay three steps behind her husband/man when walking together so that she does not step on his shadow (*sampou sagatte shi/shujin no kage o fumanai*).

Naomi summarized the discussion by saying that there are many Japanese people like this. Anna concluded by saying that this was why she disliked that sort of person, returning to her reason for not wanting to marry a Japanese person. Finally, when I asked if there are Japanese people who are *not* like this, one of the girls acknowledged that there are.

In the above two extracts, it was shown how the girls discursively construct, celebrate and value the notion of the symbolic and cultural capital of femininity and the staking of a feminist stance. It should be noted here that this kind of discussion would also not be unusual these days to be heard among a group of Japanese girls who were not of mixed-ethnicity. These implicit feminist values have become commonsensical and widespread among this generation of young girls in Japan.

Summary

In this chapter, I have examined how these girls place value on various resources available to them in their worlds as mixed-ethnic adolescent girls growing up in Japan. This valuing, which I refer to as a *celebration* of their ethnicity, amounts to their creation of cultural capital in which they are able to legitimate, through their discursive valuing, various forms of accumulative, convertible, exercisable and investable capital (Bourdieu, 1977; Bourdieu & Passeron, 1977).

While to a large extent they take their Japaneseness as unremarkable and ordinary, it is their mixed-ethnicity, with the privileges it affords them, which they celebrate as valuable and special. They are Japanese, but they are also more than just Japanese. They identify themselves not as being deficient in cultural capital, but as being abundant in it.

I have shown in this chapter how the girls construct and legitimate the cultural capital of bilingualism and biliteracy. They positioned themselves as privileged and advantaged in possessing English proficiency. They celebrated their linguistic capital as highly valued in today's globalized society where English is legitimated as one of three major academic subjects in the educational system. They constructed their knowledge of English as more than just knowledge of high-school and college entrance-examination skills; their English ability gives them intercultural access to information, greater maturity, and knowledge and literature not available to most of their Japanese peers. Within their homes, they have a parent who was raised outside of Japan who can provide them with connections, opportunities and overseas experiences.

They have special relationships within the Japanese community where they reside, including mixed-ethnic girl friendships (with each other), providing them with ethnically similar peers whom they trust and mutually support. It was shown how these girls discursively create and legitimate social and cultural capital based on these relationships. Rina was seen creating the cultural capital of privileged femininity and all of the girls were seen aligning themselves within a feminist stance regarding an imagined future marriage partner. The girls' construction of cultural and symbolic capital of intercultural savvy, choice and job opportunity was also examined.

In short, these girls celebrated their ethnicity and (re)constituted their 'otherness' through their positioning within major discourses available to them. While they worked to re-position themselves away from ethnic discourses of powerlessness, at the same time, they created and celebrated their mixed-ethnic cultural capital within alternative discourses of empowerment in the construction of their hybrid identities.

In the next chapter, I further explore another type of cultural capital that these girls created for themselves based on their gendered and ethnic embodiment.

Notes

1. Parts of this chapter, Extracts 6.1, 6.2, 6.6, 6.7a–d, 6.14 and Extract 7.4, in the following chapter, and earlier versions of the analysis have been previously published (Kamada, 2005a) and have been reproduced here with permission from the BSIG of JALT.
2. Extract 6.6 and parts of the analysis following it have been previously published (Greer *et al.*, 2005) and have been reproduced here with permission from the BSIG of JALT.
3. Throughout the study, the girls' use of lexes to refer to their *mixed-ethnicity* went through several changes. At the first meeting, Rina used the word 'bilingual' to refer to her mixed-ethnic friends. In the following meeting (the Café meeting), the three girls present mostly referred to themselves as 'bicultural'. By the Hot Springs meeting, when all six girls were present, while continuing to use the word 'bicultural' at times, the girls started to use several other words to refer to themselves such as 'half' and 'double'. By the final meeting, most of the girls were consistently using the word 'double' to refer to themselves in both English and Japanese (*daburu*). They also used other more pejoratively nuanced words when voicing what others called them, such as *gaijin* or 'half' (*haafu*).
4. Kansai is a region of Japan, west of Tokyo in which the prefectures of Hyogo, Kyoto, Nara, Osaka, Shiga and Wakayama are located.
5. *Kansai ben* (Kansai dialect) is the name of the particular non-standard Japanese dialect spoken in the Kansai region, differing slightly between the cities within the region.

Chapter 7

Discursive 'Embodied' Identities of Ethnicity and Gender

Introduction: Intersection of Gender and Ethnicity

In the previous three chapters, I problematized how the six girls negotiated their identities in terms of constituting, contesting and celebrating their ethnicity. In this chapter, I continue to examine their identification process, but I now specifically focus on how their hybrid 'embodied' identities intersect with their gendered identities, at the site of the body. In particular, I address the third central question presented in Chapter 1, which I restate here:

> How, if at all, do children (adolescent girls) of Japanese and 'white' mixed-parentage in Japan discursively identify themselves in terms of their positioning and performances based on their *gendered* and *ethnic embodiment* (their ethnicized body selves)?

I explore how the girl participants discursively 'work' to contest being 'racialized' as *haafu* or *gaijin*, while at the same time appropriate positive constructions of their 'ethnic attractiveness'. I also investigate how they take up their ethnic embodiment in their play among each other through this period of remarkable body maturation of early adolescence.

'Doing gender' and ethno-gendering

West and Zimmerman's (1987, 2009) notion of 'doing gender' and West and Fenstermaker's (1995) 'doing difference' was defined in Chapter 2 (see the section '"Doing Gender", "Doing Difference" and Ethno-Gendering' [p. 39]) as the ways in which people manage their activities within socially accepted norms of who they are expected to be or how they are expected to act in terms of their sex category and their presumed race/ethnicity. The concept of 'doing difference' addresses social inequality not only by taking into account gender, but also considering the simultaneous accomplishment of race and class. As explained in the section 'Embodied identities' [p. 41], I have similarly conceptualized the simultaneous accomplishment of gender and ethnicity as 'ethno-gendering' – the accomplishment of ethnicity and gender together. This chapter examines how the participants accomplish their ethno-gendered identities through their 'lived-body selves', what I refer to as their 'ethnic embodiment'.

In the following section, I examine the ethnic embodiment work of the girls as they demonstrate their emergence from earlier positions of powerlessness within a limiting dominant discourse of homogeneity. Over time, they can be seen taking up more self-enhancing positions when more competing discourses of diversity become available to them as they mature.

The Dilemma of Ethnically Embodied Adolescent Girls

My decision to examine Japanese adolescent girls' talk over several years during a very rapidly changing time in their lives was largely influenced by Coates' (1999) longitudinal examination of the talk of a group of adolescent girls (ages 12–15). Coates showed that as girls mature, their talk begins to take on a wider range of voices and discourses, which constrain, rather than liberate them as these discourses come into conflict. By intertextually taking up the language of those around them, the girls were shown to experiment with a wide range of voices and discourses, which they were able to adopt or subvert. Coates (1999) showed how girls are not just shaped by discourses, but they are also social agents able to resist and subvert the discourses.

I was similarly influenced by Maybin's (2002) study on pre-adolescent girls and boys in the UK. She analyzed the movement over time of developing gender identities; in this case, from childhood into adolescence by looking at relationships with parents and family, people of authority and friendship boundaries. Maybin showed how 'children invoke and are positioned within different discourses' (Maybin, 2002: 259), and looked at how dominant gendered discourses available to these children are explored, challenged and altered. Maybin showed how pre-adolescent participants reproduce the voices of others, including reported speech of people in authority roles, popular songs and other peers, but often changed those voices to assert their control.

Early adolescence is already a sensitive phase of maturational development in terms of both mental as well as physical maturation (Finders, 1997; Orenstein, 1994). The section below looks at an extract from the data in which two of the girls from this study worked to resolve dilemmas of their halfness/doubleness.

The reflection in the mirror

The following extract looks at the talk of Hanna and Anna, which they recorded without my presence.

(Extract 7.1) Hanna/Anna (age 13): 'It's totally shocking looking in the mirror'

1	A:	yappari uchi ga iitai koto wa, yappari jibun ga dondake nihonjin no
2		tsumori demo, mou honma ni 'gaijin' ga daikkirai de, mou jibun wa
3		kanzen ni, nihonjin de, nihonjin maindo de,
4		nihonjin yatte omottemo,
5		kagami o miru to nihonjin jyanaishi, sorega meccha iya jyanai?
6	H:	demosa, oosutoraria itta toki sa,
7		kanpeki ni nihonjin yato omowareteta yona
8	A:	sou dakara, sore ga meccha ureshikatta no
9	H:	e, kedo
10	A:	atashi wa meccha ureshikatta
11	H:	bimyou, teka, donna ni nihon ni ite
12		meccha 'ano hito gaikokujin yana' toka omou,
13		daburu no hito nimo nanka
14	A:	uun, yappa kagami miru to meccha shokku yana

(Extract 7.1*) (translation)

1*	A:	*what I want to say, however much I intend to be Japanese,*
2*		*I really hate [being thought of as] 'gaijin',*
3*		*I am completely Japanese with a Japanese mind,*
4*		*but even if I think of myself as Japanese,*
5*		*when I look in the mirror I'm not Japanese, and that's really disagreeable*
6*	H:	*but, when we went to Australia,*

7*   *everyone thought that we were completely Japanese*
8*   **A:**   *yeah, so that made me really happy*
9*   **H:**   *yes, but*
10* **A:**   *I was really happy about that*
11* **H:**   *it's subtle, that is, however long you stay in Japan,*
12*   *they will totally think 'that person is a foreigner'*
13*   *or that we are doubles*
14* **A:**   *yeah, it's just totally shocking looking in the mirror*

In Anna's five-line narrative concerning her ethnicity/nationality (Line nos 1–5), she used the lexis *Nihonjin* (Japanese person) five times. Hanna also used it once, along with other lexes denoting ethnicity/nationality: Australia, Japan, *gaijin*, *gaikokujin* and *daburu*. This segment started out where Anna rejected the constitution of herself as '*gaijin*' and instead took up a self-positioning as 'completely Japanese with a Japanese mind'. In Line no. 2, Anna's strong contestation of being constituted as *gaijin* shows linguistic traces of her drawing on a discourse of homogeneity and a discourse of conformity. She can be seen acting to position and align herself outside of the category of *gaijin* and instead to position herself as Japanese. Anna's account of the 'disagreeable' feeling of looking at her face in the mirror may be due to the gap she perceived between feeling Japanese and not looking Japanese.

In Line nos 6–7, Hanna can be seen calling up a 'discourse of homogeneity', which in Japan constitutes ethnic difference negatively, but here Hanna positioned herself and Anna in an empowering way to affirm their sense of belonging. Also intersecting with these other discourses, linguistic traces can be seen of these girls co-constructing a 'discourse of interculturalism'. They positively constituted themselves based on their intercultural savvy and connections associated with another culture, which has provided them with more available discourses and repertoires than they would find within the limited context of Japan. Hanna constituted herself (and Anna) as 'Japanese' within the context of Australia, drawing on a positive 'discourse of diversity' (and of positive ethnic embodiment), which positions mixed-ethnic girls not as *protruding nails*, but as *unmarked*; not as *half*, but as *whole*; not as *foreign outsider* but as *unmarked Japanese*. Next, Anna aligned herself with Hanna's positioning (Line nos 8, 10) in her co-construction, stating that she too was happy with being constituted as 'Japanese' while in Australia.

Hanna then brought the talk back to the context of Japan (Line nos 11–13). In Hanna's discursive use of intertextual 'voices' to portray what others in Japan say to her, 'that person is a foreigner', she rejected the notion that *gaikokujin* (or *haafu/daburu*) people like herself are NOT Japanese'. Hanna contested being constituted as a protruding nail of 'a foreigner' or 'a double', instead of as unmarked and as Japanese. It is notable that in Line no. 12, Hanna used the more polite form, *gaikokujin*, for the word 'foreigner', in voicing someone 'hailing' her: 'that person is a foreigner'. Also, rather than using the standard Japanese term *haafu*, Hanna used the alternative word *daburu* to refer to and position herself and Anna in a more additive, self-affirming manner and also perhaps to establish in-group solidarity with her fellow mixed-ethnic interlocutor.

Finally, Anna positioned herself on the basis of her embodied subjectivity, 'yeah, it's just totally shocking looking in the mirror' (Line no. 14) drawing on a 'discourse of homogeneity', where she negatively positioned her ethnic embodied self as 'the other'. These 'ideological dilemmas' or shifts in positioning within intersecting discourses of homogeneity and diversity reveal the contrasting multiplicity of selves, which these girls assumed in their identification process.

Contesting Ethnic Embodiment as Inferior or 'Othered'

The extract of the girls' talk in this section (below) was preceded by my showing the girls a piece of text that came out of a Japanese children's book about the human body published by a very well known Japanese publishing company (Gakken). Personally, I felt that this book, called *Hito no Karada* (*The Human Body*) (Suzuki, 1984), was an excellent children's learning book, partly based on my personal criterion that it was my own son's favorite book for many years. This book, written in Japanese, designed for Japanese children from pre-school through elementary school, had drawings, photographs and simple text about the internal organs, skin, teeth and so forth organized in a very fun, creative and approachable manner. However, what I noticed about this highly illustrated 128-page book (with numerous illustrations, diagrams and photos on every page) was that all of the people represented were Japanese people, with just three striking exceptions in which 'white foreigners' were used. It was particularly these exceptions that I found interesting and I decided to present this 'puzzle' to the girls as stimulus for discussion and as a way of eliciting data on their positioning within ethnic discourses.

One of these exceptions was an entire double-page, highlighted and titled *Bikkuri Ningen* ('Surprising People' – which could be thought of as an euphemism for 'freaks'), which included a 'giant' woman, a man born with a jawbone which can be dislocated, an extremely obese person, a strong man pulling a truck on a rope in his teeth and so forth, all of whom were non-Japanese 'white' people. Due to space limitations, I will not go into further detail about this example. Instead, it is the two other examples of the use of foreigners in this book that I would like to examine more closely here (in Extracts 7.2 and 7.3), not through my own critical discourse analysis of the text, but by analyzing how the girls discursively positioned themselves in accordance with discourses apparent in the text.

The first of the other two examples was an illustration of a blonde-haired girl with the following text:

> **Gaijin wa Nipponjin yori kaminoke ga hosoku, ke no naka no meranin no tsubu ga sukunainode, kiiro ni mieru no desu. Nipponjin ga gaijin yorimo futokute, kuroi kaminoke o motteimasu, kamin-oke no kazu ga gaijin no hou ga takusan arimasu.**
>
> Translation: *Foreigners'* [Gaijin] *hair is thinner than Japanese people's and because the grains of melanin inside of the hair are fewer, they appear as blonde. Japanese people's [hair strands] are thicker than foreigner's* [gaijin's] *hair and [we] have black hair; foreigners* [gaijin] *have a greater number of hairs.*

Following is an extract of the girls talking about this text. It was often unclear from the recording which girl was speaking in this and some of the following extracts. I have indicated this uncertainty with a question mark [?] in the 'participant' column of the extract in several places.

(Extract 7.2) Hot Springs (age 13): 'A scientific explanation'

1	N:	kore sa, 'gaijin ikooru kiniro' ni mieruttesa
2	?:	nnnn
3	N:	nanka okashiku
4	L:	deshou?
5	?:	mmm
6	N:	'gaijin wa kinpatsu' yanentte
7	?:	watashi wa shirankatta, tsubu ga sukunaikara
8	?:	chuugokujin toka sa, kuro yashina
9	R:	kore wa ne, ano, ima wa, ima,
10		kamenoke wa somerutteiu hito ga ippai isugite
11	?:	mm
12	R:	nantoiuno, chiichai goro kara, kou, nantoiuno,
13		jibun no kaminoke sorede iin dattoiuno oshieteiru jyanaikana
14	L:	mmm

15 ?:   mmm
16 R: de so, soiu no oshieten janaikana?
17 ?:   kagakuteki ni setsumeisuru dakechau, tsubu ga sukunai
          toiu, nan

(Extract 7.2*) (translation)

1*   N: *this, looks like they are saying 'gaijin equals blonde'*
2*   ?:   *yeah*
3*   N: *this is strange*
4*   L: *don't you think so?*
5*   ?:   *yeah*
6*   N: *this says 'gaijin are blonde'*
7*   ?:   *I didn't know that the amount of melanin was less*
8*   ?:   *Chinese people [as gaijin in Japan] and others have black hair*
9*   R: *this is well, um now, now,*
10*   *this is an overstatement, lots of people dye their hair these days*
11* ?:   *yeah*
12* R: *how can I say this, since I was little, like, how do I put this,*
13*   *aren't people taught that your own hair is good [as it is]*
14* L: *yeah*
15* ?:   *yeah*
16* R: *and that, they teach that, don't they?*
17* ?:   *this is just a scientific explanation isn't it, saying that there is less*
          melanin

Both Naomi and Rina used negative adjectives to refer to the passage in the book as 'strange' (Line no. 3), and as 'an overstatement' (Line no. 10). Naomi, in stating 'this looks like they are saying "*gaijin* equals blonde"' (Line no. 1), demonstrated her recognition and contestation in the text of the blatant promotion of a discourse of homogeneity in the stereotyping of 'foreigners'. Through Naomi's voicing of this, she took a position contesting this discourse. In Line no. 7, another girl, in stating 'I didn't know that the amount of melanin was less [in blondes]', discursively accepted the 'scientific truth' (scientific discourse) put forth in the text. In the following line (Line no. 8), yet another girl also seems to be contesting a discourse of homogeneity espoused in this text by presenting the example of Chinese people (as foreigners) residing in Japan with black hair, where *gaijin does NOT equal blonde*.

Rina (Line nos 9–10) further contributed to this deconstruction of homogeneity by stating that many people today dye their hair, implying that people's hair color does not always correspond with their ethnicity (nor with the volume of melanin in their hair). Following this, Rina seemed to be trying to further build her argument (Line nos 12–13), but rather than contesting a discourse of homogeneity per se, she positioned herself based on the virtue of one's (innate or 'God-given') appearance, which could be called a *discourse of learning-to-love-yourself*, where she stated, 'aren't people taught that your own hair is good [as it is]'.

Finally, another girl recognized, named and contested a scientific discourse in the text. Challenging the construction that the book seems to have subtly produced, which equates 'more melanin' as *better*, this girl seems to be seen rejecting the positioning of 'blondes' or *gaijin* in a deficit, subtractive manner, based on their hair having *less* melanin than that of 'Japanese' hair, in her statement, 'this is just a scientific explanation isn't it, saying that there is less melanin' (Line no. 17).

The next section examines an extract in which the girls further maneuver themselves within dilemmas of ethnicity, but in this section, they relate how they have learned over time to resolve ethnic marginalization by drawing on a greater number of alternative discourses, which were not available to them earlier.

Celebrating Ethnic Embodiment as Privileged Cultural Capital

Chapter 6 explored how the girls discursively create for themselves various forms of cultural, symbolic, linguistic and social capital. Another form of cultural capital, not yet thoroughly examined, which these girls also create for themselves, is the positive embodied capital of mixed-ethnicity. Below is a discussion of another example of the use of 'white foreigners' in the children's book. Here there is a photograph of a frontal-posed shot of two blonde-haired *naked* children – a boy and a girl (apparently siblings, approximately aged 7 and 8) holding hands as they are coming out of the ocean. I felt it to be a perfectly innocent photo of young children, but I wondered why the marked use of non-Japanese children, for an example, to showcase male and female genitals. I asked the girls why they thought the authors chose to use *gaijin* children rather than Japanese children.

Naomi started off rationalizing the use of non-Japanese *gaijin* children on the basis that many underwear commercials have long used foreigners in place of Japanese people to which Hanna and other girls offered agreement. The following extract follows this when I probed for more explanation of why 'foreigners' are used here (or in underwear commercials) instead of Japanese people.

(Extract 7.3) Hot Springs (age 13) : 'Foreigners have "good style"; Japanese are plain'

1101	L:	why?
1102	S:	sutairu ga ii karajyan
1103	L:	sutairu ga iin JYANAI to omou
1104	?:	sore wa
1105	?:	yaseta sutairu ga ii karayan
1106	?:	nn
1107	?:	datte mune toka, dekaishi, nihonjin shoboi mon na
1108	L:	demo kodomo deshou
1109	s:	(laugh)
1110	L:	kodomo deshou
1111	?:	ahhh
1112	N:	kodomo amari kankeinai na

(Extract 7.3*) (translation)

1101*	L:	why?
1102*	S:	*because their style [shape] is good, yeah*
1103*	L:	*it's NOT because their style is good, I think*
1104*	?:	*that is*
1105*	?:	*because the style of being thin is good*
1106*	?:	*yeah*
1107*	?:	*after all, their breasts and stuff are large, Japanese are plain [poor-looking, lacking]*
1108*	L:	*but these are children*
1109*	?s:	(laugh)
1110*	L:	*they're children, right*
1111*	?:	*ahhh*
1112*	N:	*it doesn't matter that they're children*

When Sara implied that the authors chose to use foreigners because their *body style* was better (than Japanese people's) (Line no. 1102), I expressed explicit disagreement (Line no. 1103). However, the girls rebutted my stance by giving several reasons why foreigners were used in the book, which further helped to co-construct this common notion in Japan of foreigners being considered attractive.

In the transcript, one of the girl's selection of Japanese words (Line no. 1107) to position both 'White' and Japanese people is interesting in the *non-flattering* connotation for the two constructions. This girl referred to the *mune* or chest/breasts of 'foriegners/whites' as *dekai*, which I have translated above as 'large', although there is a nuance of 'very large' or 'huge'. In contrast, this girl then referred to Japanese as being *shoboi*, a slang word meaning plain to the point of being poor-looking or lacking. This girl drew a connection of embodiment not only with *'foreign' ethnicity*, but also with *'ideal' femininity* (Line no. 107), where large breasts are taken as the feminine ideal (see Bloustien, 2001). This girl positioned Whites and presumably also mixed-ethnic Japanese-Whites (which would include herself and the others present) as ethnically attractive and diverse within these discourses, in contrast to Japanese whom she positioned as 'the other' and as plain or lacking. When I stated twice that these were children, it brought laughter and pause, before Naomi countered (Line no. 1112), further co-constructing a discourse that foreign or ethnic attractiveness extends to children as well as adults.

The rest of this section further examines how ethnic embodiment was discursively created as positive cultural capital during the Last Reunion meeting. Rina responded to Hanna's question, 'what is special about you being double?' with the answer, 'things like looks and stuff', and then she continued:

> R: **un, kanaa, kou, yappa, sugoi ekizochikku** (laugh) **na kaodachi (?) ni narukara, uchi wa kekkou sukidashi, nanka, nnn, soremou ijouiehen** (laugh)
> *um, what, because you would have an extremely exotic facial shape (?)* (laugh), *I really like that, somehow, umm, I can't say anything more than that* (laugh)

Rina used the Japanese adjective *ekizochikku*, a loan-word from the English 'exotic', to ascribe a positive value to the feature of 'facial shape' in her description of what was special to her about being 'double'. In Rina's usage of the word *kaodachi*, she implied the notion that the facial bone structure is not only different between Japanese and 'double' girls like herself, but that 'double' or 'foreigner' peoples' facial bone structure is *better*, drawing on a 'discourse of foreign attractiveness'. In saying that she 'really likes that', Rina can be seen creating for herself positive embodied capital. Her very abrupt completion of her turn in Line no. #3 may indicate that she felt some kind of embarrassment in her self-compliment, as speaking about oneself in Japanese culture would generally call for deference, restraint and humbleness. Her laugh in two places could also be indicative of this.

Constructing foreign attractiveness

In the final meeting for this study (the Last Reunion meeting), when the girls were 14 and 15, dramatic changes became evident. They matured not only in their discursive abilities to draw on various alternative discourses, but also in their physicality, evident not only to me, but also to each other. The final four extracts presented in this book were all taken from the Last Reunion meeting.

In the following extract, ethnic embodiment is additionally created (by Maya) as a form of cultural capital in a continuation of Hanna's question. This segment follows directly from another one presented earlier (Extract 6.14), concerning the cultural capital of having greater *choices*. Here now, the benefits of being 'double' suddenly shifted from job opportunity and choice to a new topic as Maya introduced into the conversation the notion of *ethnic embodiment*.

(Extract 7.4) Last Reunion (age 14): 'Hori ga Fukai'

32	L:	did you answer yet? (to Maya)
33	M:	**hori ga fukai, kawaiisa ga deru (?)**
34	L:	huh?
35	M:	**hori ga fukakunatte**
36	L:	**ah, hana ga takai?**
37	M:	**etto, Nihonjin dattara kou** (gesture)
38	S:	**amari sukijanai**
39	M:	**hori ga fukaku naru, nanto ittetara ii**
40	R:	because, just,
41		**nantoiu kana**
42		people in Japan always like deep set, deep set
43		**deyone, hori ga fukai toiu no wa**
44		deep set, they think that's beautiful so
45		**hori ga fukai toiu ii imeji deya**
46	L:	uh-huh
47	R:	**hori ga aru, hori ga fukai mo ne**
48		Sara has got beautiful deep-set eyes so

(Extract 7.4*) (translation)

32*	L:	did you answer yet? (to Maya)
33*	M:	*hori ga fukai [nicely sculptured face] the cuteness comes out (?)*
34*	L:	*huh?*
35*	M:	*a nicely sculptured face*
36*	L:	*ah, a prominent nose?*
37*	M:	*um, if [they're] Japanese, [they're] like this* (gesture)
38*	S:	*I don't really like that*

39*	M:	*coming to be well-sculptured, how can I say that*
40*	R:	because, just,
41*		*how do I say that*
42*		people in Japan always like deep set, deep set
43*		*isn't it so, 'hori ga fukai' means*
44*		deep set, they think that's beautiful so
45*		*hori-ga-fukai has a good image*
46*	L:	uh-huh
47*	R:	*having prominence, hori-ga-fukai is just*
48*		Sara has got beautiful deep-set eyes so

In the English translation (Extract 7.4*), in some places, I did not translate the word *hori ga fukai* for the purposes of coherency. Literally meaning 'a deeply cut (face)' or 'a well sculptured (face)', this expression implies a facial feature often associated with Euro-American or Caucasian features, with the nuance of exoticness and often 'foreignness'.

In answer to Hanna's question of what is special about being double, this extract began with Maya introducing a new topic: *hori ga fukai*. With this, Maya brought to the discussion the notion of 'foreign attractiveness' as she positioned 'doubles' – a category to which she and the other girls belong – as cute, exotic or good looking.

Maya asked for help in explaining the meaning of *'hori ga fukaku'* (an adverbial form), in response to my appeal for clarification (#34) with 'huh?'. Maya's initial explanation (Line no. 35) was most likely primarily directed to me, the English speaker, as the other girls would presumably already know the meaning of this Japanese word. Maya gestured to show how people, not fortunate enough to have a *hori ga fukai* face, might appear (Line no. 37), positioning herself away from Japaneseness and instead as 'exotic *haafu/daburu* with a deeply sculptured face'. Sara helped to co-construct this positioning in saying, 'I don't really like that'.

Rina, the most proficient English speaker among the girls, self-selected to fulfill Maya's request (in Line no. 39) to define this term. In Line nos 40–45, Rina offered an account of how *hori ga fukai* is perceived 'in Japan'. Drawing on a discourse of foreign attractiveness, she confirmed that this having a 'deep-cut' face or deep-set eyes was considered a sign of beauty in Japan. Linguistic traces of a 'discourse of diversity' can also be seen in Rina's talk, in her placing positive value on ethnic difference. Rina began using English and then proceeded to alternate codes between Japanese and English numerous times in explaining *hori ga fukai*. Rina's four lines spoken in English carried a message saying, 'people in Japan like deep set eyes and they think it is beautiful'. Rina's four interspersed alternations into Japanese partially functioned to index the topic *hori ga fukai* and to seek clarification from her Japanese-speaking peers of her English renditions of *hori ga fukai*. These code-switches perhaps also served the purpose of pulling in the attention of the three among the six girls in attendance who were less proficient in English. These Japanese sections did not provide much semantic relevance, except in Line no. 45, where Rina assigned positive value to the notion of *hori ga fukai*. Rina revealed proficient intercultural ability to alternate languages for the discursive purpose of negotiating better communication between Japanese monolingual interlocutors and an English speaker (me). In helping Maya explain the meaning of this term, Rina placed value on the embodied capital of their 'doubleness'.

Up until Line no. 48, the girls had been discussing the topic of *ethnic embodiment* in general terms. Rina then suddenly personally focused the talk on one of the girls present among us, abruptly switching back into English,[1] 'Sara has got beautiful deep-set eyes'. As demonstrated above, Rina here again could be seen as positioning Sara personally as the exotic 'idealized other' (Bloustien, 2001) in her co-construction of three discourses: 'diversity', where *being different* is taken as good, 'interculturalism', where Sara's exoticism is placed within a globalizing context broader than just Japan and 'foreign attractiveness'.

In this section, the girls' statements seem to buy into a popular media discourse where women's bodies are objectified as the sum of their parts, and into another related discourse, certainly within the Japan context, in which ethnic differences in beauty are commodified. Within the context of these strong influences, these girls were seen to celebrate their ethnicity in their creation of the cultural capital of 'attractive' ethnic embodiment.

While the girls of this study worked to contest marginalization due to their 'othered' appearance during their elementary school years, as they entered into adolescence, more empowering discourses of ethnicity became available to them, allowing them now to discursively take up their physical embodiment positively as *exotic* and self-enhancing. They created and celebrated embodied cultural capital of hybrid attractiveness – another form of transferable capital contributing to the positive constitution of their ethnic identities. They personally positioned themselves and each other within this 'discourse of ethnic attractiveness', while at the same time, they also disassociated themselves from the 'ordinariness' of Japanese who do not enjoy this *special* capital.

Yearning to be Embodied Like Another: The Idealized Other[2]

In the data, the girls often talked about other girls, most often about others that they admired or yearned to be like. In this section, an extract is presented exemplifying this yearning, but it is particularly interesting and relevant here in that it brings up issues of not only ethnicity, but also of gender and embodiment.

What influenced whether these girls positioned themselves as *haafu*, *daburu*, *gaijin* or Japanese, was often a result of how their identities were both ascribed by others and achieved by themselves. More than any of the other girls, Sara's (good) 'looks' emerged repeatedly in the data. At the very start of the Last Reunion meeting, before we formally began, the girls talked among themselves with the tape recorder running about another mixed-ethnic girl named Jasmine (a pseudonym), who Hanna constituted as extremely cute. Then one of the girls compared Jasmine's 'cuteness' with 'the-even-cuter' Sara, who was present among us, by stating that Jasmine was about as cute as Sara. Then Rina co-constructed this idea by stating, *'kawaii kedo Sara no tsugi gurai ni kawaii'* ('She [Jasmine] is really cute, about second after Sara'). As well, in several other instances during the last meeting, Rina discursively positioned Sara as exotic or beautiful by virtue of her mixed-ethnicity.

Sara's 'exotic ethnic looks' became the topic of discussion again during the Last Reunion meeting when we were discussing the advantages of being 'double', centering on choices and job opportunities. Directly following that segment (Extract 6.14), suddenly Rina positioned Sara as ethnically exotic, within a discourse of foreign attractiveness, stating:

R: Sara yattara geinoukai de sugu shigoto mitsukerareru
as for Sara, she would be able to find a job in the entertainment business right away

Another girl present positioned Sara as cute enough that she could get a job modeling, while another girl suggested that Sara could be the cover girl of a teen magazine. When I asked Sara if she wanted to work in the modeling or entertainment business, she rejected this positioning by referring to such kinds of work as 'a waste'.

As seen above, Sara's friends on several occasions positioned her as exotic and attractive, an attribute of her mixed-ethnicity which they all share. These adolescent girls created the notion of an 'idealized other' in Sara, whose 'cuteness' they set as a standard to achieve in their own emerging embodied subjectivities. Bloustien (2001), in her study of teen-age girls, looked at how women and girls come to view their own bodies against a model of those they aspire to look like and be like, within a discourse of femininity, which constantly portrays the 'idealized other' through such means as the media. Bloustien states, 'It is an important dimension of "self-making" ... an important aspect of emulating and "being" the other that one admires' (Bloustien, 2001: 112).

The next extract looks at another example of how these girls created this 'idealized other' in their searches to realize their own subjective ethnically embodied selves. I mentioned above that before the start of the Last Reunion meeting, while I was preoccupied, the girls were talking among themselves about a girl named Jasmine. Inadvertently, I had rather abruptly cut off this talk when I called for the start of the meeting. Much later in the session, while I was again preoccupied setting up some materials, this earlier conversation was initiated anew by the girls. Again, as before, this conversation ensued without any notice or input from me. It was only later when I began to transcribe the tape recording that I first became aware of this interaction. I had given the girls a task to draw portraits of their own faces and had set out materials for this. While they were working on their drawings, they were chatting as follows:

(Extract 7.5) Last Reunion (ages 14 and 15): 'For an Asian her eyes are really big'

1	H:	uchi na Jazumintte namae ni shitaitte iwaretena,
2		Jazumintte namae sukiyashi, demo tomodachi ga na Jazumin yanenka
3	?:	sore pakutta to omowareru de
4	H:	seyaro dakara iya yanen kedona
5	?:	nihonjin?
6	H:	unn, chuugokujin demo nihonjin
7	?:	meccha kawaii nenka sonohito
8	H:	dena nanka na chuugokujin ppokunai no seikaku,
9		chou nihonjin yashi, dakara naka yoku naretashi
10	?:	a, meccha kizuitara ketteta (unrelated talk)
11	H:	mata shashin okutteageruwa meccha kawaiishi
12		me chou dekai nenka
13	?:	e, anohito wa dare? ano shashin okuttekitayan
14	?:	are tabun Tsubasa yato omou
15	?:	e, sono mae ni nanka chuugokujin no hito

16   ?:   me okkii? hada shiroi?
[…]
24   H: dena, Jazumintte hito na chou hada shirokute,
25   hada meccha kirei yanenndena,
26   juuhassai nanyakedona,
27   muccha na suppin yanon ni chou kirei yanenka hada ga,
28   dena, me ga na, konna Ajiajin yanoni meccha dekakutena,
29   me no shita kou (?) natteyan meccha kawaii, dena,
30   kuchibiru wa na usukute na,
31   hana wa takai nenka,
32   takai tteiuka meccha kireide totonottennen,
33   chou kawaii de, shashin no toki zettai kore yanenka, dena,
34   tomodachi ga Tsubasatte hito yakara meccha nihonjin no eikyou uketeru
35   kara chou kawaii fukusou mo kekkou kawaii
36   kaminoke maccha de itanden nenkedo kawaiinen
[…]
39   ?:   nani, fande nutten no fande nuttehande Sara

(Extract 7.5*) (translation)

1*   H: *people say that I want to be called Jasmine,*
2*   *I like the name Jasmine, but I have a friend named Jasmine*
3*   ?:   *people would think you were copying her*
4*   H: *that's right, so I don't want to do that*
5*   ?:   *is she Japanese?*
6*   H: *yeah, Chinese, but Japanese*
7*   ?:   *that girl is very cute*
8*   H: *and her personality doesn't seem Chinese-like,*
9*   *she's really Japanese-like, so we got close*
10*   ?:   *(unrelated talk) ah, I kicked you, I just totally realized it*
11*   H: *I'll send you her picture again, she's extremely cute*
12*   *her eyes are very big*
13*   ?:   *oh, who was that person? that picture you sent arrived*
14*   ?:   *I think that was probably Tsubasa*
15*   ?:   *uh, before that, a Chinese person*
16*   ?:   *[does she have] big eyes? white skin?*
[…]
24*   H: *and that girl, Jasmine, has extremely white skin,*
25*   *her skin is really beautiful,*
26*   *and she is eighteen,*

27*	but her skin is really beautiful without using make-up,
28*	and her eyes, for an Asian her eyes are really big,
29*	and under her eyes (?) it's like this, like that, totally cute,
30*	and her lips are thin,
31*	her nose is high [prominent],
32*	not just high but extremely pretty and well-featured,
33*	she's extremely cute, she always poses like this in photos (gesture),
34*	and she has a friend, Tsubasa, who has a great Japanese influence on her,
35*	so she's extremely cute in her rather cute clothes
36*	her hair has become brown [damaged] but she is still cute

[...]

39*	?:	what, are you applying foundation [make-up] are you putting foundation [on your picture], Sara?

This extract is interesting in that the girls were performing ethnic embodiment in their talk. I had asked the girls to sign their portraits with their pseudonyms, which I had already selected for each of them for use in this study. While the girls were drawing portraits of their own faces, Hanna began to speak of the features of another girl, Jasmine, whose name she had wanted to claim for her own. The other girls expressed interest in Jasmine by commenting on and asking questions about her, the first of which concerned her ethnicity, 'is she Japanese?' (Line no. 5). Hanna answered that she is 'Chinese, but Japanese', leaving her ethnicity vague. Also earlier, during the segment on Jasmine at the beginning of the day, Rina had said of Jasmine, *'nihonjin rashii kedo, bimyou'* ('she's kind of Japanese-like, but it's subtle'). Is she half Chinese? All Chinese? Japanese in nationality, but Chinese in ethnicity? Half Chinese and half Caucasian? It was not made totally clear. These matters were not of importance to them, however. More importantly for them, Hanna positioned Jasmine as 'very cute' and not totally Japanese, showing linguistic traces of a discourse of ethnic or foreign attractiveness.

However, in contrast to this positive positioning of Jasmine, Hanna also unconsciously placed Jasmine's 'Chineseness' in an inferior position to 'Japaneseness' in her statement, 'and her personality doesn't seem Chinese, she's really Japanese-like, so we got close' (Line nos 8–9). Linguistic traces can be seen of Hanna drawing on a discourse of Japanese conformity and an intersecting discourse of homogeneity to position Jasmine. Hanna stated that they were able to get close because Jasmine's personality was not Chinese-like, as she conforms to expectations of Japaneseness rather than the stereotype of ethnic Chineseness (Line nos 8–9).

Hanna seemed enamored by Jasmine's cuteness – her big eyes (Line nos 12, 16, 28) and her white skin (Line nos 16, 24) – within a discourse of foreign attractiveness. Hanna looks up to Jasmine, who is four years older (18 years old) than her, as an idealized role model. Hanna keeps a photo of Jasmine in her mobile phone memory and had sent it to some of the other girls as well. Bloustien (2001) reported on the scrutinizing and commenting on the physical features of others as a commonplace, universal practice of adolescent girls. Hanna went into quite a bit of detail to describe Jasmine's beauty – a person she constructed as exceptionally attractive, even without the use of make-up (Line no. 27). In the earlier segment, Hanna had also remarked, '*meikyappu toka tsukaenai, kawarehenshine*' ('she doesn't use things like make-up, it wouldn't make any difference anyway'), drawing attention to Jasmine's *natural* beauty. Revealing traces of a discourse of foreign (*gaijin*) attractiveness, she pointed out Jasmine's exceptional *gaijin*-like features of allurement (big eyes, thin lips, high-bridged nose, white skin), *in spite of* her Asian ethnicity. Hanna stated, 'for an Asian, her eyes are really big ...' (Line no. 28), in her account of Jasmine, positioning people with more Asian-like features (in general) as less beautiful than people with more Anglo-American features.

Finally, Hanna again discursively seems to have unconsciously positioned Japanese as superior to Chinese in some aspects by attributing Jasmine's (good) sense of dress style on the Japanese influence of a friend named Tsubasa (Line nos 34–35). In spite of Hanna's constituting Jasmine as the 'ideal', she nonetheless also did not fail to notice her physical flaws, 'her hair has become brown' (referring to hair damage caused by bleaching and dying) (Line no. 36). However, Hanna dismissed it as incidental to her overall attractiveness, 'but she is still cute' (Line no. 36), in order for her to maintain the construction of Jasmine as the ideal.

At the end of this extract, one of the girls brought the talk back to the present situation, where they were sketching their self-portraits. While the above conversation was going on, Sara had taken a small tube of real make-up foundation from her purse and was applying it to her self-portrait. One of the girls asked 'what, are you applying foundation [make-up]; are you putting foundation [on your picture], Sara?' (Line no. 39). Not only was their gendered play 'serious' (Bloustien, 2001), but it was also at times 'fun'. In the 'doing' of their embodied gendering, these girls were having fun as they experimented with adult discourses and performances (see Coates, 1999; Maybin, 2002). In applying real foundation make-up to her self-portrait, Sara was performing the 'fun play' of femininity. The representation of herself, as she would like to be portrayed, in her self-portrait, was not complete without the touch-up work of make-up. The section below further examines the self-portraits of each girl.

The self-portraits

In a continuation of the above examination of Sara's work on her self-portrait, this section briefly focuses attention on each girl's drawing that they sketched of themselves during part of the final meeting (see the portraits in Appendix 3). The choices these girls made in portraying their own face can be seen as constructions of their identity. I provided them with ample white paper and various kinds of crayons, regular and colored pencils and marker pens, and allowed them as much time as they wanted.

As shown above in Sara's self-portrait, she not only used crayons and colored pencils, which I had provided, but she also produced from her bag actual make-up foundation, which she applied to her picture just before completion, as a kind of final touch-up. Sara sketched a serious, but cute face with one of her eyes partially hidden behind her straight hair. While Sara's hair is naturally wavy, she had gotten it professionally straightened several months earlier.

Rina also portrayed her face with a lock of hair partially hiding one eye. Her self-portrait is the most realistic looking of the six and is sketched totally in pencil. Rina used a lot of fine detail, including a few identifying moles (or beauty marks). She also emphasized the waviness of her hair.

Hanna's self-portrait is drawn distinctively in a *manga/anime*-style caricature, which does not really look much like her. The large eye-lashed eyes looking off to one side and tongue protruding out the side of her mouth distinctively imitates the style of 'Peko-chan' – a popular mascot girl figure of Fujiya confectionary. Nevertheless, Hanna included a few bits of detail to personally identify her, including her cross necklace and details on her dress. Large ring earrings adorn her ears, accessories that she was indeed wearing that day. Hanna accentuated her drawing with colors, mostly featuring pink.

Naomi was the only one among the six girls who asked for more than one sheet of paper and drew four rather quick sketches of her face. At completion, she selected the one she preferred for use in this book. Her lines are simple and her picture lacks a lot of detail. Like Rina, Naomi depicted her hair as wavy.

In contrast to Naomi's and Rina's wavy hair, Anna, who had mentioned above that she does not like seeing her Anglo-American features when she looks in a mirror (see Extract 7.1), drew her portrait with very straight

Japanese-like hair, which in my view resembles her actual appearance. Her face looks out straight ahead and she has drawn her name (pseudonym) in large letters colored in pink.

Maya drew her face slightly smaller than any of the other girls, by using less of the available space on the paper. She used various colors to design a frame of hearts and flowers around her face. It seems that she focused most of the detail in the hair and eyes.

While all of the girls captured their Asian and Anglo-American ancestry in their portraits to some extent, it seems that Naomi and Rina (the two most fluent English speakers) highlighted such mixed features more than the others. However, it is also interesting to note that Anna, Hanna, Maya and Sara have all combined black and brown lines to color their hair, while Rina has depicted her hair as dark black and Naomi has only used black in drawing the outline of her hair. When I examined their photos taken on that day, Anna, Hanna, Maya and Naomi are captured with dark, blackish hair while Rina's and Sara's hair are a bit lighter, brownish color. In the photos, Anna, Hanna and Sara are captured with very straight hair and Maya, Naomi and Rina are seen with wavy hair.

While this section looked at how the girls *contested* various discourses of ethnicity and gendering, the next section looks at how the girls *celebrate* their ethnic embodiment within positive discourses of empowerment.

Adolescent Girls' Changing Bodies: Performing Embodiment and 'Fun' Femininity

This final section particularly looks at how these adolescent girls positioned themselves within the intersection of various discourses of gender and ethnicity during a period of rapid embodied maturation. Not only do I examine how these girls discursively position themselves in terms of their ethnic and gendered 'lived-body selves', but I also analyze how they enact these identities through their 'serious play' (Bloustien, 2001) and their 'fun play' with each other. This particular performance and play, which included 'body work' (Bloustien, 2001) of teasing, touching and laughter, continued on-and-off throughout the entire (three-hour) session of the Last Reunion meeting, from the start of the session until the finish.

The theme of the final meeting was to be a reunion between the girls who had not assembled all together for at least four months since Naomi and Hanna had left for Australia where they had attended a local state (public) school. They returned home to Japan a few days before the meeting – Hanna for good and Naomi for a temporary vacation before her planned return. From the very start of this final meeting, Rina, who was sitting next to Naomi, showed great interest in Naomi's recently acquired cleavage and larger breasts.

Naomi was wearing a low-cut, sleeveless shirt that she had purchased in Australia. In contrast to Australia, this kind of 'sexy' attire is only just beginning to be worn by adolescent girls in Japan. Even today, however, the under garments adorning the female body clothed in the traditional Japanese dress, the kimono, are tightly bound around the upper body in order to flatten the breasts. This is thought to enhance the beauty of the costume. Thus the more elegant kimono-wearer is not someone with large breasts or an hourglass figure (large breasts and hips with a small waist), but rather someone with a straight, svelte figure. However, young girls today generally very seldom wear kimonos; most girls these days wear their first adult-style kimono at the Coming-of-Age ceremony at age 20, which is formally held in large public halls every January.

The traditional notion of Japanese female beauty, promoted in the first two beauty contests in Japan prior to WWII, was a construction of a young feminine, fertile, healthy girl who was also pure of spirit (Robertson, 2001). In post-war Japan, the most commonly used word to refer to a desirable young girl/woman has been *kawaii* (cute). The notion of a 'sexy' hourglass figure has been thought of by Japanese as a Western-woman's body type. Only recently has the word *sekushii* (sexy) come to be heard of as a positive descriptor of young girls in Japan, disseminated through such mass-media routes as television, fashion magazines and advertising, promoting a discourse of female desirableness (and beauty) as full-breasted and sexy. Many young girls recently want to portray themselves not only as cute, *but also* as full-breasted and sexy (often without replacing cuteness with sexiness). Taken up like the newest 'fad', this newly 'imported' concept has resulted, over the last several years, in girls in Japan beginning to show more skin by wearing low-cut, spaghetti-strap clothing, or underwear-like garments, similar to that seen among youths in Western countries.

From the very start of our three-hour discussion at the Last Reunion meeting, sitting on the *tatami* mat floor around a low table, nearly every time Naomi took the floor to speak, Rina reached out and pushed Naomi's breasts from her side to accentuate them, often to the laughter of all, including Naomi, who only partially expressed annoyance by it, as will be shown in the following extract. Bloustien refers to this kind of touching 'play' as constituting, 'different forms of exploration with the body, with space, with relationships' (Bloustien, 2001: 109). Naomi, having returned from an absence overseas with a more 'feminine' body shape, attracted the attention of the other girls in the form of this playful teasing.

At the beginning of the session, Naomi responded with *'urusai'* ('you're annoying') to the laughter of all the girls. Rina asked her, *'bura shiteiru, sore'* ('are you wearing a bra, there'). Naomi answered in the affirmative and then attempted to seriously address my question as to the advantages of her participation in my project, but was again interrupted by Rina's touching and commenting *'uchi ichiban chiisai'* ('mine are the smallest'), positioning herself as less 'femininely' embodied than the other girls, particularly Naomi.

In the following extract, which occurred much later in the session, by this time all of the girls had come to focus on Naomi's newly acquired cleavage and began to playfully tease her by seeing if they could get a pencil to stand up between the cleavage of her breasts.

(Extract 7.6) Last Reunion (ages 14 and 15): 'Her cleavage can hold up pencils'

1488	**R:**	(R pushes N's breasts to accentuate them. Everyone laughs, including N)
1495	**?:**	**hasameta**
1496		(The girls try to stick a pencil into the cleavage of N's breasts to see if it holds up without dropping through)
1497	**?:**	**mou ha ha ha** (laugh)
1498	**?:**	**misetteru kara**
1499	**H:**	**nanbo hasameru ka?**
1500	**?:**	**misetteru kara**
[…]		
1508	**?:**	**yattemiteyo**
1509	**?:**	**yattemite**
1510	**?:**	**yatte, yatte, yatte** (clapping hands in rhythm as they chant)
1511	**R:**	**Sara, (?) muriyone, wa uchi to onnajide muriyanen**
1512	**?:**	**muri**
1513	**L:**	I should take a picture of it right now.
1514	**N:**	no, no (laugh) no, no, no (laugh)
1515	**?:**	**zettai kyacchiyade** (?)
1516	**N:**	**saiaku** (laugh)
1517	**?:**	**yameteyo, tokatte**
1518	**?:**	**yatteyo**
1519	**?:**	**iya**
1520	**L:**	can't find my camera
1521	**S:**	**henna puraido**
1522	**S:**	**henna puraido**

1523 S: **henna puraido**
[...]
1535 ?:   **saiakuya**
1536 L: with Rina touching it
1537 R: **Sa, S, Sara kochikara oo, oshite, tanima tsukutteageyou**
1538 L: wait, **chottomatte**
1539 R: (?) **OK sei, no, Sara sochirakara oshite**
1540 ?s: **aaaa**
(The girls yell as S and R simultaneously push N's breasts to accentuate
the cleavage)
1541 ?:   **arie hentte**
1542 L: **yokuitte, OK, chotto mouikkai** (L clicks a photo)
1543   I'm not sure how
1544 ?:   **mouikkai toka iushina**
1545 ?:   **pen hasame**
1546 N: **iya ha, ha, ha** (laugh)
1547 ?:   **kore demo hasamareruyaro**
1548 L: I'm not sure if that came out (about the photo)
1549 ?:   **mouikkai**
1550 N: **iya, yamette**
1551 S: **nani sonna henna puraido**
1552 ?s: (laugh)

(Extract 7.6*) (translation)

1488* R: (R pushes N's breasts to accentuate them. Everyone laughs,
             including N)
1495* ?:   *it holds it [the pencil]*
1496*   (The girls try to stick a pencil into the cleavage of N's breasts
             to see if it holds up without dropping through)
1497* ?:   *that's too much, ha ha ha* (laugh)
1498* ?:   *because you're showing it*
1499* H: *it will hold up many of them [pencils]*
1500* ?:   *because you're showing it*
[...]
1508* ?:   *let's try it*
1509* ?:   *let's try it*
1510* ?:   *do it, do it, do it* (clapping hands in rhythm as they chant)
1511* R: *Sara, (?) you couldn't do it, right, you are the same as me, we can't
             do that*
1512* ?:   *impossible*

1513* **L:** I should take a picture of it right now.
1514* **N:** no, no (laugh) no, no, no (laugh)
1515* **?:** *you can definitely catch it [on camera] (?)*
1516* **N:** *this is the worst [possible thing]* (laugh)
1517* **?:** *she said to stop it*
1518* **?:** *do it*
1519* **?:** *yuk*
1520* **L:** can't find my camera
1521* **S:** (to Naomi) *you have a strange pride*
1522* **S:** (to Naomi) *you have a strange pride*
1523* **S:** (to Naomi) *you have a strange pride*
[...]
1535* **N:** *it's the worst [possible thing]*
1536* **L:** with Rina touching it
1537* **R:** *Sa, S, Sara, you pu-push from that side, let's give her a cleavage*
1538* **L:** wait
1538* **L:** *wait a minute*
1539* **R:** *(?) OK, one, two, Sara, push from that side*
1540* **?:** aahhhh
(The girls yell as S and R simultaneously push N's breasts to accentuate the cleavage.)
1541* **?:** *that's strange*
1542* **L:** *that's good,* (L clicks a photo), *OK, one more time*
1543* **L:** I'm not sure how
1544* **?:** *she said to do it one more time*
1545* **?:** *stick a pen in there*
1546* **N:** *yuk, ha ha ha* (laugh)
1547* **?:** *this could be stuck this in there too*
1548* **L:** I'm not sure if that came out (about the photo)
1549* **?:** *take another one*
1550* **N:** *no, stop*
1551* **S:** *why do you have such a strange pride [about it]*
1552* **?s:** (laugh)

Analyzed within a FPDA framework in which gender is focused on as a site of struggle (Baxter, 2003), the extract above depicts performances of these adolescent girls drawing on gendered discourses (provisionally identified and named in Chapter 2) of *if you've got it, flaunt it* along with *if you flaunt it (some attribute), you deserve whatever reaction you get from people.* Also here these girls enact the gendered performance of *fun femininity* in their 'serious' and 'fun' play. Moving out of childhood discourses and into more serious and mature discourses of adulthood, these girls are beginning to explore and challenge the limitations and potentialities of their embodied identities (see Coates, 1999; Maybin, 2002).

The girls took interest in Naomi's recently developed breasts, which were very conspicuously noticeable, partly due to Naomi's choice of clothing for that day and also her posture of leaning over the low table, not to mention her actual physical maturation, which occurred during her absence. One of the girls stated two times (Line nos 1498, 1500) 'because you're showing it', positioning Naomi as deserving of such teasing due to her purposeful flaunting of herself within a discourse of 'if you flaunt it (some attribute), you deserve whatever reaction you get from people'.

The other girls discursively took up subject positions for themselves on the basis of their own embodied identities in relation to a generalized (media-produced) 'ideal' and to Naomi's body, which they constructed as 'the ideal'. Rina, who is Naomi's closest friend among the girls and who was seated next to her, instigated much of the performance. As the girls were playfully trying to see if a pencil would hold up between Naomi's breasts, Rina said, 'Sara, you couldn't do it, right, you are the same as me, we can't do that' (Line no. 1511). Rina was implying that if she or Sara were to *try* to hold up a pencil between their 'smaller' breasts, it would just drop to the ground, positioning them as less *femininely* embodied than Naomi, based on the smaller size of their breasts.

I entered the play by producing my camera and preparing to take a photo. When Naomi began to protest, Sara stated, three times, 'you have a strange pride' (Line nos 1521–1523). While the Japanese word, *puraido*, derives from the English word 'pride', it has the nuance of shame or embarrassment here. Linguistic traces can be seen of Sara drawing on a discourse of *if you've got it, flaunt it* in her positioning of Naomi as 'strangely proud', implying that Naomi *should be* proud of her feminine embodiment, and not ashamed of it. Sara positioned Naomi as *strange* for not recognizing and demonstratively celebrating and freely flaunting the cultural capital of her (feminine) embodied self.

Again, I entered to help co-construct the interactions here by jokingly asking Naomi to remove her glasses. This action on my part was contextualized by an event that took place earlier in the session that day when we had taken a recess to go outside so that Naomi's mother and I could take some photos of the girls. As Naomi had forgotten to remove her glasses for the photos, she had insisted that we take them all over again. This was what prompted me above to request that she take off her glasses. Naomi accepted my request and removed her glasses. Then, just as I was getting ready to take the photo, Rina told Sara to 'push from that side, let's give her a cleavage' (Line no. 1537). Just as they did so, I snapped a photo. I then called for one more photo, but Naomi refused to pose for a second shot. Then Sara asked for the fourth time, 'why do you have such a strange pride about it?' (Line no. 1551) again positioning Naomi as 'strangely proud' within a discourse of *if you've got it, flaunt it*, where according to Sara, Naomi should be proud to flaunt what she's got. At the same time, Sara also implicitly positioned herself as being less femininely embodied compared with Naomi. Some tension in the 'serious play' may have been created as Sara, Rina and some others may have felt themselves to be in a position of powerlessness in comparison to Naomi's greater 'feminine endowments'.

Looking at this passage within a discourse analytic framework (Edley, 2001; Edwards & Potter, 1992; Horton-Salway, 2001; Wetherell, 1986, 1998), this co-constructed play among the girls reveals two juxtaposed gendered interpretive repertoires used in the talk of these girls:

> you have a strange pride (Line nos 1521–1523, 1551) [for not flaunting yourself more]
> ('if you've got it, flaunt it' discourse)

and

> because you're showing it (Line nos 1498, 1500) [you're asking for this foul-play]
> ('if you flaunt it [some attribute], you deserve whatever reaction you get from people' or 'blame the victim' discourse).

These two repertoires interact as an ideological dilemma if we interpret this positioning as a co-construction, as it is not always clear who used which repertoires or if they were even expressed by the same person or not. While this ideological dilemma, paradox or nexus of 'competing discourses' (Baxter, 2003) can be said to occur for all girls in general, here we witness it, as it occurred, in the speech of these girls. One commonsensical notion expressed here states that one should be proud of one's good points and one should show them off so that others can see them. Generally, this repertoire is used to refer to the flaunting of physical features, particularly one's attractive or 'sexy' attributes. The other commonsensical notion contradicts this. If you are not careful to hide your attractiveness (or sexiness), you risk being the brunt of aggression or foul play, of which *you* will be responsible. In its extreme form, this is the quintessential defense of the rapist, 'She was asking for it'. One of the girls present has produced a much less threatening, but similar commonsensical repertoire in order to justify her (and everyone else's) teasing of Naomi. Bloustien (2001) also observed this 'paradox' of adolescent girls who work hard to be in the public gaze – to be attractive and to gain attention, while at the same time who must maintain 'vigilance' in not attracting the unsolicited gaze of sexual harassment or violence. Bloustien writes:

> The moral dimension within the discourse of femininity is particularly powerful and circulates through the cultural texts that target young women. It places the responsibility of sexual control firmly on the young women herself ... If she is too daring in self-presentation then she runs the risk of social condemnation. To be acknowledged as attractive equates with being regarded as 'sexy' but this immediately becomes an area of conflict in terms of a girl's appearance. (Bloustien, 2001: 119)

This gendered play took place within a *safe* atmosphere involving a gendered performance of 'fun femininity' which is mainly closed to in-groups of (heterosexual) girls only. It was a discursive celebration of their femininity and their solidarity as femininely self-positioned girls. Naomi, while being the brunt of the joke, also celebrated this 'fun femininity' as she appeared to be only very slightly annoyed at times by the attention focused on her, laughing throughout and resisting only ever so subtly. This playfulness was not limited to these few selected extracts, but continued from time to time throughout the entire meeting in which discussion of breasts and performance of embodiment emerged between our other more focused talk. Bloustien (2001: 107), in referring to the 'joy of physicality' among adolescent girls, noted how girls of this age, compared with adult women, are much more free, relaxed, silly and uncontrolled with their physicality in their individual body movements and in contact with each other.

Several turns later, this 'fun femininity' continued with Rina remaining attentive to the embodied changes of Naomi in relation to her own less-changed body, focusing on Naomi's body, instead of her words. Rina again stated, 'we used to be the same size', showing her envy as well. A few minutes later, Rina again repeatedly brought up the same point:

R: uchi, uchi onaji ookisa yatten de, Ausutoraria iku mae wa
I, I was the same size as her, before she went to Australia

Rina was emphasizing a connection between Naomi's newly embodied attractiveness (and physical maturation) and her (four-month) outside-of-Japan residence. Several lines after this, another girl positioned herself as 'small'. Finally, Naomi began to protest, saying '*sawanna, sawanna, sawanna*' ('don't touch, don't touch, don't touch') as she came to more explicitly contest being objectified in this manner, toward the end of the final session that day.

Underlying this play, these girls were performing their gendered identities while at the same time positively constituting their ethnic identities. Rina repeatedly made mention of Naomi having returned from overseas with larger breasts, which she enviously constituted as positive and valuable. Linguistic traces of a discourse of foreign attractiveness (particularly, white-Western beauty) were examined earlier where the girls were seen constituting their white heritage as endowing them with bigger (and thus better) breasts, in comparison to Japanese who they positioned as plain (see Extract 7.3; Line no. 1107).

I have given much space here to this teasing play among the girls, which focused on their changing bodies partly because of the prominence of their actions occurring throughout the entire last meeting. While there were no explicit references to ethnicity in the extract above, the girls implicitly constituted their ethno-gendered identities through various references to the outside-of-Japan influence on Naomi's embodied attractiveness. This occurred within the context of their earlier constructions, which revealed linguistic traces of a discourse of foreign attractiveness in connection with the 'nice body style' of having large breasts. These earlier positionings might suggest that Naomi's sudden 'sexy' embodiment was not only constructed by these girls as a mere result of maturation over the passage of time, but also as a consequence of her being ethnicity associated with a culture outside of Japan.

The participants' self-reflections of change

This final extract taken from the final meeting examines the girls' self-reflections of change. They were reflecting on what they had gained through the process of this study in assembling together and talking about themselves. In the following extract, they talked not only about the meetings, but also how they felt they had changed in general over that time.

(Extract 7.7) Last Reunion (ages 14 and 15): 'I had never thought about how I felt before'

320	H:	minna ga jibun no jinshu, toiuka, nanka,
321		sono jibun ga haafu yatte koto ni tsuite
322		douiu fuu ni omottenno ka shiru no ga omoshirokatta
323	L:	umm, uh-huh
324	H:	owari (laugh)

325   L: OK, hai, OK, hai, Maya
326   M: hee (..) heee, mou Rina to meccha isshode, nanka ima made
327   jibun ga kangaeta you no ga kangaehenkatta you na koto
328   bakkari o nanka atsumatte, minna de
329   S: minna de ki point dayone
330   M: mmm, minna de, hanashi aeta no wa yokattashi
331   ?:   itsumo
332   M: nanka mawari no hito no mite,
333   mirarekata to ka
334   amari kangaeta koto nakatta kara
335   ?:   [(?) watashi mo so] na kanji ya

(Extract 7.7*) (translation)

320*   H: *everyone, their own race, that is, somehow,*
321*   *about ourselves being half*
322*   *it was interesting knowing how we [all] feel about that*
323*   L: *umm, uh-huh*
324*   H: *that's all* (laugh)
325*   L: *OK, yes, OK, yes, Maya*
326*   M: *yah (..) yaaa, I feel completely like Rina, somehow, until now*
327*   *I had never thought about how I felt before,*
328*   *talking about these things, getting together with everyone*
329*   S: *the key point was [that it was] all of us*
330*   M: *mmm, with everyone, I am glad that we could all get together*
             and talk
331*   ?:   *always*
332*   M: *like looking at those around us*
333*   *and how they view us, and things*
334*   *because I had never thought much about those things before*
335*   ?:   (?) *it was that way with me too*

In expressing what she had gained from our meetings together, Hanna used the word *jinshuu* (race) (Line no. 320), a word that did not appear elsewhere throughout the entire dataset. Then in the same turn (Line no. 321), as if to correct herself, she switched to the word *haafu* in referring to herself and the other girls. The girls here seemed to be co-constructing the notion that up until these arranged meetings, they had not really thought deeply about their being half/double and what it meant to them.

When I called on Maya to respond to my question concerning what, if anything she had gained from the meetings, Maya explicitly referred to a statement Rina had made earlier (not shown here) about not having really thought about her ethnicity until now (Line nos 326–328). Then Sara stated that the key point of the meetings for her was that it created an opportunity for them to all get together (Line no. 329). Then Maya quickly agreed, co-constructing that she was glad to be able to talk about issues which were relevant to them, but which they had not really discussed in great detail before, such as how they were viewed in society and how they viewed society and themselves.

It seems that these meetings had a positive effect on the girls as they reflected upon not only their chance to get together and meet their best friends, but also to talk about issues specifically relevant to their lives and the society in which they reside. While during the time-span of the study, as the girls went through tremendous physical, mental and emotional changes, their ethnic identities also seemed to have gone through a significant process of maturation and change.

This chapter, focusing on how the girls identified themselves in terms of their gendered and ethnic embodiment, mostly featured data from the latter meetings. The theme of body consciousness took prominence in the final meeting. The topic of discussion often turned to ethno-gendered assertions of their identities, which had not been expressed to this degree in earlier meetings.

Summary

In this chapter, I have focused on how these girls discursively identified themselves by means of their positioning and performances based on their *gendered* and *ethnic embodiment* (ethnicized body selves), and how they *combined gender with ethnicity* in the construction of their identities in response to the third central question.

As the girls moved, over time, out of childhood and into adolescent girlhood and underwent rapid physical and maturational development, they came to draw on a wider range of available ethnic and gendered discourses. Constantly attracting the stare of others, they at times enacted their Japaneseness within a 'discourse of conformity', calling up the Japanese proverb: 'The nail that sticks up gets hammered down'. At other times, they celebrated their diversity and constructed for themselves the privileged 'embodied' positioning of ethnic exoticness while simultaneously rejecting being constituted as the marked 'outsider'. There was not always a clear separation of gender and ethnicity in how they positioned themselves within gender and ethnic discourses, especially in regard to their embodied identities at the site of the body.

Drawing on the tools and terminologies of both DP (Edley, 1997, 2001; Edley & Wetherell, 2008; Horton-Salway, 2001) and FPDA (Baxter, 2003), I showed how the gendered embodied identities of these girls are inextricably intertwined with their ethnic embodied selves. We examined, through the frame of FPDA, how these girls drew on various discourses of both ethnicity and gender. Also, within DP, we explored how they used interpretive repertoires and ideological dilemmas in their speech as well as other discursive tools in order to give accounts and to position themselves positively. Furthermore, we conceptualized the construction of identity by drawing on the overlap between these two frameworks.

As adolescent girls constantly confronting issues of 'how they look', the issue of their ethnic embodiment could not be denied. The multiperspective examination of their discursive interactions of talk, performance and play allowed a window into how these girls constituted their ethnogendered embodied identities.

The question of how these girls discursively gave accounts, represented and positioned themselves and others in their identification of their ethnic selves was also addressed in this chapter. I showed how these girls moved from their earlier dilemmas within less empowering limited discourses of homogeneity and conformity to more self-enhancing alternative discourses of diversity and interculturalism in the constitution of their ethnogendered embodied selves. The girls had to work hard over time in order to overcome controlling social discourses. But the girls showed that they were at times able to resist being *interpellated* (Althusser, 1971) as subjects positioned within limiting discourses by asserting their agency to break through and deconstruct the structures holding together the dominant discourses (Derrida, 1976). They often accomplished this by re-positioning themselves in other more empowering alternative discourses.

Analysis of the data revealed how these girls created and positioned their own embodied identities in relation to others whom they constructed as the 'idealized other'. Within this construction, Hanna was also seen in the process of unconsciously othering others. She did so even as she contested her own marginalization as 'the ethnicized other', and while also at the same time constituting a 'Chinese' girl as 'ideally' ethnically attractive. She drew on intersecting and conflicting discourses of homogeneity and Japanese conformity (in her positioning of Chinese) as well as ethnic diversity and *gaijin* attractiveness.

Furthermore, I investigated the question of how these girls discursively *celebrated* their ethnicity. In their talk about the representation of the referent *gaijin* in a children's book, the girls revealed their recognition and knowledge of the occurrence of racializing and deficit discourses of ethnicity in society. Not only were these girls shown here to contest such representations, but they were also shown to celebrate their ethnic embodied cultural capital within a discourse of ethnic attractiveness.

Finally, I examined the gendered play of 'fun femininity' as these girls celebrated and constructed their hybrid embodied cultural capital. An ideological dilemma appeared in the interaction between the girls over the representation of their embodied capital. While discursively revealing some serious play, this interaction also involved femininity, which was performed as fun 'body' play as these girls confronted their ever maturing embodied identities.

Notes

1. Rina's switch into English may be explained in terms of Japanese adult norms where complimenting someone directly in this manner would come across as an interpersonal *faux pas*. Such behavior may be interpreted as a negative violation of 'moderation' and *enryo* (restraint) documented as characteristic behaviors in Japanese interpersonal communication (LoCastro, 1990: 121). In the context of her mixed-ethnic peers, Rina may have seemed comfortable drawing on this intercultural form of interpersonal communication, but perhaps it felt more natural switching into an English frame to deliver a direct compliment.
2. Parts of the sections 'Yearning to be Embodied Like Another: The Idealized Other' and 'Adolescent Girls' Changing Bodies: Performing Embodiment and 'Fun' Femininity' (parts of Extracts 7.5 and 7.6, and earlier versions of the analysis; also parts of Extract 4.16b) have been previously published (Kamada, 2008) and have been reproduced here with permission from Palgrave Macmillan.

Chapter 8

Discursive Construction of Hybrid Identity in Japan: Where has it Taken Us?

Introduction

This final chapter highlights the relationship between the questions posed at the beginning of this book, the theoretical framework upon which this study is based and the results of the data analysis. The 'truth' that is represented here is contextualized on the basis of the talk of six participants and me, situated within a certain site at a particular moment in time. It was stimulated by my search for answers to several research questions that grew out of my own personal experiences and previous research within this community. Within this context, in this concluding chapter, I present to my readers both limitations, as well as important implications of this study. I examine questions originally elicited by myself, but co-constructed in the voices of my participants. In summarizing the findings of this study here, I point out the weaknesses and strengths. Most importantly, I situate this study within the fields of PDA, gender and feminist studies, DP, and hybridity studies in general, and in particular, within the specific site of Japan. Furthermore, I also draw attention to the growing interest in multiperspective approaches to discourse analysis.

Limitations and Reflexivity

One of my main purposes throughout this book has been to allow the voices of the participants to be heard, who otherwise might not have been noticed, a component central to FPDA theory (Baxter, 2003). While my voice too has appeared throughout the data in this research as the seventh participant, I have tried to remain reflexive in reporting how I have obtained the data and how I have come to analyze it. Within a constructionist framework, I acknowledge that these same data could potentially have been analyzed with a different view.

With this in mind, I recognize that the study has some limitations and weaknesses regarding the interpretation of the data that need pointing out. First of all, the limited scope of this work warrants mention. As this study only involved six participants, I do not try to make general sweeping arguments for all mixed-ethnic (*haafu/daburu*) adolescent girls in Japan. This study was conducted in a particular location, at a particular point in time, to a particular group of six girls and under certain circumstances that may contribute to making this study unique to these conditions. Having said that, I do not see these six middle-class Japanese/white girls as atypical of the 'population' from which they were drawn, in terms of socio-economic status, access to opportunities and choices, and the type of spread-out English-speaking foreign community within the larger Japanese community in which they reside.

I have contributed to the co-construction of ethnic identity along with these participants in the interaction of our talk. Throughout, I have taken account of my input and the intentional suggestions and questions, which I posed to the group in order to stimulate discussion. While to a large extent, I was able to collect extremely rich data by guiding the discussion in ways that 'naturally occurring data' might not have provided, my unreserved approach in which I occasionally spoke out as another participant may be viewed by some as a drawback of the study. Throughout, however, I have not tried to diminish the role that I myself played in this co-construction and I have attempted to analyze my own discursive input and interaction in the data.

My own particular subject positioning based on my ethnic, linguistic, generational and historical background, which I brought to the study, must also be mentioned as influencing factors in my contextualized search for 'truth' and 'knowledge' as I see it. While trying to remain as reflexive as possible throughout in examining the data, I acknowledge that at times my analysis of the data may be challenged on the grounds of reading into the data what might not be interpreted in the same way by someone else. This is one of the biggest challenges of qualitative research methodology where it is important to clearly show the reader not only *what* knowledge was gleaned from the analysis of the data, but also *how* the knowledge was attained (Hertz, 1997a). Where I have failed to convince my reader of how I analyzed a certain section of the data, I have fallen short.

Where this Study has Taken Us

This study was conducted in order to understand how mixed-ethnic adolescent girls in Japan discursively constitute their ethnic identities. It was intended that this study shed more light not only on hybrid identity in Japan, but also the *approaches* to analyzing discourse in the assessment of this ethnic identity. The three central questions of this study have been problematized: the dilemmas and tensions of hybridity, the celebration of hybridity and the intersection of hybridity and gender (at the site of the body). By re-addressing these central questions, this section examines where this study has taken us in terms of hybrid identity studies, gender and feminist studies and discourse analytic approaches.

Studies of hybrid identity

This book has explored hybridity (also referred to in other contexts as studies of children/people of 'mixed racial descent', 'mixed-ethnicity', 'multiethnicity', 'multi-/biraciality', 'mixed-parentage'), first, by examining a non-European/non-North American model: Japan. While various research studies using discursive approaches to analyzing ethnic identities have appeared in non-Asian contexts (e.g. Katz, 1996; Mama, 1995; Phoenix & Owen, 2000; Sebba, 1993; van Dijk, 1987, 1991, 1993; Wetherell & Potter, 1992), this study has led the way into research on hybrid identity within Japan.

The first central question asked: 'Are there any tensions or dilemmas in the ways children (adolescent girls) of Japanese and "white" mixed-parentage in Japan identify themselves in terms of their ethnicity? If so, what are they and how do these girls constitute themselves?' This study has shown how mixed-ethnic adolescent girls come to draw on a wider range of discourses of ethnicity available to them as they mature. But they do this through a process of struggle and tension in their shifting self-positionings within various intersecting discourses of ethnicity constituting their multiplicity of selves. We witnessed a range of ethnic subject positionings taken up by these six girls. In Hanna and Anna's talk among themselves (Extract 7.1), we saw them working to position themselves as 'Japanese' in their rejection of being constituted as *gaijin* as they co-constructed their ethnicities within discourses of homogeneity and conformity. At the same time, Anna, 'disgusted' and 'shocked' by the view of herself in the mirror, positioned her own ethnically embodied self as 'the other'.

This has shown how the constitution of hybrid identity is not a clear and simple unchanging aspect of one's being, but a difficult process of struggle and hard work, which can alter and shift depending on the context and interactions with others.

This book also clarified how these girls negotiated their identities in terms of their managed control over their *difference* when constituted as 'bad difference'. Some of them claimed 'good difference' for themselves by constituting themselves as *different* in a *good* sense within discourses of diversity and interculturalism. Naomi reclaimed this word *difference* for herself and turned it into *good* difference in her constitution of her ethnic identity. In her 'doing difference', she positioned herself as 'better' than her Japanese 'friends' at school on the basis of this good difference which was not accessible to her Japanese peers. Naomi self-positioned herself as peripheral within her school in her performance of difference where she distanced herself from seeking to become popular. Here it was shown how *popularity*, which was made inaccessible to her, also became 'undesirable' to her, as she came to appropriate her differentness as her independence (see Eckert, 1993).

The question of *who/what they are* did not come with a ready answer for these girls. The various memberships that these girls held were either foregrounded or backgrounded depending on contextual situations and the communities in which they were engaged. It was not always easy for them to articulate exactly what they were, but what was demonstrated was that they did not want to be constituted by others, especially as 'the marked outsider'. *What they are* was something they wanted to determine by themselves as the situation arose. Even as Naomi consistently performed her difference within Japanese society, she did not deny her Japaneseness. She positioned herself as 'two people ... one of them in Japan and the other one in America'. She did not try to privilege one of her identities over the other, as her identity was clearly unfixed and contingent on the context in which she interacted with others. This study has shown how mixed-ethnic adolescent girls in Japan constituted and categorized themselves within *multimemberships* in complex and diverse ways in the negotiation of their identities, which could not be narrowly defined in singular terms.

The second central question asked: 'How, if at all, do children (adolescent girls) of Japanese and "white" mixed-parentage in Japan celebrate their ethnicity? How, if at all, do they construct ethnic (and gendered) cultural, symbolic, linguistic and social capital for themselves on the basis of their hybrid identities?' While I have been influenced by various earlier studies of ethnic and hybrid identity, this study is original in looking at participants whose subjectivities were simultaneously constituted as 'othered'/marginalized on the one hand, and also on the other hand as *celebrated* in terms of a *double dominance*. As demonstrated in this book, these girls created and enjoyed a constructed social positioning of dominance in terms of the double aspects of their native nationality/heritage dominance along with their foreign and white-Western dominance. This uncommon positioning gave these girls a means to take control of 'othering' and to create privileged cultural, symbolic, linguistic and social capital for themselves on the basis of their two ethnicities, both of which they constituted (and were constituted by others) as dominant. This study has helped us to realize that even girls marginalized as 'the other' or positioned as deficient or different (in a bad way), can re-negotiate this positioning to one of triumph and empowerment, which integrates their 'double dominance' into an unfixed subjectivity of their 'double' selves.

Even though many of the participants were not particularly proficient in English, they nevertheless positioned themselves as privileged in their possession of cultural and linguistic capital of English proficiency and its attendant high-status position. They took up the opportunity to demonstrate their English abilities when given the chance among their other mixed-ethnic peers. Their 'Englishing' (Joseph, 2002) or their 'doing English' (Pennycook, 2007) was a means through which they were able to create and celebrate positive linguistic capital. They worked to constitute themselves and each other as 'owners' of this capital, which for them was more than just knowledge of entrance-examination skills; their English ability gave them access to information, knowledge and literature, which was not available to most of their Japanese peers. It allowed them to positively position themselves as special, more fluent and more mature, and to connect their bilinguality with higher thinking skills such as the ability to comprehend difficult and complex stories in a second language.

Their outside-of-school friendship with one another was another form of important cultural and social capital for them, giving them a world larger than school and neighborhood associations. Through these friendships, they were able to open up to each other and to share similar experiences and feelings of solidarity as they dealt with issues of marginalization and othering in society. It was shown in their talk together, how they co-constructively overcame situations of disempowerment through their mutual support. These girls also discursively created the cultural and symbolic capital of choice and job opportunity as they positioned themselves as having an option of 'two nationalities' and of being in a situation where things were 'not already decided'.

I have also addressed a gap in the limited studies conducted on hybrid identity in Japan by examining girls who attend Japanese schools, rather than immersion (Bostwick, 1999, 2001) or international schools

(Greer, 2001, 2003). Within this context of regular Japanese schools, this book examined how mixed-ethnic girls in Japan avoid standing out as different or peculiar. They were shown to negotiate their identities in their daily lives among their Japanese peers at their schools not only on the basis of their ethnic identity, but also identities of gender, class and popularity within school-group dynamics.

While group identity at school is an important aspect of life also in America, Europe and elsewhere (Finders, 1997; Orenstein, 1994; Simmons, 2002), some particular features of this phenomenon in the context of Japan and in the talk of these girls appeared. The Japanese notion of *hamideru*, which emerged many times during the early part of the data collection period, epitomized the importance of being included in groups at school. This notion of *hamideru* took on several nuances from *standing out, being left out, being yourself* to *being the odd one out*. The commonplace Japanese proverb (or repertoire): 'the nail that sticks up, gets hammered down', was shown to be linked to this notion of *hamideru*, which binds social behavior in terms of social status, gender and ethnicity for these girls. Rina and Naomi equated 'being yourself' with 'standing out', implying that one has to hide one's 'real self' in order to avoid standing out. However, for these girls, it was impossible for them to hide their physical selves – the way they look. They had to constantly work to negotiate their identities within the anti-social behavior of 'being different' and of standing out at school, especially to avoid censure and bullying by boys. Hanna related how she was unable to break free of the disempowering control of the boys at school who had forced her, for fear of bullying, to join one of two groups at school, both of which she constituted negatively.

In order to deconstruct marginalizing dominant discourses of ethnicity, particularly Rina and Naomi were shown in many instances to position themselves within other alternative discourses, which privileged them over their Japanese peers. They tended to create an us–them frame with themselves as the *haafu/daburu* privileged insider and Japanese people as 'the other'. Rina constituted her Japanese girl peers at school as mentally less mature, engaging in the 'low-level stuff' of playing outdoors and playing in the snow, compared with the more 'mentally mature' mixed-ethnic girls who stay inside and listen to music and talk. Naomi positioned her peers at school as 'really sad', 'disgusting' and 'below' her. Clearly invoking a globalizing discourse of interculturalism, Naomi applauded and privileged her 'good difference', which has allowed her to 'see a lot more of the world'.

While to a large extent they took their Japaneseness as unremarkable and ordinary, it was their mixed-ethnicity (including its non-Japanese exotic white-Westernness), which they celebrated as exceptional and special, by virtue of the various forms of capital resources to which they have privileged access. They are Japanese, but they are also more than just Japanese. They positioned their mixed-ethnic selves *not* as being deficient in ethnic cultural capital, but as being abundant in it. These girls also created the cultural capital of positive femininity and attractive *ethnic embodiment* as they co-constructed discourses of diversity and 'foreign' attractiveness in their self-enhancing personal positioning based on their physicality. They positioned themselves, each other and other *haafu/ daburu* girls, in general, as ethnically attractive with nicely sculptured faces (*hori ga fukai*).

In this book, I have identified several, as yet, unnamed discourses of ethnicity in Japan, which affect this group in question. A discourse of interculturalism was one of several discourses identified and named in this book. Reconceptualized from earlier discourses of 'openness to the outside world' and 'internationalization' (*kokusaika*), this post-modern discourse of interculturalism has come into being in Japan in recent years. Impacted by the effects of globalization, this discourse encompasses a scope extending beyond national boundaries and ideologies.

It was shown how these girls draw on this discourse in their talk and how they created positive aspects of interculturality and *intercultural savvy* for themselves as a result of having greater access to information (in more than one language); relatives, connections and experiences beyond the borders of Japan; mixed-ethnic girl friendships in outside-of-school settings; access to a greater array of available choices and opportunities; and parental support and understanding concerning intercultural and international activities. Not only did they create forms of capital resources in a general sense in their categorizations of hybridity, but also they co-constructively and personally positioned themselves and each other in positive discourses of ethnicity, as they distinguished themselves from the 'ordinariness' of 'Japanese' people who do not enjoy this *special* capital.

Gender and feminist studies

Along with ethnic studies, this book is also situated within gender and feminist studies that examine *embodiment* at the site of the body. The third central question asked: 'How, if at all, do children (adolescent girls) of Japanese and "white" mixed-parentage in Japan discursively identify themselves in terms of their positioning and performances based on their gendered and ethnic embodiment (their ethnicized body selves)?' While interest in recent years in gender and feminist studies on *embodiment* has been increasing, as yet there have been few studies that have set out to problematize aspects of both gendered and ethnic embodied identities of ethnic minorities in a Far-East-Asian context, as this study has done. This study found that while the participant girls of this study worked hard to conform to the *norms of Japanese behavior*, conforming to the *norms of physical appearance* was something that was beyond their agency and out of their control, as they recurrently attracted the stare and notice of others due to their conspicuous hybrid features.

In several extracts, the girls were seen taking up both ethnic and gendered identities at the same time – a concept referred to in this study as 'ethno-gendering'. An example was presented where Rina constructed mixed-ethnic boys, in the example of her brother, as being more socially restricted, in that as boy and as mixed-ethnic, her brother has less room to 'be himself' compared with girls, like her. Rina, as a mixed-ethnic girl, is allowed to 'stand out' without having to face bullying to the degree that she would have to endure if she had been born a boy. As girl, she does not have to try to be as 'Japanese' as her brother, and can exert her 'ethnic difference' with more freedom.

In search of their own subjective ethnically embodied selves, the girls of this study created the notion of the 'idealized other'. They were seen creating and emulating the idealized *ethnically embodied* other, at times idealizing others among themselves and at times others outside of their group. Particularly during the last meeting, these girls often spoke about Sara as the idealized mixed-ethnic beauty with her deeply sculptured face and deep-set eyes (*hori ga fukai*), facial features and 'good body style'. Naomi, having returned from overseas with a newly acquired cleavage, was likewise constituted as the embodied 'idealized other'. Hanna also talked at length about a girl named Jasmine, her ethnically embodied 'idealized other' – a Chinese/Japanese girl, four years her senior. Even though Jasmine was Asian, Hanna constituted her as attractive and Caucasian-like, with features of big eyes, thin lips, high-bridged nose and white skin. In this study, we examined a clear example, occurring in the talk of the girls, of what Bloustien (2001) referred to as the importance of the role of emulating and 'being' the 'idealized other' in the process of understanding one's own self.

Throughout this book, we looked at how these girls constituted their ethnic identities not only in terms of their use of discursive tools to privilege themselves and to create positive cultural capital, but also in the ways in which they positioned and performed their ethnic embodied selves. The 'body work' (Bloustien, 2001) of teasing, touching and laughter was played out by these girls through a blending together of their ethnic and gendered identities. Over this period of rapid embodied maturation, these girls underwent visible changes, some sooner and more pronounced than others, of which they were eager to explore, not just in the language of words, but in a physical, bodily, touching way. These girls eagerly engaged in 'the joy of physicality' (Bloustien, 2001) in a non-sexual, free, relaxed and fun play in coming in contact with and touching each other physically. This was particularly evident during the entire session of the last meeting when the girls were 14 and 15 years old. Rina was seen throughout the data unabashedly and freely touching Naomi every time the attention turned to Naomi when it was her turn to speak. Whereas in earlier sessions, Rina had constituted Sara as ethnically attractive on the basis of her 'deep-set' (Caucasian-like) eyes, later she constituted Naomi as having 'a nice body', while at the same time positioning herself as less femininely embodied.

Change in the girls over time

Another point of significance in this book was the examination of how these girls changed over time. While many studies have taken up how, as girls mature, they become better at contesting and mitigating various subject positions and instead take up alternative positions (Bloustien, 2001; Coates, 1999; Eckert, 1993, 2000; Maybin, 2002), this study investigated how this group of mixed-ethnic girls in Japan discursively matured as they learned to cope with ethnic slurs and name-calling (see Chapter 6). The data collection period, which covered several years, followed these girls out of childhood and into the rapid physical and mental growth period of early adolescence. It coincided with a time when they were highly conscious of being in the public gaze and a time when they often were confronted with issues of acceptance and popularity at their schools.

At the Birthday meeting (ages 13 and 14), I noted in field notes my impression of dramatic changes seen in these girls since our previous meeting six months earlier. This project started with a group of girls mainly associated through Rina's network of friends who only very rarely all met together at the same time. However, through the process of this study, they may have become a *community of practice* (see Lave & Wenger, 1991; Wenger, 1998) where their shared identities and practices have come to unite them into a community and impel them to want to continue meeting. If this study has helped in some way to shape the attitudes and self-images of the girls positively, in ways that might not have developed had these get-togethers not occurred, then I feel that this is another important contribution and fruitful outcome of this type of research. My purpose throughout has been to forefront their voices, which might have not been otherwise heard, to illuminate how these girls search for ways to empower themselves, and to contribute to empowering them during this extremely sensitive and changing time of their early adolescence. Over the several-year span of this study, I was able to follow these girls out of childhood and into their early adolescence. A window was opened into the ways in which these girls' gender and ethnic identities developed and changed, and was documented in an unfolding storyline narrated in the girls' own voices.

Multiperspectival approaches to discourse analysis: FPDA and DP

This study is situated within the growing genre of multiperspectival research frameworks that combine more than one discourse analytic approach. By analyzing the data both through the lens of DP as well as FPDA, a broader understanding of the dynamics behind the constitution of hybrid identity was gained through the unique contributions of each of these approaches. As well, I have integrated CDA into part of the analysis in explaining discourses and the 'order of discourse' surrounding non-Japanese (foreign) ethnicity in Japan. The complementary nature of these approaches, which overlapped each other in similar basic theoretical and methodological features, allowed further insight into hybrid identity.

First, from a FPDA point of view – which emphasizes how people position themselves within competing discourses based on fluctuating contextual situations – we witnessed linguistic traces of these girls moving away from reliance on a more limited array of discourses. The girls spoke of being constrained during elementary school within discourses of homogeneity, Japanese conformity, 'halfness' and *gaijin* 'otherness'. Later, the girls were able to break out of these constraints as they came to access more empowering alternative gendered and ethnic discourses of diversity and interculturality as they began to mature both mentally and physically. For example, in several data extracts, we witnessed the girls' narratives of how during elementary school they were helpless to empower themselves when marginalized as *gaijin* within a singular ethnic discourse of homogeneity and then how they were later able to re-position and empower themselves by gaining access to alternative discourses of diversity and interculturalism.

Within DP – which particularly focuses on the discursive functions and tools employed in the construction of ethnic identities – we examined how these girls utilized various rhetorical stances in order to re-position themselves from being marginalized by others. It was shown how these girls were able to shift the marginality onto the name-callers and marginalizers as they progressively worked through their negotiations of identity. They showed how they were able to stand up to the 'bullies' who had tried to marginalize them and instead position those people as the 'sickening' and 'stupid' *others*. They were also seen positioning themselves in elevated positions of 'better' and 'more mature' as they worked to break free from being bullied and to positively empower themselves. Rina recounted how she was able over time to re-position a 'bully' into 'a really nice guy' and hold on to the friendship. Naomi came to the situation already empowered by brushing off ethnic slurs in which she saw the bullies as just using it 'as an excuse' or to try to find a weak point where they could intimidate her in a fight. Naomi showed how she could stand her ground, already knowing their strategy in advance.

The simultaneous use of these two complementary approaches of FPDA and DP has been helpful in deepening our understanding of hybrid identity. Both approaches, based on social constructionist poststructuralist (Foucauldian) theoretical frameworks, were shown to use the notion of subjectivity and subject positioning to explain the non-fixed nature of human identity construction. This study explored how these two approaches apply both micro- and macro-analysis to spoken data in order to gain a more integrated picture of how identities are discursively constructed and simultaneously constituted within historically produced discourses. It was shown how such discourses may be taken up, challenged, contested or changed in the present within contextualized interactions between people.

What DP refers to as 'repertoires', FPDA refers to as 'discourses', and may be simply described as 'ways of seeing the world' (Sunderland, 2004: 6). In the data of this study, we saw the participants drawing on the *competing gendered discourses* of 'if you've got it, flaunt it' and 'if you flaunt it (some attribute), you deserve whatever reaction you get from people' (or 'a blame the victim discourse'). Within DP, this was explained as two gendered interpretive repertoires: 'you have a strange pride [for not flaunting yourself more]' and 'because you're showing it [you're asking for this foul-play]'. These two interpretive repertoires represented an ideological dilemma – two commonsensical notions that express different ideological views of the situation at the same time. While both approaches of FPDA and DP are still in a process of development, this study has shown the complementariness of the simultaneous use of these two compatible frameworks.

Increasingly, studies are beginning to appear, which utilize and promote multiperspective approaches in analyzing discourse. A particular form of DP that strongly promotes integration with *conversation analysis* is gaining impetus (see Kitzinger, 2008; Speer, 2005; Stokoe, 2008). However, outside of this present study, few studies have combined aspects of DP with *(F)PDA* (others include Edley, 2001; Edley & Wetherell, 2008; Kamada, 2008). This present study has contributed to the set of studies that are only just beginning to appear in which these two approaches of (F)PDA and DP are combined with fruitful results and few tensions into a viable multiperspective methodology. Here the emphasis is on the analysis of how people use discursive tools to perform their identities and position themselves, and also how competing discourses (also repertoires or ideological dilemmas) appear as linguistic traces in their talk.

In this study, the viability of incorporating the notion of *ethnicity* into Baxter's (2003) FPDA, as a methodological and theoretical discourse analysis approach has been substantiated. Whereas Baxter's FPDA specifically focuses on how women or girls are multiply positioned, I have adapted and extended this theoretical notion by exploring not only gender identities, but also ethnic identities. One of the central outcomes of this study has been to elucidate the ways in which these girls are not only positioned powerlessly within a singular dominant marginalizing discourse of ethnicity in Japan, but how they also are relatively powerful within other competing alternate discourses of ethnicity. While these girls struggled to contest ethnic marginalization during their elementary school years within more limited discourses of homogeneity, conformity, 'foreignness' and 'halfness', this study has highlighted how over time, they came to be able to position themselves within a wider array of more empowering discourses of diversity, interculturalism and ethnic attractiveness enabling them to create and celebrate positive cultural capital based on their ethnicity.

I feel that I have overcome many challenging obstacles in getting a single group of adolescents to assemble and cooperate consistently over an extended period of time over several years, without the convenience of an already established venue where they regularly meet. It was difficult planning for the meeting at a distance and assembling them together over long distances throughout the expansive Morita region where they lived, far from one another. The venues, discussions and activities had to be arranged so that the girls would be motivated to attend again and again, in spite of their usually hectic schedules and priorities in their lives. I managed this by addressing their agendas of having fun and enjoying the company of each other.

Other Hybrid Ethnicities in Japan: Extending the Research Scope

From here, an important question warrants consideration concerning how this study might be relevant to identities of peoples in Japan of mixed-ethnicities other than only that of English-speaking children of Japanese and 'white foreign' mixed-parentage. Other more marginally placed ethnic groups in Japan might be faced with added challenges such as social and economic obstacles – something that was less problematic for the participants of this study. For many less privileged children, their two (or more) ethnicities might not afford them the 'double dominance' that the participant girls of this study enjoy by virtue of having one insider, indigenous Japanese parent and another parent from a super-power nation who speaks a high-status foreign language.

Nevertheless, while warranting future empirical study, I would argue that children of other such marginally placed mixed-ethnicities and of other less socially valued minority home-languages, would still have access to various privileging forms of cultural, symbolic, linguistic and social capital, which is generally not readily available to their Japanese peers. Like the girls of this study, these other mixed-ethnic children in Japan *do* have access to positive forms of cultural capital such as intercultural savvy and outside-of-Japan connections and family, access within the home to bi-/multilinguality, friends in the community of similar mixes of ethnicities and an ethnic community within a larger Japanese community, which allows them to enjoy their rich home cultures – including language, music, dance, story-telling, festivals, religion and social interaction. Although these people might often find themselves marginalized on the basis of their minority ethnicity, based on the same theoretical framework as that of this study, I argue that they would be similarly multiply positioned. While they may at times be positioned as powerless within certain dominant discourses of ethnicity in Japan, at other times and in other contexts, they would be positioned as powerful within a range of alternative, competing discourses of ethnicity, similar to the girl participants of this study.

Implications for Future Research

There are a number of future directions which this research could take in order to further contribute to our understanding of hybrid identity in Japan.

First, as addressed above, the question of hybrid identity in Japan needs to be further researched and analyzed with more numbers and a greater variety of participants, not only of adolescent Japanese-white girls, but of other groups of ethnically mixed peoples in Japan seen in increasingly growing numbers such as Brazilian-Japanese, Chinese-Japanese, Filipino-Japanese and Afro-Japanese children, as well as non-English-speaking (white/Japanese and other) multi- or mixed-ethnicities comprising more than just two distinct ethnicities. Also, examination of non-mixed *gaijin* children of two foreign parents coming to live in Japan would further provide much insight into other questions of ethnic identity in Japan. While not a concern of the participants of this study, there is a growing population of non-Japanese school-aged children in Japan whose only language is a minority mother-tongue, which severely restricts their access to a proper education (of any kind) in a country that fails to make educa-tion compulsory for 'foreign' children. Even in places where Japanese education is made available to such children, minority-language educa-tional needs have not yet been addressed.

While I have specifically looked at adolescent girls in this study, other studies that look also at boys or boys and girls would contribute to fill-ing a gap in this area. Due to space limitations and concerns beyond the scope of this book, I was unable to include the analysis of data that I had collected and analyzed on adolescent *haafu/daburu* boys in Japan of Japanese and white mixed-parentage, which contained promisingly interesting and rich findings (see Kamada, 2009). As a topic of research for future work, of particular interest in these boys' data was the revela-tion of mixed-ethnic boys in Japan drawing on the same discourse of ethnic attractiveness as girls. The data suggested that within a 'discourse of foreign attractiveness', it was not only girls, but also boys who constructed the 'idealized other' (Bloustien, 2001), where adolescents view their bodies against a model of those they aspire to be like, as portrayed in the media. Boys seemed to express a feminized, narcissistic body consciousness in which they struggled to resist a 'discourse of foreign grotesqueness' and instead worked to position themselves within a positive 'discourse of foreign attractiveness', as did the girls of this study. To mention a specific example, boys used the same expression *hori ga fukai* (well-sculptured face) to celebrate their embodied capital of hybridity, just as the girls had done (Kamada, 2009). This may lead us to question whether ethnicity is more salient than gender. As an interesting direction for more extensive research, in contrast to the dominant 'male–female differences' model of gender, an unconventional gender model could be theorized in which we have both 'differences within gender' as well as 'commonalities across gender' of mixed-ethnic adolescent girls and boys.

Other comparative studies would also be worth conducting, such as studies that matched up similar groups of adolescent Japanese girls and mixed-ethnic girls in Japan. Also, while adolescence is an extremely fascinating period to focus on in terms of the dramatic maturational changes occurring over a short period of time, research on mixed-ethnic identity of other age groups (including pre-adolescent and toddler children, as well as adults) has so far received little attention, especially in the context of Japan.

It would also be worth conducting further research that more specifically focused on the influence of languages (including monolinguality, bilinguality and multilinguality) on hybrid identity in the context of Japan. While this study touched on some issues of language and bilinguality, this area is in need of further exploration.

This study has raised some new questions concerning the possibility of determining other ethnic discourses in Japan, which go beyond those already identified, named and examined in this book. It would be worth conducting further research to look at not only how *mixed-ethnic* children and adults in Japan manifest linguistic traces of various ethnic discourses, but to also explore how *Japanese* children and adults discursively draw on various discourses and repertoires *in their talk about minorities in Japan*. In line with Wetherell and Potter's (1992) investigation of how the white-Pakeha people in New Zealand talk of the minority Maori people, such a study in Japan that problematized how Japanese people draw on various discourses and interpretive repertoires and ideological dilemmas in their talk of ethnic minorities would be a valuable contribution.

Finally, extending beyond the data of this small group of six girls in Japan, it is hoped that this study will further contribute to more research and actual changes in policy and practice by having an influence on the general consciousness in society concerning these issues. The voices of these six participants that normally go unheard in Japanese society need to be recognized by the wider public in order for schools and other social institutions to acknowledge these issues and to work to eliminate the use of damaging discourses of ethnic marginality in an ever-diversifying Japanese society.

From an educational policy point of view, perhaps pre-knowledge of how existing dominant and alternative discourses of ethnicity within Japanese society (and specifically within the Japanese school system) is manipulated and used might help educators, policy-makers and teachers to better understand the feelings and needs of the rapidly increasing numbers of children of mixed-ethnicity and other non-Japanese children in the state schools. Furthermore, this knowledge might also help Japanese children develop a broader intercultural consciousness of acceptance of differences and diversity of people within their midst.

I also hope that this study stimulates further research and discussion from a variety of angles in order for these normally unheard voices to be known beyond their local networks, not only throughout the community of Japan, but also beyond those borders.

Final Words

This book has highlighted the contradictions and tensions of cultural expectations that adolescent girls of mixed-parentage in Japan are faced with. These adolescents must struggle to learn how to negotiate their constantly changing positionings in their various contexts. Not only do such young people work to take on multiple identities, but this has also come to be taken for granted. In an expedient, globalized, media-driven, multicultural world, the chameleon ability to assume different and competing identities, to appreciate diverse perspectives and to appropriate different forms of cultural capital as advantageous, might be seen as a vital means of survival and strength, rather than as victimhood.

In all its complexities, Japan is a dynamic place I have come to love and chosen to call home, and for this reason, I hope to see it socially develop even further than it already has. The journey over several years that I have traveled with these six girls spanning their early adolescence has not only revealed to me many unexpected aspects of hybrid identity that differ greatly from my own ethnic identity as a *gaijin* in Japan, but this expedition has also been extremely rewarding and exciting as a parent of a mixed-ethnic child and a veteran member of this proliferating community, where I plan to continue residing.

Appendix 1: Transcript of Rina's Think Aloud Protocol (Uncorrected)

(March 14, 2001: 3 days before the end of elementary school, sixth grade: 12 years old)

Why my Life is Special

I feel my life is special because I am bilingual. Being bilingual has many benefits. I can speak, read and write in both English and Japanese, which helps me make friends in both cultures. I also feel that being bilingual expands my future. Meaning that there are many jobs that only people like I can do. For example, translating tourist guides etc.

I also feel my life is special because I have at least five very close bilingual girlfriends. Because we are all bilingual, we all know how eachother feels about problems at school. For instance, if someone at school says something mean to a friend A, we all listen and give her and eachother advice and share our own similar stories. Leaving us all feeling well informed for when we are in similar situations. We can also trust eachother and we are all very close, which I think plays an important role in special lives.

(Note: The English errors in this transcript have not been corrected.)

Appendix 2: Descriptions of Materials Used for Discussion

I used the following materials in order to stimulate discussion:

(1) A picture where I asked the girls: 'Have you ever felt like this before?'

Permission was received from *Time* magazine and Cecelia Wong (illustrator) to print this illustration, which is also used on the cover of this book. (This illustration originally appeared in *Time Asia* on March 11, 2002: 22.)

(2) Photos from a Japanese glossy magazine (*Nikita*) of which all of the models were non-Japanese, or of Japanese and white mixed parentage (see the section 'A "discourse of foreigner attractiveness"' [p. 42]).

(3) A cover photo from *Time Asia* magazine (April 23, 2001) featuring three 'Eurasian' girls with the headline 'All Mixed Up' and with the article inside entitled 'Eurasian Invasion'.

(4) A picture from *Time Asia* (March 4, 2002) of a newly debuted brown-skinned 'multiethnic' Barbie doll (see Extract 5.5). The picture below of the multiethnic Barbie doll, named 'Kayla' is similar to that of the photo that appeared in *Time Asia*.

(5) A copy of a Japanese police report about illegal foreigners in Japan (see Figures 2.1–2.4).

(6) Three photos from a Japanese children's book on the human body entitled: *Hito no Karada* (Suzuki, 1984) (see the sections 'Contesting Ethnic Embodiment as Inferior or "Othered"' [p. 185] and 'Celebrating Ethnic Embodiment as Privileged Cultural Capital' [p. 188] and Extracts 7.2, 7.3).

Appendix 3: Self-Portraits (in Alphabetical Order)

Anna's Self-Portrait

Hanna's Self-Portrait

Maya's Self-Portrait

Naomi's Self-Portrait

Rina's Self-Portrait

Sara's Self-Portrait: With Real Make-Up Foundation Applied

Glossary of Japanese Words

aho. ([E] stupid, idiot.) Kansai area slang for the more common word in standard Japanese usage, *baka*, also meaning stupid or idiot.

ainoko. ([E] cross-breed [in-between] kid.) Derogatory term denoting a mixed-ethnic or hybrid person.

anime. ([E] animation.)

chou. ([E] super, to exceed, surpass.) A relatively new slang usage to mean extreme or super.

daburu. ([E] 'double'.) This is a reconstruction of the term *haafu* (half). It refers to mixed-ethnic people in Japan who have Japanese and non-Japanese (usually white) mixed-parentage.

deru kui wa utareru. ([E] 'The nail that sticks up gets hammered down'.). A Japanese proverb illustrating the disagreeableness of standing out, being different or acting in an individual manner in Japanese society.

du yua besuto. ([E] do your best.)

ekizochikku. ([E] exotic.)

enryo. ([E] reserve, restraint.)

gaijin. ([E] foreigner, outsider.)

gaikoku no kata. ([E] a person from a foreign country.) This is an honorific expression of respect used to refer to a foreigner.

gaikokujin. ([E] a person from a foreign country.)

gaijin na kuse ni. ([E] because you're a *gaijin* [foreigner], or 'even though you're a foreigner ...'.)

gaikokujin yakara. ([E] That's because you're a *gaijin* [foreigner].)

haafu. ([E] 'half'.) This is a short form of 'half-Japanese'. This (usually neutral) term refers to mixed-ethnic people in Japan who have Japanese and non-Japanese (often 'white') mixed-parentage.

hamideru. ([E] to stand out, to protrude, to stick out.)

hamigo. ([E] a kid who stands out or protrudes.) (slang)

hamiru. ([E] to stand out, to be isolated out.) (slang)

hamitteiru hito. ([E] a person who stands out or protrudes.) (slang.)

hana ga takai. ([E] a high-bridged nose.) This expression connotes a person's face that is considered attractive and is often used to refer to features thought to resemble an Anglo-American type of facial structure. A person with a high-bridged nose is also thought to have deep-set eyes, a prominent nose, or a well-sculptured face.

hori ga fukai. ([E] a deeply sculptured face.) This expression connotes a person's face that is considered attractive and is often used to refer to features thought to resemble an Anglo-American type of facial structure.

ibunka. ([E] interculturalism, intercultural, interculturalization.)

ijime. ([E] bullying.) (also *ijimerareru* = to be bullied [by someone].)

jinshuu. ([E] race [of people].)

kakkou ii. ([E] good style.) An informal expression equivalent to 'cool looking'.

kaodachi. ([E] facial [bone] structure.)

kawaii. ([E] cute.)

kitanai, kiken, kitsui. ([E] dirty, dangerous, demanding.) Referred to as the three Ks (or the three Ds, in English) of conditions describing unskilled jobs in the labor sector that Japanese youths have come to shun in recent years.

kokusaika. ([E] internationalization.)

konketsu. ([E] mixed-blood.) Derogatory term for a mixed-ethnic (hybrid) person.

konketsuji. ([E] mixed-blood kid.) Derogatory term for a mixed-ethnic (hybrid) person.

komakai. ([E] picky, trivial.)

korosu, koroshite. ([E] to kill, kill.)

kuyashi namida. A Japanese idiom indicating the shedding of tears with anger, regret or shame. It is rendered into English in this book as 'it's enough to make you weep'.

manga. ([E] comic, comic book, cartoon illustration.)

minna chigatte, minna ga ii. ([E] 'All people in their differences are all good', or 'Everyone's different, and everyone's okay'.)

Mombushou. ([E] The Japan Ministry of Education.) This ministry was created by the Meiji Government in 1871. It was combined with several other ministries in 2001 to form what is popularly referred to as the MEXT or the Monkashou (see below).

Momotarou. ([E] literally: 'Peach Boy'.) Momotarou is the name of a boy hero from a classic Japanese fairytale. In the story, Momotarou is born from a huge peach that an old woman plucks from a river.

Monkashou. (MEXT or The Japan Ministry of Education, Culture, Sports, Science and Technology.) This was formed in 2001 by combining the Mombushou (see above) with other ministries.

moteru. ([E] literally, to have, to possess.) *Moteru* (as used by the participants of this study) has been used since the Edo period to refer to a person who has 'cool style' or who is 'good looking' – a person who really 'has it'.

Nihonjinron. ([E] literally, theories on the Japanese people.) This is a genre of literature and other media-produced discourse on the topic of Japaneseness which peaked during Japan's bubble economy in the 1980s.

otaku. In recent years, this word has been adopted in many western cultures to commonly refer to people who are overly indulged in some pastime such as games, comic books (particularly Japanese comics [*manga*]), animation [*anime*]) and so on. However, the meaning in Japan sometimes goes beyond this to include people who are extremely focused on a wider range of singular (often marginal) pastimes including, among others, train watching, collecting cards or other objects, or engaging in some kind of on-line activities.

oni. ([E] ogre or devil.) *Oni* have been depicted since Japan's earliest written recordings as a beastly sub-human, but anthropomorphic, character with horns, large teeth, a large belly and a big nose.

puraido. ([E] pride.) *Puraido* carries the nuance of shame or embarrassment and often refers to a 'loss of pride'.

sampo ushiro ni aruite koi. ([E] woman, stay three steps behind the man when walking.) (*sampou sagatte shi [shujin] no kage o fumanai* = walk behind your lord [husband] without stepping on his shadow.)

sekushii. ([E] sexy.)

shimaguni konjou. ([E] island disposition.) This refers to the notion of Japan as having an insular worldview based on its geographical features as an island country in contrast to, for example, China with a broader continental disposition.

shinu, shinde, shine. ([E] to die, die, die.)

shouji. A Japanese sliding door made with a thin wooden frame backed with opaque Japanese rice paper.

sutairu ga ii. ([E] good style.) In the context in which this is used in this book, this 'good style' refers to body style, such as someone who is slim, well-proportioned, 'hunky' (in the case of males), or 'busty' (in the case of females).

tan'itsu minzoku. ([E] literally, one people.) A 'one-people' Japan refers to the notion of the Japanese people (nation, society) as consisting of a homogeneous race.

tatami. A mat flooring used in Japanese houses made of woven rice sheaths and placed side by side to construct living and sleeping spaces. Shoes or slippers are not worn on tatami.

teishu kampuku. ([E] the husband as ruler of the house.) This term refers to the stereotypical 'male chauvinist' Japanese husband (often portrayed as a 'salaryman') who returns home from work late, sits down and orders his wife to bring him a drink and food, fix his bath and prepare his bed. In the morning, he expects his wife to have his work clothes laid out for him and to serve him a hot breakfast and prepare his home-made boxed lunch. Such a patriarchical-type (bread-winner) husband yields total authoritarian power in the family with the wife doing all of the household chores, childcare and care-giving to his elderly parents.

zasshu. ([E] literally, mongrel.) Derogatory term for a mixed-ethnic (hybrid) person. This word is generally used to refer to 'mongrel' dogs.

References

Aguirre, Jr., A. and Turner, J. (2001) *American Ethnicity: The Dynamics and Consequences of Discrimination* (3rd edn). Boston: McGraw-Hill.

Althusser, L. (1971) *Lenin and Philosophy and Other Essays*. London: New Left Books.

Antoni, K. (1991) Momotaro (The Peach Boy) and the spirit of Japan: Concerning the function of a fairy tale in Japanese nationalism of the early Showa Age. *Asian Folklore Studies* 50, 155–188.

Bakhtin, M. (1984) *Problems in Dostoevsky's Poetics*. Minneapolis: University of Minnesota Press.

Bakhtin, M. (1986) *Speech Genres and Other Late Essays* (V.W. McGee, trans.). Austin, TX: University of Texas Press.

Barbour, R. and Kitzinger, J. (eds) (1999) *Developing Focus Group Research: Politics, Theory and Practice*. London: Sage.

Baxter, J. (2002a) A juggling act: A feminist post-structuralist analysis of girls' and boys' talk in the secondary classroom. *Gender and Education* 14 (1), 5–19.

Baxter, J. (2002b) Competing discourses in the classroom: A post-structuralist discourse analysis of girls' and boys' speech in public contexts. *Discourse and Society* 13 (6), 827–842.

Baxter, J. (2003) *Positioning Gender in Discourse: A Feminist Methodology*. Hampshire: Palgrave Macmillan.

Baxter, J. (2008) Feminist post-structuralist discourse analysis – a new theoretical and methodological approach? In K. Harrington, L. Litosseliti, H. Sauntson and J. Sunderland (eds) *Language and Gender Research Methodologies* (pp. 243–255). Basingstoke: Palgrave Macmillan.

Befu, H. (2001) *Hegemony of Homogeneity: An Anthropological Analysis of 'Nihonjirnron'*. Melbourne: Trans Pacific Press.

Bhabha, H. (1990) The third space. In J. Rutherford (ed.) *Identity: Community, Culture, Difference*. London: Lawrence and Wishart.

Bhabha, H. (1994) *The Location of Culture*. London/New York: Routledge.

Billig, M. (1987/1996) *Arguing and Thinking: A Rhetorical Approach to Social Psychology* (new edn). Cambridge: Cambridge University Press.

Billig, M. (1991) *Ideology and Opinions: Studies in Rhetorical Psychology*. London: Sage.

Billig, M. (1997) Discursive, rhetorical and ideological messages. In C. McGarty and A. Haslam (eds) *The Message of Social Psychology*. Oxford: Blackwell.

Billig, M. (2001) Discursive, rhetorical and ideological messages. In M. Wetherell, S. Taylor and S. Yates (eds) *Discourse Theory and Practice: A Reader* (pp. 210–221). London: Sage.

Billig, M., Condor, S., Edwards, D., Gane, M., Middleton, D. and Radley, A. (1988) *Ideological Dilemmas: A Social Psychology of Everyday Thinking*. London: Sage.

Blackledge, A. (2002) The discursive construction of national identity in multi-cultural Britain. *Journal of Language, Identity and Education* 1 (1), 67–87.

Blackledge, A. and Pavlenko, A. (2001) Negotiation of identities in multilingual contexts. *International Journal of Bilingualism* 5 (3), 243–257.

Bloustien, G. (2001) Far from sugar and spice: Teenage girls, embodiment and representation. In B. Baron and H. Kotthoff (eds) *Gender in Interaction: Perspectives on Femininity and Masculinity in Ethnography and Discourse* (pp. 99–136). Amsterdam/Philadelphia: John Benjamins Publishing Co.

Bostwick, M. (1999) Nihon ni okeru imaazyon kyoiku [Immersion education in Japan]. In Y. Yamamoto (ed.) *Bairingaru no Sekai (The World of the Bilingual)* (pp. 181–218). Tokyo: Taishukan.

Bostwick, M. (2001) Bilingual education of children in Japan: Year four of a partial immersion programme. In M.G. Noguchi and S. Fotos (eds) *Studies in Japanese Bilingualism* (pp. 272–311). Clevedon: Multilingual Matters.

Bourdieu, P. (1977) *Outline of a Theory of Practice* (R. Nice, trans.). Cambridge: Cambridge University Press.

Bourdieu, P. (1984) *Distinction: A Social Critique of the Judgment of Taste*. Cambridge, MA: Harvard University Press.

Bourdieu, P. (1991) *Language and Symbolic Power* (G. Raymond and M. Adamson, trans.). Cambridge, MA: Harvard University Press.

Bourdieu, P. (1993) *The Field of Cultural Production: Essays on Art and Literature*. New York: Columbia University Press.

Bourdieu, P. (1999) Language and symbolic power. In A. Jaworski and N. Coupland (eds) *The Discourse Reader* (pp. 502–521). London/New York: Routledge.

Bourdieu, P. and Passerson, J.S. (1977) *Reproduction in Education, Society, and Culture*. Beverly Hills: Sage.

Bucholtz, M. (1999) 'Why be normal?': Language and identity practices in a community of nerd girls. *Language and Society* 28, 203–223.

Budgeon, S. (2003) Identity as an embodied event. *Body and Society* 9 (1), 35–55.

Charmaz, K. and Mitchell, Jr., R.G. (1997) The myth of silent authorship: Self, substance, and style in ethnographic writing. In R. Hertz (ed.) *Reflexivity and Voice* (pp. 193–215). London: Sage.

Ching, L. (1998) Yellow skin, white masks. In K-H. Chen, H.O.L. Kuo, H. Hang and H. Ming-Chu (eds) *Trajectories: Inter-Asia Cultural Studies* (pp. 65–86). London/New York: Routledge.

Ching, L. (2001) *Becoming 'Japanese': Colonial Taiwan and the Politics of Identity Formation*. Berkeley/LA: University of California Press.

Chouliaraki, L. and Fairclough, N. (1999) *Discourse in Late Modernity: Rethinking Critical Discourse Analysis*. Edinburgh: Edinburgh University Press.

Christian, M. (2000) *Multiracial Identity: An International Perspective*. London: Macmillan Press, Ltd.

Clark, K. (1998) The linguistics of blame: Representations of blame in the *Sun's* reporting of crimes of sexual violence. In D. Cameron (ed.) *The Feminist Critique of Language* (pp. 183–197). London: Routledge.

Coates, J. (1999) Changing femininities: The talk of teenage girls. In M. Bucholtz, A.C. Liang and L.A. Sutton (eds) *Reinventing Identities: The Gendered Self in Discourse* (pp. 123–143). New York/Oxford: Oxford University Press.

Cummins, J. (1991) Interdependence of first- and second-language proficiency in bilingual children. In E. Bailystok (ed.) *Language Processing in Bilingual Children* (pp. 70–89). Cambridge: Cambridge University Press.

Darling-Wolf, F. (2003) Media, class, and western influence in Japanese women's conceptions of attractiveness. *Feminist Media Studies* 3 (2), 153–172.

Davies, B. and Harré, R. (2001) Positioning: The discursive production of selves. In M. Wetherell, S. Taylor and S. Yates (eds) *Discourse Theory and Practice: A Reader* (pp. 261–271). London: Sage.

Day, D. (1998) Being ascribed, and resisting, membership of an ethnic group. In C. Antaki and S. Widdicombe (eds) *Identities in Talk* (pp. 151–170). London: Sage.

Debito Arudou (2006) Immigration to Japan is already happening and it will not stop. On WWW at http://debito.org/ (January 2006).

Debito Arudou (2009) On WWW at http://debito.org/. See also at http://www.debito.org/?p=2466 (March 2009).

Denoon, D., Hudson, M., McCormack, G. and Morris-Suzuki, T. (eds) (1996) *Multicultural Japan: Paleolithic to Postmodern*. Cambridge: Cambridge University Press.

Derrida, J. (1973) *Speech and Phenomenon*. Evanston: North-western University Press.

Derrida, J. (1976) *Of Grammatology*. Baltimore: John Hopkins Press.

Derrida, J. (1978) *Writing and Difference*. London: RKP.

Diene, D. (2006) Racism, racial discrimination, xenophobia and all forms of discrimination. Report of the special Rapporteur on contemporary forms of racism, racial discrimination, xenophobia and related intolerance, addendum: MISSION TO JAPAN. UN Commission on Human Rights.

Dillon, T. (2004) Hitting the nail on the head. *The Japan Times*, February 29, p. 10. Tokyo.

Donahue, R.T. (2002a) Guideposts for exploring Japaneseness. In R.T. Donahue (ed.) *Exploring Japaneseness: On Japanese Enactments of Culture and Consciousness* (pp. 3–27). Westport, CN: Ablex Publishing.

Donahue, R.T. (ed.) (2002b) *Exploring Japaneseness: On Japanese Enactments of Culture and Consciousness*. Westport, CN: Ablex Publishing.

Dower, J. (1986) *War Without Mercy*. New York: Pantheon Books.

Eckert, P. (1993) Cooperative competition in adolescent 'girl talk'. In D. Tannen (ed.) *Gender and Conversational Interaction* (pp. 32–61). New York/Oxford: Oxford University Press.

Eckert, P. (2000) *Linguistic Variation as Social Practice: The Linguistic Construction of Identity in Belten High*. Cambridge/Oxford: Blackwell Publishers.

Edley, N. (1997) Jockeying for position: The construction of masculine identities. *Discourse and Society* 8 (2), 203–217.

Edley, N. (2001) Analysing masculinity: Interpretative repertoires, ideological dilemmas and subject positions. In M. Wetherell, S. Taylor and S. Yates (eds) *Discourse as Data: A Guide for Analysis* (pp. 189–228). London: Sage.

Edley, N. and Wetherell, M. (1996) Masculinity, power and identity. In M. Mac An Ghaill (ed.) *Understanding Masculinities: Social Relations and Cultural Arenas*. Buckingham: Open University Press.

Edley, N. and Wetherell, M. (1997) Jockeying for position: The construction of masculine identities. *Discourse and Society* 8 (2), 203–217.

Edley, N. and Wetherell, M. (1999) Imagined futures: Young men's talk about fatherhood and domestic life. *British Journal of Social Psychology* 38, 181–194.

Edley, N. and Wetherell, M. (2008) Discursive psychology and the study of gender: A contested space. In K. Harrington, L. Litosseliti, H. Sauntson and J. Sunderland (eds) *Language and Gender Research Methodologies* (pp. 161–173). Basingstoke: Palgrave Macmillan.

Edwards, D. and Potter, J. (1992) *Discursive Psychology*. London: Sage.

Fairclough, N. (1992) *Discourse and Social Change*. Cambridge: Polity Press.

Fairclough, N. (1995) *Critical Discourse Analysis*. London/New York: Longman.

Fairclough, N. (1999) Linguistic and intertextural analysis within discourse analysis. In A. Jaworski and N. Coupland (eds) *The Discourse Reader* (pp. 183–211). London: Routledge.

Fairclough, N. (2000) *New Labour, New Language?* London: Routledge.

Fairclough, N. (2001) The discourse of new labour: Critical discourse analysis. In M. Wetherell, S. Taylor and S.J. Yates (eds) *Discourse as Data: A Guide for Analysis* (pp. 229–266). London: Sage.

Fairclough, N. (2003) *Analysing Discourse: Textual Analysis for Social Research*. London/New York: Routledge.

Fenton, S. (1999) *Ethnicity: Racism, Class and Culture*. London: Macmillan.

Finders, M. (1997) *Just Girls: Hidden Literacies and Life in Junior High*. New York/London: Teachers College Press.

Foucault, M. (1972) *The Archeology of Knowledge and the Discourse on Language*. London: Routledge.

Foucault, M. (1979) *The History of Sexuality, Vol. 1: An Introduction*. London: Allen Lane.

Foucault, M. (1980a) The history of sexuality. In C. Gordon (ed.) *Power/Knowledge: Selected Interviews and Other Writings 1972–1977* (pp. 183–193). New York: Pantheon Books.

Foucault, M. (1980b) Truth and power. In C. Gordon (ed.) *Power/Knowledge: Selected Interviews and Other Writings 1972–1977* (pp. 109–133). New York: Pantheon Books.

Gergen, K. (1985) Social constructionist inquiry: Context and implications. In K.J. Gergen and K.E. Davies (eds) *The Social Construction of the Person*. New York: Springer.

Gergen, K. (1999) *An Invitation to Social Construction*. London: Sage.

Gergen, K. (2001) Self-narration in social life. In M. Wetherell, S. Taylor and S. Yates (eds) *Discourse Theory and Practice: A Reader* (pp. 247–260). London: Sage.

Gillis-Furutaka, A. (ed.) (1999) Bullying in Japanese schools: International perspectives. *Japan Association for Language Teaching, Bilingualism SIG Monograph*, Japan.

Gottfried, H. (2003) Temp(t)ing bodies: Shaping gender at work in Japan. *Sociology* 37 (2), 257–276.

Greer, T. (2001) Half, double, or somewhere in-between? Multi-faceted identities among biracial Japanese. *Japan Journal of Multilingualism and Multiculturalism* 7 (1), 1–17.

Greer, T. (2003) Multiethnic Japanese identity: An applied conversation analysis. *Japan Journal of Multilingualism and Multiculturalism* 9 (1), 1–23.

Greer, T., Kamada, L., Ascough, T. and Shi J. (2005) Four studies into multi-ethnic identity in Japan. In K. Bradford-Watts, C. Ikeguchi and M. Swanson (eds) _JALT2004 Conference Proceedings_ (pp. 949–961). Tokyo: JALT.

Hanazaki, K. (2000) Decolonialization and assumption of war responsibility. _Inter-Asia Cultural Studies_ 1 (1), 71–83.

Have, P.X. (1998) _Doing Conversational Analysis: A Practical Guide._ London: Sage.

Hayes, J. and Flower, F. (1983) Uncovering cognitive processes in writing: An introduction to protocol analysis. In P. Mosenthal, L. Tamor and S.A. Walmsley (eds) _Research on Writing: Principles and Methods._ New York/London: Longman.

Heller, M. (1999) _Linguistic Minorities and Modernity: A Sociolinguistic Ethnography._ New York: Addison Wesley Longman Limited.

Heller, M. (2001) Gender and public space in a bilingual school. In A. Pavlenko, A. Blackledge, I. Piller and M. Teutsch-Dwyer (eds) _Multilingualism, Second Language Learning, and Gender_ (pp. 257–282). Berlin/New York: Mouton de Gruyter.

Hertz, R. (1997a) Introduction: Reflexivity and voice. In R. Hertz (ed.) _Reflexivity and Voice_ (pp. 7–18). London: Sage.

Hertz, R. (ed.) (1997b) _Reflexivity and Voice._ London: Sage.

Hoffman, M. (2005) _Ero-manga_ got the blues. _The Japan Times,_ June 6, p. 9. Tokyo.

Hollway, W. (2001) Gender difference and the production of subjectivity. In M. Wetherell, S. Taylor and S. Yates (eds) _Discourse Theory and Practice: A Reader_ (pp. 272–283). London: Sage.

Horton-Salway, M. (2001) The construction of M.E.: The discursive action model. In M. Wetherell, S. Taylor and S. Yates (eds) _Discourse as Data: A Guide for Analysis_ (pp. 147–188). London: Sage.

Howson, A. (2005) _Embodying Gender._ London: Sage.

Iino, M. (1996) 'Excellent foreigner!': Gaijinization of Japanese language and culture in conflict situations – an ethnographic study of dinner table conversations between Japanese host families and American students. Unpublished PhD thesis, University of Pennsylvania.

Ivanic, R. (1998) _Writing and Identity: The Discoursal Construction of Identity in Academic Writing._ Amsterdam/Philadelphia: John Benjamins Pub. Co.

Japan Ministry of Justice and Immigration (2008) 平成１９年末現在における外国人登録者統計について平成20年6月 (2007 Census Report) (June 2008). Also Statistics for Registered Foreigners in Japan for 2006 at http://www.stat.go.jp/english/index/official/202.htm, Change of number of registered aliens by country of origin at http://www.mofa.go.jp/policy/human/race_rep1/attach2.html.

JINF (Japan Institute for National Fundamentals) (2008) _Proposal No. 2._ Subcommittee on Voting Rights for Foreigners (March). On WWW at http://www.en.jinf.jp/pdf/english2.pdf.

Joseph, J. (2002) Is language a verb? Conceptual change in linguistics and language teaching. In H. Trappes-Lomax and G. Ferguson (eds). _Language in Language Teacher Education_ (pp. 29–47). Amsterdam: John Benjamins Pub. Co.

Jurik, N. and Siemsen, C. (2009) 'Doing gender' as canon or agenda. _Gender and Society_ 23 (1), 72–75.

Kamada, L. (1995a) _Bilingual Family Case Studies (Vol. 1). Monographs on Bilingualism No. 3._ Tokyo, Japan: Japan Association for Language Teaching, Bilingualism SIG.

Kamada, L. (1995b) Bilingual family case studies in Japan: Significant factors. _Bunkei Ronsou_ 30 (3), 113–129.

Kamada, L. (1997) *Bilingual Family Case Studies (Vol. 2). Monographs on Bilingualism No. 5.* Tokyo, Japan: Japan Association for Language Teaching, Bilingualism Special Interest Group.

Kamada, L. (2004) Conceptualizing multilingual and multi-ethnic 'othering' in Japan. In *JALT 2003 at Shizuoka: Conference Proceedings* (pp. 1–8). Tokyo: Japan Association for Language Teaching.

Kamada, L. (2005a) Celebration of multi-ethnic cultural capital among adolescent girls in Japan: A post-structuralist discourse analysis of Japanese-Caucasian identity. *Japan Journal of Multilingualism and Multiculturalism* 11, 19–41.

Kamada, L. (2005b) Interpretive repertoires and ideological dilemmas of gender: Japanese-Caucasian girls in Japan. *Aomori Akenohoshi Tanki Daigaku Research Reports* 31, 31–43.

Kamada, L. (2006a) Multiethnic identities of '*haafu/daburu*' girls in Japan. In K. Bradford-Watts, C. Ikeguchi and M. Swanson (eds) *JALT2005 at Shizuoka: Conference Proceedings* (pp. 102–113). Tokyo: Japan Association for Language Teaching.

Kamada, L. (2006b) Yasuko Kanno plenary – bilingual education in Japan: Unequal access to bilingualism. In *Bilingual Japan* (pp. 9–12). Tokyo: JALT Bilingualism Special Interest Group.

Kamada, L. (2008) Discursive 'embodied' identities of 'half' girls in Japan: A multiperspective approach. In K. Harrington, L. Litosseliti, H. Sauntson and J. Sunderland (eds) *Language and Gender Research Methodologies* (pp. 174–190). Basingstoke: Palgrave Macmillan.

Kamada, L. (2009) Mixed-ethnic girls and boys as similarly powerless and powerful: Embodiment of attractiveness and grotesqueness. *Discourse Studies* 11 (3), 329–352.

Kang, S. (2001) Post-colonialism and diasporic space in Japan. *Inter-Asia Cultural Studies* 2 (1), 137–144.

Kanno, Y. (2004) Sending mixed messages: Language minority education at a Japanese public elementary school. In A. Pavlenko and A. Blackledge (eds) *Negotiation of Identities in Multilingual Contexts* (pp. 316–338). Clevedon: Multilingual Matters.

Kanno, Y. (2008) *Language and Education in Japan: Unequal Access to Bilingualism.* London: Palgrave Macmillan.

Katz, I. (1996) *The Construction of Racial Identity in Children of Mixed Parentage: Mixed Metaphors.* London/Bristol/Pennsylvania: Jessica Kingsley Publishers.

Kawai, H. (1996) *The Japanese Psyche: Major Motifs in the Fairy Tales of Japan.* Woodstock, CT: Spring Publications.

Kitzinger, J. (2008) Conversation analysis: Technical matters for gender research. In K. Harrington, L. Litosseliti, H. Sauntson and J. Sunderland (eds) *Language and Gender Research Methodologies* (pp. 119–138). Basingstoke: Palgrave Macmillan.

Kitzinger, J. and Barbour, R. (1999) Introduction: The challenge and promise of focus groups. In R. Barbour and J. Kitzinger (eds) *Developing Focus Group Research: Politics, Theory and Practice* (pp. 1–20). London: Sage.

Klaus, A. (1991) Momotaro (The Peach Boy) and the spirit of Japan: Concerning the function of a fairy tale in Japanese nationalism of the early Showa Age. *Asian Folklore Studies* 50, 155–188.

Kowner, R. (2002) Deconstructing the Japanese national discourse: Laymen's beliefs and ideology. In R.T. Donahue (ed.) *Exploring Japaneseness: On Japanese Enactments of Culture and Consciousness* (pp. 169–182). Westport, CN: Ablex Publishing.

Krueger, R. (1998) *Moderating Focus Groups*. London/New Delhi: Sage.

Kubota, R. (1999) Japanese culture constructed by discourses: Implications for applied linguistics research and ELT. *TESOL Quarterly* 33 (1), 9–35.

Kubota, R. (2002) Japanese identities in written communication: Politics and discourses. In R.T. Donahue (ed.) *Exploring Japaneseness: On Japanese Enactments of Culture and Consciousness* (pp. 293–315). Westport, CN: Ablex Publishing.

Laclau, E. and Mouffe, C. (1985) *Hegemony and Socialist Strategy: Towards a Radical Democratic Politics*. London: Verso.

Lave, J. and Wenger, E. (1991) *Situated Learning: Legitimate Peripheral Participation*. Cambridge: Cambridge University Press.

LeCompte, M. and Schensul, J. (1999) *Designing and Conducting Ethnographic Research*. Walnut Creek: AltaMira Press.

Le Page, R. and Tabouret-Keller, A. (1985) *Acts of Identity: Creole-Based Approaches to Language and Ethnicity*. Cambridge: Cambridge University Press.

Lie, J. (2001) *Multiethnic Japan*. Cambridge: Harvard University Press.

Litosseliti, L. and Sunderland, J. (eds) (2002) *Gender Identity and Discourse Analysis*. Amsterdam/Philadelphia: John Benjamins Pub. Co.

LoCastro, V. (1990) Intercultural pragmatics: A Japanese–American case study. Unpublished PhD thesis, University of Lancaster.

Lovering, K.M. (1995) The bleeding body: Adolescents talk about menstruation. In S. Wilkinson and C. Kitzinger (eds) *Feminism and Discourse: Psychological Perspectives* (pp. 10–31). London: Sage.

Maher, J. (1995) Multilingual Japan: An introduction. In J. Maher and K. Yashiro (eds) *Multilingual Japan* (pp. 1–17). Clevedon: Multilingual Matters.

Maher, J. and Yashiro, K. (1991) *Nihon no Bairingarizumu [Japan's Bilingualism]*. Tokyo: Kenkyusha.

Maher, J. and Macdonald, G. (1995a) Culture and diversity in Japan. In J. Maher and G. Macdonald (eds) *Diversity in Japanese Culture and Language* (pp. 3–23). London/New York: Kegan Paul International.

Maher, J. and Macdonald, G. (eds) (1995b) *Diversity in Japanese Culture and Language*. London/New York: Kegan Paul International.

Maher, J. and Yashiro, K. (eds) (1995) *Multilingual Japan*. Clevedon: Multilingual Matters.

Makoni, S. and Pennycook, A. (2007) Disinventing and reconstituting languages. In S. Makoni and A. Pennycook (eds) *Disinventing and Reconstructing Languages* (pp. 1–41). Clevedon: Multilingual Matters.

Mama, A. (1995) *Beyond the Mask: Race, Gender and Subjectivity*. London/New York: Routledge.

Mason, J. (2002) *Qualitative Researching* (2nd edn). London: Sage.

Maybin, J. (2002) 'What's the hottest part of the Sun? Page 3!': Children's exploration of adolescent gender identities through informal talk. In L. Litosseliti and J. Sunderland (eds) *Gender Identity and Discourse Analysis* (pp. 257–273). Amsterdam/Philadelphia: John Benjamins Pub. Co.

McCormack, G. (1996a) Introduction. In D. Denoon, M. Hudson, G. McCormack and T. Morris-Suzuki (eds) *Multicultural Japan: Paleolithic to Postmodern* (pp. 1–14). Cambridge: Cambridge University Press.

McCormack, G. (1996b) Kokusaika: Impediments in Japan's deep structure. In D. Denoon, M. Hudson, G. McCormack and T. Morris-Suzuki (eds) *Multicultural Japan: Paleolithic to Postmodern* (pp. 265–286). Cambridge: Cambridge University Press.

Miller, R.A. (1982) *Japan's Modern Myth: The Language and Beyond*. New York/ Tokyo: Weatherhill.

Minami, H. (1994) *Nihonjinron: Meiji kara konnnichi made* [Nihonjinron: *From Meiji to Today*]. Tokyo: Iwanami Shoten.

Myers, G. and Macnaghten, P. (1999) Can focus groups be analysed as talk? In R. Barbour and J. Kitzinger (eds) *Developing Focus Group Research: Politics, Theory and Practice* (pp. 173–185). London: Sage.

Noguchi, M. (2001) Introduction: The crumbling of a myth. In M. Noguchi and S. Fotos (eds) *Studies in Japanese Bilingualism* (pp. 1–23). Clevedon: Multilingual Matters.

Noguchi, M.G. (1996) *Adding Biliteracy to Bilingualism: Teaching Your Child to Read English in Japan. Monographs on Bilingualism No. 4*. Tokyo, Japan: Japan Association of Language Teachers Bilingualism Special Interest Group.

Noguchi, M. and Fotos, S. (eds) (2001) *Studies in Japanese Bilingualism*. Clevedon: Multilingual Matters.

Norton, B. (1997) Language, identity, and the ownership of English. *TESOL Quarterly* 31 (3), 409–429.

Norton, B. (2000) *Identity and Language Learning: Gender, Ethnicity and Educational Change*. Essex: Pearson Education Limited.

O'Hearn, C. (ed.) (1998) *Half and Half: Writers on Growing Up Biracial and Bicultural*. New York: Pantheon Books.

Onishi, H. (1989) The iconography of demons in Japanese art: A few modest proposals. *Asian Cultural Studies* 17, 13–19.

Orenstein, P. (1994) *Schoolgirls: Young Women, Self-Esteem, and the Confidence Gap*. New York: Anchor Books.

Parmenter, L. (1997) Becoming international in a Japanese junior high school: An ethnographic study. Unpublished PhD thesis, Department of Education, University of Durham.

Passeron, J.C. (2000) Theories of socio-cultural reproduction. In D. Robbins (ed.) *Pierre Bourdieu* (pp. 174–186). London: Sage.

Pavlenko, A. and Blackledge, A. (2004) Introduction: New theoretical approaches to the study of negotiation of identities in multilingual contexts. In A. Pavlenko and A. Blackledge (eds) *Negotiation of Identities in Multilingual Contexts* (pp. 1–33). Clevedon: Multilingual Matters.

Pennycook, A. (2007) The myth of English as an international language. In S. Makoni and A. Pennycook (eds) *Disinventing and Reconstructing Languages* (pp. 90–115). Clevedon: Multilingual Matters.

Phillips, L. and Jorgensen, M. (2002) *Discourse Analysis: As Theory and Method*. London: Sage.

Phoenix, A. and Owen, C. (2000) From miscegenation to hybridity: Mixed relationships and mixed parentage in profile. In A. Brah and A.E. Coombes (eds) *Hybridity and its Discontents: Politics, Science, Culture* (pp. 72–95). London/ New York: Routledge.

Potter, J. (2003) Discursive psychology: Between method and paradigm. *Discourse and Society* 14 (6), 783–794.

Potter, J. and Mulkay, M. (1985) Scientists' interview talk: Interviews as a technique for revealing participants' interpretive practices. In M. Brenner, J. Brown and D. Canter (eds) *The Research Interview: Uses and Approaches*. New York: Academic Press.

Potter, J. and Wetherell, M. (1987) *Discourse and Social Psychology: Beyond Attitudes and Behaviour*. London: Sage.

Ramanathan, V. (2005) *The Engish-Vernacular Divide*. Clevedon: Multilingual Matters.

Ratcliffe, P. (1994) Conceptualising 'race', ethnicity and nation: Towards a comparative perspective. In P. Ratcliffe (ed.) *Race, Ethnicity, and Nation: International Perspectives on Social Conflict* (pp. 2–25). London: UCL Press.

Reischauer, E. (1978) *The Japanese*. Cambridge, MA: Harvard University Press.

Robertson, J. (2001) Japan's first cyborg? Miss Nippon, eugenics and wartime technologies of beauty, body and blood. *Body and Society* 7 (1), 1–34.

Rohlen, T. (1983) *Japan's High Schools*. Berkeley: University of California Press.

Sacks, H. (1972) On the analyzability of stories by children. In J. Gumperz and D. Hymes (eds) *Directions in Sociolinguistics* (pp. 325–345). New York: Holt, Rinehart and Winston.

Said, E. (1978) *Orientalism*. New York: Pantheon Books.

Schilling, C. (1993) *The Body and Social Theory*. London: Sage.

Sebba, M. (1993) *London Jamaican: Language Systems in Interaction*. London/New York: Longman.

Silverman, D. (2005) *Doing Qualitative Research* (2nd edn). London: Sage.

Simmons, R. (2002) *Odd Girl Out: The Hidden Culture of Aggression in Girls*. New York: Harcourt, Inc.

Singer, J. (2000) Japan's singular doubles. *Japan Quarterly* 47 (2), 76–82.

Skutnabb-Kangas, T. (1981) *Bilingualism or Not: The Education of Minorities*. Clevedon: Multilingual Matters.

Skutnabb-Kangas, T. (1999) Education of minorities. In J. Fishman (ed.) *Handbook of Language and Ethnic Identity* (pp. 43–59). New York: Oxford University Press.

Smits, J. and Gunduz-Hosgor, A. (2003) Linguistic capital: Language as a socio-economic resource among Kurdish and Arabic women in Turkey. *Ethnic and Racial Studies* 26 (5), 829–853.

Speer, S. (2005) *Gender Talk: Feminism, Discourse and Conversation Analysis*. London/New York: Routledge.

Stokoe, E. (2008) Categories, actions and sequences: Formulating gender in talk-in-interaction. In K. Harrington, L. Litosseliti, H. Sauntson and J. Sunderland (eds) *Language and Gender Research Methodologies* (pp. 139–157). Basingstoke: Palgrave Macmillan.

Sunderland, J. (2004) *Gendered Discourses*. London: Palgrave Macmillan.

Sunderland, J. (2006) *Language and Gender*. London/New York: Routledge.

Sunderland, J. and Litosseliti, L. (2002) Gender identity and discourse analysis: Theoretical empirical considerations. In L. Litosseliti and J. Sunderland (eds) *Gender Identity and Discourse Analysis* (pp. 1–39). Amsterdam/Philadelphia: John Benjamins Pub. Co.

Suzuki, T. (1975) *Kotoba to Shakai*. Tokyo: Chuo Kouron-sha.

Suzuki, T. (1978) Why teach Nihongo [Japanese] to foreigners? Unpublished lecture (March 18). Tokyo, Japan.

Suzuki, T. (1984) *Hito No Karada* [*The Human Body*]. Tokyo: Gakken.

Swartz, D. (1997) *Culture and Power: The Sociology of Pierre Bourdieu*. Chicago/ London: University of Chicago Press.

Talbot, M. (1995) *Fictions at Work*. London: Longman.

Thapan, M. (1997a) Introduction: Gender and embodiment in everyday life. In M. Thapan (ed.) *Embodiment: Essays on Gender and Identity* (pp. 1–34). Delhi: Oxford University Press.

Thapan, M. (ed.) (1997b) *Embodiment: Essays on Gender and Identity*. Calcutta: Oxford University Press.

The Japan Times (newspaper) (2008) *Chinese Now No. 1 Foreign Group* (July 4).

Trechter, S. and Bucholtz, M. (2001) Bringing language into whiteness studies. *Journal of Linguistic Anthropology* 11 (1), 3–21.

Tsunoda, T. (1978) *Nihonjin no Nou* [*The Japanese Brain*]. Tokyo: Taishuukan.

van Dijk, T.A. (1987) *Communicating Racism: Ethnic Prejudice in Thought and Talk*. Beverly Hills/London: Sage.

van Dijk, T.A. (1991) *Racism and the Press: Critical Studies in Racism and Migration*. London/New York: Routledge.

van Dijk, T.A. (1993) Analyzing racism through discourse analysis: Some methodological reflections. In J. Stanfield II and R. Dennis (eds) *Race and Ethnicity in Research Methods* (pp. 92–134). London: Sage.

Vogel, E. (1979) *Japan as Number One: Lessons for America*. Cambridge, MA: Harvard University Press.

Walton, M.D., Weatherall, A. and Jackson, S. (2002) Romance and friendship in pre-teen stories about conflicts: 'We decided that boys are not worth it'. *Discourse and Society* 13 (5), 673–689.

Wasserfall, R. (1997) Reflexivity, feminism and difference. In R. Hertz (ed.) *Reflexivity and Voice* (pp. 150–168). London: Sage.

Weedon, C. (1987) *Feminist Practice and Poststructuralist Theory*. Cambridge/ Oxford: Blackwell.

Weiner, M. (1997a) Introduction. In M. Weiner (ed.) *Japan's Minorities: The Illusion of Homogeneity* (pp. 11–18). London/New York: Routledge.

Weiner, M. (ed.) (1997b) *Japan's Minorities: The Illusion of Homogeneity*. London/ New York: Routledge.

Wenger, E. (1998) *Communities of Practice: Learning, Meaning, and Identity*. Cambridge: Cambridge University Press.

Werbner, P. (1997) Introduction: The dialectics of cultural hybridity. In P. Werbner and T. Modood (eds) *Debating Cultural Hybridity: Multi-Cultural Identities and the Politics of Anti-Racism* (pp. 1–26). London/New Jersey: Zed Books.

Werbner, P. and Modood, T. (eds) (1997) *Debating Cultural Hybridity: Multi-Cultural Identities and the Politics of Anti-Racism*. London/New Jersey: Zed Books.

West, C. (2002) Peeling an onion: A critical comment on 'competing discourses'. *Discourse and Society* 13 (6), 843–851.

West, C. and Zimmerman, D. (1987) Doing gender. *Gender and Society* 1 (2), 125–151.

West, C. and Fenstermaker, S. (1995) Doing difference. *Gender and Society* 9 (1), 8–37.

West, C. and Zimmerman, D. (2009) Accounting for doing gender. *Gender and Society* 23 (1), 112–122.

Wetherell, M. (1986) Linguistic repertoires and literary criticism: New directions for a social psychology of gender. In S. Wilkenson (ed.) *Feminist Social Psychology*. Milton Keynes: Open University Press.

Wetherell, M. (1998) Positioning and interpretive repertoires: Conversation analysis and post-structuralism in dialogue. *Discourse and Society* 9, 387–412.

Wetherell, M. and Potter, J. (1992) *Mapping the Language of Racism: Discourse and the Legitimation of Exploitation*. New York/London: Harvester.

Wetherell, M. and Edley, N. (1998) Gender practices: Steps in the analysis of men and masculinities. In K. Henwood, C. Griffin and A. Phoenix (eds) *Standpoints and Differences: Essays in the Practice of Feminist Psychology*. London: Sage.

Wetherell, M., Taylor, S. and Yates, S. (eds) (2001a) *Discourse Theory and Practice: A Reader*. London: Sage.

Wetherell, M., Taylor, S. and Yates, S. (eds) (2001b) *Discourse as Data: A Guide for Analysis*. London: Sage.

Wolcott, H. (1999) *Ethnography: A Way of Seeing*. Walnut Creek: AltaMira Press.

Yamaguchi, M. (2005) Discursive representation and enactment of national identities: The case of Generation 1.5 Japanese. *Discourse and Society* 16 (2), 269–299.

Yamamoto, M. (1995) Bilingualism in international families. *Journal of Multilingual and Multicultural Development* 16 (1/2), 63–85.

Yamamoto, M. (2001a) *Language Use in Interlingual Families: A Japanese–English Sociolinguistic Study*. Clevedon: Multilingual Matters.

Yamamoto, M. (2001b) Japanese attitudes towards bilingualism: A survey and its implications. In M.G. Noguchi and S. Fotos (eds) *Studies in Japanese Bilingualism* (pp. 24–44). Clevedon: Multilingual Matters.

Young, R.J.K. (1995) *Colonial Desire: Hybridity in Theory, Culture and Race*. London/New York: Routledge.

Young, L. (2000) Hybridity's discontents: Rereading science and 'race'. In A. Brah and A.E. Coombes (eds) *Hybridity and its Discontents: Politics, Science, Culture* (pp. 154–156). London/New York: Routledge.

Yuval-Davis, N. (1997) Ethnicity, gender relations and multiculturalism. In P. Werbner and T. Modood (eds) *Debating Cultural Hybridity: Multi-Cultural Identities and the Politics of Anti-Racism* (pp. 193–208). London/New Jersey: Zed Books.

Index